A Chorus of Faith

A Chorus of Faith

A Festschrift in Honor of Vigen Guroian

Edited by
CARRIE FREDERICK FROST

☙PICKWICK *Publications* · Eugene, Oregon

A CHORUS OF FAITH
A Festschrift in Honor of Vigen Guroian

Copyright © 2025 Wipf and Stock Publishers. All rights reserved. Except for brief quotations in critical publications or reviews, no part of this book may be reproduced in any manner without prior written permission from the publisher. Write: Permissions, Wipf and Stock Publishers, 199 W. 8th Ave., Suite 3, Eugene, OR 97401.

Pickwick Publications
An Imprint of Wipf and Stock Publishers
199 W. 8th Ave., Suite 3
Eugene, OR 97401

www.wipfandstock.com

PAPERBACK ISBN: 978-1-6667-5882-5
HARDCOVER ISBN: 978-1-6667-5883-2
EBOOK ISBN: 978-1-6667-5884-9

Cataloguing-in-Publication data:

Names: Frost, Carrie Frederick, editor.

Title: A chorus of faith : a festschrift in honor of Vigen Guroian / edited by Carrie Frederick Frost.

Description: Eugene, OR: Pickwick Publications, 2025. | Includes bibliographical references and index.

Identifiers: ISBN 978-1-6667-5882-5 (print). | ISBN 978-1-6667-5883-2 (print). | ISBN 978-1-6667-5884-9 (epub).

Subjects: LSCH: Guroian, Vigen. | Theology, Doctrinal. | Orthodox Eastern Church.

Classification: BX260 C22 2025 (print). | BX260 (epub).

Unless otherwise noted, Scripture quotations are from New Revised Standard Version Bible, copyright © 1989 National Council of the Churches of Christ in the United States of America. Used by permission. All rights reserved worldwide.

Scripture quotations marked (RSV) are taken from the Revised Standard Version of the Bible, copyright © 1946, 1952, and 1971 National Council of the Churches of Christ in the United States of America. Used by permission. All rights reserved worldwide.

In chapter 13 one stanza of the hymn "Christ Is Alive" is quoted. Words: Brian Wren © 1975, rev. 1995 Hope Publishing Company, www.hopepublishing.com. All rights reserved. Used by permission.

Contents

List of Illustrations | vii

Acknowledgments | ix

Editor's Foreword: Vigen Guroian: The Icon and the Axe | xi
    Carrie Frederick Frost

List of Contributors | xvii

PART ONE: **Ethics and Reality**

1. Orthodoxy and the Transformation of Marriage | 3
    David Bradshaw
2. Eschatological Tension and Transfiguration: Guroian as an Exemplar of Orthodox Christian Ethics in America | 18
    Philip LeMasters
3. Notes Toward an Eastern Orthodox Disability Ethic | 32
    Katherine Karam McCray

PART TWO: **Inheriting Paradise**

4. The Wondrous Garden in Early Christian Imagining | 49
    John Anthony McGuckin
5. Love God, Love Thy Neighbor, Love the Trees: Ecological Justice in Orthodox Christianity | 61
    Perry Hamalis
6. A Garden Grows Around Him | 74
    Winn Collier
7. Return to the Garden: Vigen Guroian's Christian Ecological Ethics | 81
    Jonathan Elliott

Part Three: **Tending the Heart**

8 A Wardrobe of Images: Children's Stories
  and the Moral Imagination | 93
    Daniel B. Coupland and Rebecca Schwartz
9 Spontaneous Grace: Vigen Guroian as Teacher and Friend | 105
    William M. Wilson
10 Tiller of Significant Soil: Vigen Guroian
   as Teacher, Mentor, Gardener, Friend | 109
    Brian Martin Lapsa

Part Four: **Faith, Church, Mission**

11 The Earliest Surviving Armenian Betrothal Prayers | 125
    Michael Daniel Findikyan
12 The Truly Human Things: Virtues, Stories, & Teachers | 138
    Ani Shahinian
13 The Right Time and the Fullness of Time: "Timefulness"
   in Orthodox Interpretations of Scripture | 158
    Edith Mary Humphrey
14 Vigen Guroian in the Armenian Church | 173
    Shant Kazanjian

Index | 187

Illustrations

Figure 12.1: Yovhan Orotnecʻi teaching his student Grigor Tatʻewacʻi from the Gospel of Matthew. Matenadaran, image from WikiCommons | 141

Figure 12.2: Grigor Xlatʻecʻi, teaching from the Psalms: "Blessed is the man who . . ." Matenadaran, Image from reddit.com | 154

Figure 12.3: Photo at Oriel College Chapel, University of Oxford, May 2018 | 156

Acknowledgments

THIS PROJECT WAS INSPIRED by a book panel held at the Orthodox Theological Society in America (OTSA) conference in 2018 on Vigen Guroian's book *Rallying the Really Human Things: Moral Imagination in Politics, Religion, and Everyday Life.* My gratitude goes to both OTSA and to the Western Washington University Office of Vice-Provost of Research for assistance in the preparation of this manuscript.

Editor's Foreword
Vigen Guroian: The Icon and the Axe

CARRIE FREDERICK FROST

VIGEN GUROIAN WAS MY teacher and dissertation advisor during my doctoral study at the University of Virginia. Vigen was the reason, in fact, that I did my PhD at the University of Virginia; his presence allowed me to focus on the theology and ethics of the Christian East. He continues to be a mentor and a friend, and I am grateful for his presence in my life.

While I was in graduate school in the mid aughts, the undergraduate Orthodox Christian Fellowship (OCF) partnered with a Catholic group to host an evening of conversation on the Orthodox and Catholic churches today. The two speakers were both from the University of Virginia's Religious Studies department: the great church historian Robert Louis Wilken and the man we celebrate with this volume, Vigen Guroian. Those of us who had taken classes with Professor Wilken felt the comfortable assurance of a venerable elder telling us the stories with which we were familiar. He gave a wonderful talk that, even though typically critical of the state of Catholic worship post-Vatican II, ended on a hopeful note.

When Vigen's turn to speak came, he grinned for a few seconds before beginning—an inimitable grin that is so essential to his gestalt that it is referenced by several contributors to this volume. The first words out of his mouth were, "I've come with an axe." An OCF student behind me audibly gasped. Vigen proceeded to walk the audience through the poor state of affairs of the Orthodox Church's presence in America today. At one point I heard one of the OCF organizers whisper to the other, "What have we

Editor's Foreword

done?" The Q&A was lively. The Orthodox students looked rather shaken as they left the chapel. Accustomed to the sort of speaker that would showcase only the triumphal delights of Orthodoxy in an ecumenical context, they were brought up short.

Over time though, I watched these undergraduates, whom I knew well, grapple with some of what Vigen had said. Ultimately his words that evening and their other encounters with him led them to a more sophisticated relationship with their faith and its current realities in America. Which is not to say that all of them came around to Vigen's "Orthodox reality"—to reference a title of one of his books—but his vision made them question and adjust theirs in productive ways. At a dinner party I recently attended, I saw two of those students. They were still talking about what Vigen said that evening, more than fifteen years later.

I tell this story because it illustrates a quality of Vigen's work that has influenced my own work, but more than that, has left its mark on a number of fields to which he has contributed. Namely, that the endeavor of theology—and indeed of being a Christian—is not to be comfortable but instead to treat every aspect of the faith as a deep and salvific mystery, no matter how challenging or uncomfortable that is. Vigen will not make a specimen of Christian theology and life. He brings the axe.

But along with the axe he also brings the icon. When Vigen said he came with an axe that evening, James Billington's Russian cultural history *The Icon and the Axe* came to mind. Billington's title refers to the icon and the axe that literally hung over every Russian peasant's doorway. The icon embodied the sense of holiness and beauty and the axe, as tool and weapon, testified to the pragmatic functionality and capacity of the Russian people.

The icon also stands for the rich, beautiful, and inspiring sources that remind us of who we are, that heal us, that call us to a higher standard, that we can offer to those inside and outside the Church, knowing that world craves this sort of beauty and order. But we also need the axe; we need the cutting critique; we need the willingness and ability to speak frankly about our flaws and shortcoming and the threats to our world and to our church and to rebuild—the axe is ultimately a constructive, not a destructive, tool. Vigen Guroian brings both icon and axe to his work.

To characterize Vigen Guroian's career is a mighty task. Vigen has significantly contributed to many fields: ethics, politics, theology, culture, literature, education, and gardening as is seen in his dozens and diverse publications in academic and non-academic publications and his dozen-plus

Editor's Foreword

books. Therefore, I will not attempt to do his work justice, but will instead offer a gloss, encouraging the reader to engage with his many offerings.

Vigen attended the University of Virginia as an undergraduate and Drew University as a graduate student, where he studied with Will Herberg and wrote his dissertation (with Russell Kirk on his committee) on "Politics and the Moral Life in the Writings of Edmund Burke and Reinhold Niebuhr," commencing a lifelong engagement with religion and politics with the theme of a Burkean conservatism.

Very soon Vigen branched into other topics. In his early career, he began to make a mark in the world of Christian Ethics with his first publication *Incarnate Love: Essays in Orthodox Ethics* (1987) the influence of which cannot underestimated, followed by *Ethics After Christendom: Toward an Ecclesial Christian Ethic* (1994). Other books followed, including two beloved works that are ostensibly about Vigen's true love of gardening but offer an introduction to Eastern Christianity in general and a unique perspective on Christian eco-spirituality in particular: *Inheriting Paradise: Meditations on Gardening* (2000) and *The Fragrance of God* (2006). These two volumes are so poignant and profound that dear friends of mine have an annual tradition of listening to Vigen's related interview on Krista Tippet's popular podcast on Easter afternoon while they rest in their garden ("Restoring the Senses: Gardening and Orthodox Easter" recording for *On Being*, 2012).

Concurrent to these publications and no less important were Vigen's many and ongoing contributions to Armenian Orthodox theology and ethics, including his writings on the Armenian Genocide, including *How Shall We Remember?: Reflections on the Armenian Genocide and Church Faith* (2005). Vigen also continued to contribute to Eastern Christian theological conversation with *The Melody of Faith: Theology in an Orthodox Key* (2010) and *The Orthodox Reality: Culture, Theology, and Ethics in the Modern World* (2018).

Perhaps most beloved of his books is *Tending the Heart of Virtue: How Classic Stories Awaken a Child's Moral Imagination* (1998; 2023), which explores various subjects and themes that belong to virtue ethics in the classical and Christian traditions and is influenced by his reading of Josef Pieper and G. K. Chesterton.

In addition to his many books, Vigen has lectured all over the world at prestigious universities including Oxford, Durham, and Princeton and seminaries including St. Nersess Armenian Seminary and St. Vladimir's

Editor's Foreword

Orthodox Seminary. He belongs to all manner of professional organizations, offering papers and holding offices at places including the Center for the Study of Law and Religion of Emory University as the Distinguished Fellow of the John Jay Institute, Permanent Senior Fellow of the Russell Kirk Center for Cultural Renewal, and Board of Directors of the Society of Christian Ethics. He has served on editorial boards of distinguished journals including *Pro Ecclesia: A Journal of Catholic and Evangelical Theology*, *St. Nersess Armenian Seminary Theological Review*, and *The Journal of Religious Ethics*.

I have not attempted to mention and address all of Vigen's books, lectures, memberships, or honors. But I will note that a few features run through them all, even in their diversity: beautiful prose, a deep love of liturgy and conviction of its formative role in theology and ethics, and a willingness to engage with a diversity of sources not only from Eastern Christianity (both Eastern Orthodox and "Oriental" Orthodox), but also with the Western Christian tradition and all manner of poetry, music, iconography, hymnography, and liturgy. Readers will also find the icon and the axe across Vigen's work; both his doxological appreciation for Creation and Creator and also his uncompromising lack of triumphalism that urges his readers to both celebrate and lament the state of the paradise we have inherited.

I chose to divide this book into four parts, each based on the title of one or more of his books. These is much overlap across the parts, but I hope they will serve the reader well in considering his legacy. Part One: Ethics and Reality deals with topics of theology and ethics. David Bradshaw writes of the tensions between the idols and ideals of marriage in the church and the productive possibilities of these tensions. Vigen's influential legacy as an ethicist is taken up by Philip LeMasters, and Katherine Karam McCray develop's Vigen's work on disability ethics.

Part Two: Inheriting Paradise includes contributions that, in one way or another, engage with Vigen's vocation as a gardener and an eco-spiritual/ethical visionary. John Anthony McGuckin explores the theme of garden in the early Christian imagination. Perry Hamalis considers concepts of ecological justice from the Orthodox tradition. Two of Vigen's students muse on Vigen's work on creatures and creation and on their own relationships with him; Winn Collier reflects on Vigen's commitment to understanding the world as God-saturated, and Jonathan Elliott remembers his personal

Editor's Foreword

time in Vigen's garden and the influence Vigen's ecological ethics have had on his path as a farmer.

Part Three: Tending the Heart addresses Vigen's work on caring for the flourishing of human beings—children in general and longtime friends and students in particular. Coupland and Swartz extend Vigen's work on the development of the moral imagination that is possible through children's literature. Longtime friend William M. Wilson reflects on his early impressions of Vigen and their friendship, former student Brian Martin Lapsa revisits his formative years spent in Vigen's classroom and garden.

Part Four: Faith, Church, Mission takes up matters of ecclesiology, liturgy, and scripture in both the Eastern and Armenian Orthodox contexts. Former student Michael Daniel Findikyan offers insight into Armenian betrothal prayers. Ani Shahinian characterizes Armenia's ecclesiastical history and hagiographical tradition. Edith Humphrey works with time and Orthodox interpretation and scripture, and Shant Kazanjian testifies to Vigen's extensive work with, and effect on, the contemporary Armenian Church.

It is a pleasure and an honor to edit this festschrift for Vigen, who is worthy and deserving of gratitude and tribute from his students, his colleagues, and his friends. I, along, with the volume's contributors thank him for his role in our lives and work, and we wish him many years!

Contributors

David Bradshaw is Professor of Philosophy at the University of Kentucky. He is the author of *Aristotle East and West* (2004) and *Divine Energies and Divine Action* (2023) as well as numerous articles on ancient, patristic, and medieval philosophy. He also edited the section on "The Greek Christian Tradition" in *Medieval Philosophy: A Multicultural Reader* (2019) and co-edited *Natural Theology in the Eastern Orthodox Tradition* (2021). He and his wife attend St. Athanasius Orthodox Church in Nicholasville, Kentucky. Their daughter Marian is a co-founder of Draw Near Designs, a company that produces calendars and other materials for Orthodox children.

Winn Collier, a pastor for twenty-eight years, is an Episcopal priest and now teaches pastoral theology and directs the Eugene Peterson Center for Christian Imagination at Western Theological Seminary in Holland, Michigan. Winn holds a PhD in Religion & Literature from the University of Virginia, where he studied with Vigen Guroian and wrote on the sacramental vision of Wendell Berry's fiction. Winn has written five books (*Restless Faith*; *Holy Curiosity*; *Let God: Spiritual Conversations with François Fénelon*; *Love Big, Be Well*; and *A Burning in My Bones, The Authorized Biography of Eugene Peterson*) and for numerous periodicals, including *Christian Century*, *Christianity Today*, and *Washington Post*. Winn, his wife, two college-age sons, and their dog Gus live near Lake Michigan.

Daniel B. Coupland is the Dean of the Graduate School of Classical Education and Professor of Education at Hillsdale College, where he regularly teaches courses on English grammar, classical pedagogy, and classic children's literature. He earned a BA in Spanish from Liberty University, an MA in Linguistics from Oakland University, and a PhD in Education from Michigan State University. Dr. Coupland has written for a variety of

Contributors

publications including *Academic Questions, Virtue, National Review, The Chicago Tribune, The Detroit News,* and *The Washington Examiner.* He is the author of *Tried & True: A Primer on Sound Pedagogy* (2022). He, his wife, and their three children live in Michigan.

Jonathan Elliott and his wife, Ellen, own and operate Living Pastures Farm in Marshall, Virginia. He was an undergraduate student of Vigen Guroian at the University of Virginia where he earned a BS in Mechanical Engineering before completing an MA in theology at the Dominican House of Studies in Washington, DC.

Michael Daniel Findikyan is Research Ordinary Professor of Armenian Liturgy at The Catholic University of America in Washington DC, and Director of the Doctoral Program of the Gevorgyan Seminary of the Holy See of the Armenian Orthodox Apostolic Church in Etchmiadzin, Armenia. He received his doctoral degree in Eastern Church Studies (Liturgiology) at the Pontifical Oriental Institute, Rome, under the direction of the late Robert F. Taft, SJ. His research and writings concern the historical development, theology, and interpretation of the liturgical traditions of the Armenian and other eastern churches. Findikyan is a bishop and vartabed of the Armenian Church. He has served as Dean and Professor of Liturgy at St. Nersess Armenian Seminary (New York), Director of the Krikor and Clara Zohrab Information Center of the Eastern Diocese of the Armenian Church of America, and Primate of the Eastern Diocese.

Carrie Frederick Frost, editor of this volume, is Assistant Professor of Religion and Culture at Western Washington University. She received a PhD in Theology, Ethics, and Culture from the University of Virginia under the tutelage of Vigen Guroian. She attends to matters of women and mothers in the church, sacraments and practice, Christian material culture, and contemplative prayer. Frost is the author of *Maternal Body: A Theology of Incarnation from the Christian East* (2019) and *Church of Our Granddaughters* (2020) and Editor of Book Reviews for *Journal of Orthodox Christian Studies.* She is the mother of five, the grandmother of one, and lives in Washington State.

Perry Hamalis is Cecelia Schneller Mueller Professor of Religion at North Central College in Naperville, Illinois. He earned a BA in Philosophy from Boston College, an MDiv from Holy Cross Greek Orthodox School of Theology, and a PhD in Theological Ethics from the University of Chicago.

In 2015, he was awarded a Fulbright Senior Research Fellowship and was appointed as Underwood Visiting Professor of Theology at Yonsei University in Seoul, South Korea. During his year in Korea, he was ordained a deacon by His Eminence Metropolitan Ambrosios of Korea (Ecumenical Patriarchate). Fr. Perry is a frequent lecturer on topics pertaining to Eastern Orthodoxy, Ethics, and Social Thought. He has over forty academic publications, including the book he co-edited with Dr. Valerie Karras, *Orthodox Christian Perspectives on War* (2018).

Edith Mary Humphrey is the William F. Orr Professor Emerita of New Testament at Pittsburgh Theological Seminary. She is the author of articles on topics as diverse as the rhetorical analysis of vision reports, C. S. Lewis, theological anthropology, and justification in St. John Chrysostom and Calvin. Her eleven published books include *Mediation and the Immediate God: Scripture, the Church, and Knowing God* (2023); *The Ladies and the Cities: Apocalyptic Identity in Joseph and Aseneth, 4 Ezra, the Apocalypse and the Shepherd of Hermas* (1995; 2018); *Further Up and Further In: Orthodox Conversations with C. S. Lewis on the Bible and Theology* (2017); and *Scripture and Tradition: What the Bible Really Says* (2013). An Orthodox Christian, she is active in her parish, and speaks widely both in Orthodox contexts as well as among other faith communities. Her three married daughters and sons-in-law have given her twenty-three grandchildren, all of whom are in the Orthodox faith. In her retirement, she has completed two fantasy novels for them (and others) to enjoy—*Down the Valley* (2024) and *Beyond the White Fence* (2021).

Shant Kazanjian is the Director of Christian Education for the Eastern Prelacy of the Armenian Apostolic Church of America. He holds a MDiv degree from St. Vladimir's Orthodox Theological Seminary. Deacon Shant has developed, supervised, coordinated, and conducted Christian educational programs at both local and national levels for all segments of the Armenian Church community. He has translated the *Commentary on the Nicene Creed* by Archbishop Zareh Aznavorian from modern Armenian (2013) and is the author of *Praying with the Armenian Apostolic Orthodox Church* (2019), a translation of all the prayers from the Book of Hours of the Armenian Church from the original classical Armenian. He serves as the archdeacon at St. Illuminator's Cathedral of the Armenian Apostolic Church in New York City.

Contributors

Brian Martin Lapsa is Director of UK and European Operations for Memoria Press, Assistant Researcher in Roman History at the University of Latvia, and Latin Teacher at the Catholic High School of Riga. As an undergraduate at the University of Virginia he took courses in theology with Vigen Guroian. Lapsa wrote his doctorate in Classics, focusing on fourth-century pagan and Christian education theories, in Oriel College of the University of Oxford. There he also taught a bit of Latin and Greek. He now divides his time between Riga, Oxford, and Louisville.

Philip LeMasters is Professor of Religion and Director of the Honors Program at McMurry University in Abilene, Texas, where he is also the pastor of St. Luke Orthodox Church. An archpriest of the Antiochian Orthodox Christian Archdiocese of North America, he is a member of the Board of Trustees of St. Vladimir's Orthodox Theological Seminary, where he has taught adjunctively. Having received a PhD in Christian Theology and Ethics from Duke University, he studies applied issues in Orthodox ethics, including the implications of the Eucharist for peacemaking, marriage, and other aspects of Christian social witness. LeMasters' publications include *The Goodness of God's Creation* (2008); *The Forgotten Faith* (2013); and *Sex and Salvation* (forthcoming, 2025). He is married and has two daughters.

Katherine Karam McCray is a research fellow at Trinity College, University of Toronto. She holds a ThM from St. Vladimir's Orthodox Theological Seminary and an MDiv from Princeton Theological Seminary. She specializes in disability ethics and Eastern Orthodox moral philosophy. Her doctoral research focuses on negative representations of disability in global Christianities and symbolic alternatives from within the Eastern Christian tradition. Her work has received funding from the Louisville Institute, the Redemptorists of Canada, and the National Endowment for the Humanities through the Orthodox Christian Studies Center at Fordham University. She also serves as the Facilitator of Mental Health Ministries for the Assembly of Canonical Orthodox Bishops of the United States.

John Anthony McGuckin is the Nielsen Professor Emeritus of Early Christian and Byzantine Church History at UTS and Columbia University, New York, and currently a member of the Theological Faculty of Oxford University. He is a senior Professorial Fellow of Emory Law School, and of St. Irenaeus' Orthodox Institute at Radboud University, Nijmegen. He has written extensively on Patristic and Byzantine matters and is a Fellow of the

Royal Historical Society of Great Britain. He serves as an Archpriest of the Romanian Orthodox Patriarchate at St. Anne's in England.

Rebecca Schwartz is an MA student in the Graduate School of Classical Education at Hillsdale College with interests in literature, literacy, and the importance of stories to human life. She previously earned a BA in English at Hillsdale College and spent several years teaching high school literature and coaching volleyball at a classical school in Kentucky. She and her husband live in Michigan.

Ani Shahinian is an Assistant Professor in Armenian Christian Art and Theology, holding a post in Grace and Paul Shahinian Lectureship, at the St. Nersess Armenian Theological Seminary in New York. Dr. Shahinian earned her doctorate in History and Theology at the University of Oxford. She holds an MA degree in Near Eastern and Languages and Cultures from UCLA, and diplomas in Philosophy and Theology from the University of Oxford. She received her BA in Philosophy, Ethics, Public Policy, and Professional Writing from the University of California, Santa Barbara (UCSB). Her doctoral research addressed the question of Christian martyrdom in the context of political, socio-economic, and ecclesiastical history in Late Medieval Armenia. More broadly, Dr. Shahinian's research interests address questions of what it means to be human in a technological age, focusing on virtue-ethics and the freedom of the human will.

William M. Wilson is Professor Emeritus at the University of Virginia, where he taught Philosophical Theology and Religion and Literature for thirty-two years. During this time, he served as academic Dean and Director of the University's undergraduate Honors Program (Echols Scholars) and of the Graduate Fellowship at the Jefferson Scholars Foundation. Before Virginia, he was Assistant Professor of Theology at Loyola College (now University) where his prior acquaintance with Vigen Guroian became a lasting friendship.

Part One

Ethics and Reality

1

Orthodoxy and the Transformation of Marriage

David Bradshaw

Orthodox views of marriage and the family fall into two broad camps. Some find in these institutions the opportunity for a rich spiritual life shaped by love, self-sacrifice, and (ideally) the begetting and raising of godly children. They emphasize the spiritual benefits of the disciplines imposed by marriage and the capacity of love to move us beyond narrow and self-centered forms of thought and feeling. The family on this view constitutes a kind of "little church" that finds its fullest realization in the creation of new life and the shared love and service of God.

Others caution against the dangers of viewing any earthly institution through such spiritually-charged lenses. They observe that marriage and family, like so many other things, can become an idol—that is, a false god that is in fact merely a way of validating one's own desires for comfort, love, and security. They emphasize the need for asceticism even in marriage and point out that the sexual drive that is at the heart of marriage is inevitably tainted, if not by sin, at least by a certain carnality and desire for pleasure. Sometimes they also express skepticism about the prominence given to the family within contemporary Christianity, particularly appeals to "family values" and the accompanying cultural politics.

Vigen Guroian is a robust proponent of the first and more positive view of marriage. This is particularly evident in his sustained treatments of the subject in *Incarnate Love* and *The Orthodox Reality*. There he begins—as any Orthodox surely must—with the creation account in Genesis. From Genesis we learn that "marriage is founded in a sexual love that, when not deviant, aspires toward perfect union with the other," and that such union is "the primary good of marriage."[1] This does not mean that marriage is an end in itself, however; on the contrary, it is "an eschatological commitment and venture in faith" that aims to prepare the married couple, and the "little church" they create, for the Kingdom of God.[2] Male and female are the "elements and symbols of transformation" in the sacrament of marriage, much as bread and wine are in the Eucharist.[3] To welcome children as a blessing from God is an integral part of this sacramental transformation. Guroian has much to say about parenthood and childhood as essential dimensions of Christian marriage. He also does not shy away from the cultural politics that these commitments often involve, offering vigorous critiques of the campus hook-up culture, same-sex marriage, and the general de-Christianization of contemporary society.[4]

This is a markedly high view of marriage. Its strength lies in the continuity it finds between our biological identity as male or female and our ultimate destiny as transformed within the Kingdom of God. Yet not all Orthodox authors agree in taking such a high view. An interesting counterpoint may be found in a recent essay by Fr. John Behr.[5] Rather more than Guroian, Behr emphasizes that marriage is like monasticism in that it is a way of realizing "the fundamental Christian vocation of martyrdom."[6] This is a difference of emphasis, for Guroian, too, recognizes that marriage often requires great sacrifice.[7] A more marked difference occurs in their

---

1. Guroian, *Incarnate Love*, 110–11.

2. Guroian, *Incarnate Love*, 114–15.

3. Guroian, *Orthodox Reality*, 135.

4. See Guroian, *Rallying the Really Human Things*; Guroian and Wilson, "Sex and Danger at UVA."

5. Behr, "From Adam to Christ," 303–19.

6. Behr, "From Adam to Christ," 310.

7. Nonetheless, there is a straightforward contradiction in their interpretations of the crowns bestowed on the bride and groom during the Orthodox wedding service. For Guroian they indicate that "the bride and groom are king and queen of this new heavenly kingdom of their marriage" (*Orthodox Reality*, 136), whereas for Behr they are strictly and solely crowns of martyrdom ("From Adam to Christ," 310).

treatments of sexuality. For Behr, the sexual dimension of marriage marks it as necessarily belonging to our fallen state: "Procreation, and sexual activity more generally, is inherently *in Adam*, not *in Christ*: *One cannot procreate 'in Christ.'*"[8] The same is true of sexual identity in general: "To the extent that we identify ourselves by our sexuality, male or female (or, as is said today, anywhere on the spectrum between), we are in Adam, not in Christ."[9] This is not to say that our sexual identity will be eliminated in the eschaton (a view Behr rejects), but only that it will no longer "register," having been transcended in Christ.[10] Notably, Behr says little about parenthood or children, other than to assert that children are not the goal of marriage; nor does he mention anything positive about either sexual desire or the ordinary, routine domesticity of married life.

Broadly speaking, where Guroian sees continuity between the married state and the Christian *telos*, Behr sees discontinuity. This difference is hardly without precedent, for it echoes a similar difference among the Greek Fathers. St. John Chrysostom, whom Guroian often cites, offers a view of marriage that finds much value in married sexuality, raising children, and forming a household. His view is in some tension (although not open disagreement) with that of the more Platonically-inclined Fathers cited by Behr, such as St. Gregory of Nyssa and St. Maximus the Confessor. For them the very existence of sexuality is a concession to our fallen nature and can in no way contribute to our ultimate salvation. Much like Behr, they have little positive to say about sexual desire, the raising of children, or domesticity, seeming to see these as little more than necessary evils.

I have elsewhere given my reasons for thinking this Platonically-inspired view is mistaken.[11] Nonetheless, we must recognize how plausible it was in light of the common experience of marriage in antiquity. Until well into the Byzantine era, marriage was widely understood as existing for the sole purpose of establishing a common household and producing and raising offspring. The idea that it might also serve higher ends took centuries to percolate into common consciousness. It did so through a long and for the most part not consciously directed process. The result has never received an explicit theological affirmation—save, perhaps, in the Orthodox wedding service—and remains even today little understood.

8. Behr, "From Adam to Christ," 311 (emphasis original).
9. Behr, "From Adam to Christ," 313–14.
10. Behr, "From Adam to Christ," 313.
11. Bradshaw, "Sexual Difference," 15–35. See also Mitchell, *Origen's Revenge*.

I will seek here to offer a contribution toward understanding the Orthodox transformation of marriage. In doing so, I have no wish to take sides between the more affirmative and more skeptical views. Both offer important truths that deserve to heard. My main goal is to point out how the more affirmative view only became possible because of the development of an Orthodox consciousness in ways that, at first glance, had *nothing to do* with marriage. The very possibility of viewing marriage as does Guroian is a remarkable (although largely unsought) cultural achievement. It deserves to be celebrated even while we remain aware of the cautions put forward by more skeptical voices.

MARRIAGE IN ANTIQUITY

Aristotle devotes a chapter of the *Politics* to the ideal age for marriage.[12] Questions of love and mutual compatibility do not enter the discussion. The issue as he frames it is that of how to maximize the couple's childbearing potential. Since a man (as he believes) remains fertile about twenty years longer than a woman, the man should be roughly that much older at marriage. It is important, too, that both be physically healthy and mature; hence he concludes that ideally the woman should be eighteen and the man thirty-seven.

Although most did not reason the matter through with such precision, this discussion illustrates well ancient attitudes toward marriage. As Demosthenes remarked, "Mistresses we keep for the sake of pleasure, concubines for the daily care of our persons, but wives to bear us legitimate children and to be faithful guardians of our households."[13] In practice Greek women married in their later teens and Greek men at about five years older.[14] No doubt this age difference alone created a certain initial inequality, but the more significant factors were differences in education and social status. A man was expected to be sexually experienced at marriage (typically with slave girls and prostitutes), whereas a woman entering her first marriage was expected to be a virgin. The man's sexual freedom continued after marriage, too, whereas Greek women generally remained sequestered if the family could afford it, and in any case would have been expected to remain strictly faithful. A modern companionate marriage of

---

12. Aristotle, *Politics* 7.16.
13. Demosthenes, "Against Neaera" 122 (445–47).
14. See Brown, *Body and Society*, 12–13.

two equals was out of the question. This is not to say that there was no love in such marriages, but the love was *philia*, the affection that comes of living and laboring together. As Plato's dialogues attest, passionate desire or *eros* was more common between an older man and a male youth. A man could have *eros* for a woman—as Paris notoriously did for Helen of Troy—but to have *eros* for one's wife was considered vulgar.

Roman women had more freedom than those of the Greeks, but in other respects Roman practices were even further removed from our own. The legal age of marriage for a Roman girl was twelve. As Rodney Stark has observed, there is evidence that some girls married even younger, although the marriage did not become legitimate until she came of age.[15] Regardless of the bride's age, the marriage was consummated without regard to whether she had passed through puberty. Roman marriage practices were thus consistent with what we would consider to be child rape.

Repugnant though such practices are, we must see them in light of the demographic realities of the age. Life expectancy was short—less than thirty at birth—and furthermore, due to the widespread exposure of female infants, there was a dearth of marriageable women.[16] Stark cites a study estimating 1.3 males per female in Rome and 1.4 in the rest of the empire.[17] There was thus immense pressure to produce children. Yet the long-term effect of Roman marriage practices was precisely the opposite of that intended, for men as well as women found marriage under such circumstances unappealing. As the classicist Beryl Rawson observed, "One theme that recurs in Latin literature is that wives are difficult and therefore men do not care much for marriage."[18] It could hardly be otherwise when girls were married as children and expected to accept without complaint their husbands' extra-marital indulgences. Despite much official encouragement of marriage and children, and legal prohibition of adultery, birth rates remained low and adultery and divorce commonplace.

It was into this world that Christianity was born. Christians were sharply critical of much that they found in society around them, including abortion, infanticide, adultery, divorce, homosexuality, and prostitution, as well the general atmosphere of licentiousness and debauchery that characterized much of ancient life. They also "voted with their feet" in less vocal

---

15. Stark, *Rise of Christianity*, 6.
16. See Brown, *Body and Society*, 6; Stark, *Rise of Christianity*, 97–98, 115–22, 155.
17. Russell, *Late Ancient and Medieval Population*, 97.
18. Rawson, *Family in Ancient Rome*, 117.

ways that over time had an immense effect. As Stark has shown, Christian girls tended to marry at an older age than their pagan counterparts, due no doubt to the expectation that the marriage would last a lifetime and must therefore be entered into freely.[19] Christian men moved in the opposite direction, marrying younger than their pagan counterparts because they did not enjoy in the meanwhile the same freedom of sexual exploration. By the Byzantine era these trends produced an average age at marriage of around fifteen for women and twenty for men.[20] This convergence worked with more explicit aspects of Christian teaching, such as the ban on adultery for both sexes, to produce what surely must have been more equal and companionate marriages.

What Christians did *not* do was offer a full-scale program for the reform of marriage. Christianity was not a social reform movement. Abortion and the other acts mentioned were ready targets because they were *acts* that could be freely renounced by individuals. The very institution of marriage as it then existed, despite its many noxious features, was not an act but simply part of the existing furniture of the world.

By the same token, although the early Christians had much to say about right and wrong sexual practices, they did not challenge prevailing assumptions about the very purpose of sex. Pagans tended to approach this subject through a few simple categories: the purpose of sex in marriage was to bear children and (for the husband, at least) sexual release; that of sex outside of marriage was pleasure. Plato had explored the potency of *eros* as a means of spiritual growth and interpersonal communion, but he had seen these as occurring precisely through the *renunciation* of sex, and in any case he focused almost exclusively on the attraction of a man to a male youth. Only in the Renaissance did Christian authors begin, with considerable hesitation, to explore how the Platonic teaching about *eros* could apply to the relation of a man and a woman.

We might be inclined to think that the early Christians should have sought to articulate a higher view of sex by drawing on biblical sources. After all, Christ based his teaching about divorce on the evocative statement of Adam when God presented him with Eve: "This is now bone of my bones, and flesh of my flesh. . . . Therefore shall a man leave his father and his mother, and shall cleave unto his wife: and they shall be one flesh" (Gen 2:23–24). The reference to becoming one flesh places sexual union

---

19. Stark, *Rise of Christianity*, 105–7.
20. Talbot, "Women," 121.

simultaneously in two lights: as a sign or token of the permanent union of marriage, and as a reunion of man with woman, who was originally taken from his side. This statement is undoubtedly important for the ontological and moral depth it gives to what might otherwise be mistaken for a merely biological act. However, that very depth means that the value thus assigned to the sexual act is decidedly two-sided. According to St. Paul, sex can also make a person of one flesh with a harlot (1 Cor 6:16). The Genesis story thus does not give *intrinsic* value to sex; sexuality is like so much else, a power we have that can be used equally for good and for evil.

Lest we overlook the obvious, let me add that Christ cites the Genesis passage to exalt not sex, but marriage. Elsewhere he warns against the corrupting power of sexual desire: "whoever looks at a woman lustfully has already committed adultery with her in his heart" (Matt 5:28). St. Paul, too, although he offers a profound interpretation of marriage in Ephesians 5, says little about its physical dimension. Husband and wife are not to deny one another without mutual consent, a commandment that did much to encourage greater equality in marriage (1 Cor 7:3–5). Yet this passage goes on to recommend celibacy for those who are capable of it and to present marriage primarily as a remedy for concupiscence. It was partly in deference to these Pauline teachings that the early Christians showed little interest in exploring the positive potentialities of marriage.

THE MONASTIC REVOLUTION

But this was far from the whole story. Rather than challenge ancient views of marriage directly, the ancient Church executed what might be seen as a kind of end run around the entire marital-procreative complex. I would emphasize that to execute such an end run was not primarily its purpose. The purpose was to seek Christ, to glorify him, and to live in obedience to his commandments. Nonetheless, the Church in pursuing these ends revolutionized human society, including how marriage was understood and experienced, as well as how sex came to be viewed in its human and ethical dimension.

Much could be said on this subject, beginning with how the Christian understanding of God as one who loves mankind and underwent suffering for our sake was itself revolutionary. However, here I will concentrate on two factors that I believe were most immediately relevant to marriage.

The first was monasticism. A long-standing prejudice holds that the aim of monasticism is to earn salvation or accumulate "merit." Whatever may have been the truth of this in some times and places, it has no bearing on early monasticism. For the early monastics the overriding goal was *the recovery of full humanity*. This is evident in the *Life of Antony* by St. Athanasius. Athanasius offers a vivid description of Antony's emergence from the abandoned fort where he spent twenty years alone wrestling with demons. At the end he remarks, "he maintained utter equilibrium, like one guided by reason and steadfast in that which accords with nature."[21] Later St. Antony himself explains that virtue is natural and is lost only when the soul departs from its natural condition:

> For the Lord has told us before, "The kingdom of heaven is within you." All virtue needs, then, is our willing, since it is in us and arises from us. For virtue exists when the soul maintains its intellectual part according to nature. It holds fast according to nature when it remains as it was made—and it was made beautiful and perfectly straight.[22]

That is the point of the fasting, the isolation, the intense prayer and warfare with demons: to return the soul to its natural state where it directly experiences the kingdom of heaven that is within. The rest of the *Life* goes on to describe in detail what Antony was like in this restored and fully natural condition, including his teachings, his miracles, and his victory in debate with pagan philosophers.

The description of Antony might seem to bear little connection to sex or marriage. As I have mentioned, we have here not a direct teaching about these subjects, but an end run around the entire way they had been conceived. The ideal Antony describes is not limited to monks alone; it is a vision of the human soul that, if it is true at all, is true for everyone. To the extent that one believes it, one will seek to live accordingly regardless of one's calling or station in life. Antony does not describe what this would look like in the case of married persons, but any married person who took his teaching seriously could not help but be affected by it. In the succeeding centuries, countless husbands and wives embraced the monastic ideal of holiness as their own—not by becoming monks or nuns, but by incorporating the monastic ethos of self-denial, humility, and constant remembrance of God into their lives as best they could. We might be tempted to think of

---

21. Athanasius, "Life of Antony," 42.
22. Athanasius, "Life of Antony," 46.

Orthodoxy and the Transformation of Marriage

this as a sort of "compromise," but that would be to fall into the mistake of thinking that the monastic life is intrinsically better and more pure than life in the world. It is not; the two are simply different.[23] Part of the difference is precisely that monastics, because they can devote themselves fully to seeking and serving God, are in a position to blaze a trail that people in the world can then follow in their own way.

It is for this reason that monastic practices such as extended periods of fasting, regular confession, and attendance at vigils took root and became normative for the Church as a whole.[24] They were not imposed from above; they grew up spontaneously from the piety of people who had encountered the holiness of the ascetics, either directly or through the reports of others, and wanted to seek it in their own lives. Likewise, the reading of saints' lives and veneration of the saints through their relics and icons became enormously popular. This was accompanied by a growth in the population of the saints to include not only martyrs and hierarchs, but outstanding ascetics (such as St. Antony himself) and others who were models of Christian virtue.

For our purposes, the details of these practices matter less than how they affected marriage. The monastic paradigm set before people in the world a new way of thinking about their married life, as the arena in which they have been called to pursue holiness. After all, one need not be a monk to practice charity, hospitality, forgiveness, and self-denial; the sacrifices of a mother in caring for her children, or of a father in providing for his family, may well take this form. The ancient way of thinking about marriage as a means of legitimizing children and providing mutual support was thus enriched by a new level of meaning. Marriage became a spiritual undertaking in a way it had not been before. This new level of meaning was eventually codified in the wedding service, which remains the most authoritative teaching of the Orthodox Church concerning marriage.[25]

Sex, as so integral a part of marriage, was naturally included in this process. But here the transformation was even more indirect, for the early Christians, living in the hypersexualized culture of antiquity, were well aware of the dangers of making an idol of sexual pleasure. Some continued

---

23. The emphatic insistence on the superiority of the monastic life in the West was a product of the Jovinianist controversy; see Hunter, *Marriage, Celibacy, and Heresey.*

24. For a survey of such developments see Chadwick, *Early Church*; McGinn and Meyendroff, *Christian Spirituality*; Ferguson, *Encyclopedia of Early Christianity.*

25. See the careful explication of this service in Ware, "Sacrament of Love."

to insist, as had some pagan moralists, that the only legitimate purpose for sex even in marriage is procreation. Yet there was an important countercurrent. St. John Chrysostom viewed sexual desire as having been given to humanity, not only for procreation, but as a way of binding husband and wife together despite the estrangement caused by the Fall.[26] He saw sexual pleasure in the same positive light, considering it as an extension of the desire for offspring:

> How do they [husband and wife] become one flesh? It is as if you were to take away the purest part of gold and mingle it with other gold; so here also the woman as it were receives the richest part fused with pleasure, nourishes and cherishes it, and contributing her own share, restores it back as a man. The child is a sort of bridge so that the three become one flesh, the child connecting, on either side, each to the other.... Therefore he said with accuracy, not "they shall be one flesh," but [they shall be joined] "into one flesh" (Gen 2:24, LXX), namely, that of the child. What then—when there is no child, will they not be two? On the contrary, their coming together has this effect, it diffuses and commingles the bodies of both. Just as one who has cast ointment into oil makes the whole one, so it is here.[27]

Elsewhere Chrysostom takes it as obvious that intercourse into old age is not blamable even though it can no longer produce children.[28] Thus in his view married sexuality, even when it is incapable of producing children, retains its value as a kind of union and reconciliation of the two sexes.

---

26. John Chrysostom, *Homilies on 1 Corinthians* 26.2 (NPNF[1] 12:151). Chrysostom comments on the sentence given to Eve, "thy turning shall be to thy husband" (Gen 3:17, LXX): "God, considering the malice of the devil, raised up the bulwark of this word; and what enmity was likely to arise from [the devil's] evil device, he took away by means of this sentence and the desire implanted in us, thus pulling down the partition wall, that is, the resentment caused by sin."

27. John Chrysostom, *Homilies on Colossians* 12.3 (NPNF[1] 13:319).

28. See John Chrysostom, *Homilies on Titus* 5.2 (NPNF[1] 13:536): "No one would blame him who comes together with his wife lawfully even into old age, but all would blame him who hoards money." The remainder of the passage goes on to contrast the attitude of St. Paul toward sex within marriage with that toward a love of wealth: "Concerning wives he says, 'Defraud ye not one another, except it be with consent,' and 'come together again' (1 Cor 7:5). And you see him often laying down rules for lawful intercourse, and he permits the enjoyment of this desire, and allows a second marriage, and bestows much consideration upon the matter, and never punishes on account of it. But he everywhere condemns him that is fond of money."

JOY SO LONG DESIRED

Despite the positive character of Chrysostom's views, they still place sex and sexual pleasure in a fundamentally biological light, as natural concomitants of the desire to reproduce. Although the Church Fathers and the wedding service say much about the need for *agape* in marriage, they say little about the personal dimension of marriage that we today tend to consider so important—the desire to love and be loved, to share intimate thoughts and feelings, and to be valued for what one truly is. And they certainly do not place sex in this context.

This brings me to the second way in which Christianity performed an end run around the complex of assumptions that governed ancient thought about marriage. It did so by presenting a model of holiness even higher and more exalted than that of the ascetics. I have in mind, of course, the Virgin Mary. Her elevation to a central place in Christian life revolutionized how men thought about women, and thereby also how women thought about men and how both thought about marriage.

Mary, of course, had been part of Christian teaching from the beginning. Prayers seeking her intercession have been found on papyri as early as the third century. However, it was only with the rise of the monastic movement that she began to play a central role in Christian devotion. Church Fathers such as St. Athanasius in the East and St. Ambrose in the West held her up as a model of a life of virginity that is devoted to God.[29] The Christological debates of the fifth century gave her further prominence. Particularly through the work of St. Cyril of Alexandria, to identify Mary as the Theotokos, the Mother of God, came to be seen as essential to affirming the full divinity of Christ. It is in the wake of the Council of Ephesus in 431, which codified this decision, that we find the first great flowering of artistic and liturgical devotion to the Theotokos. Homilists emphasized that her purity derived from the presence of God within her womb. According to Theodotus of Ancyra in a homily preached at the Council, "the stainless Virgin was, as it were, burned pure through the approach of the divine and immaterial fire . . . so that henceforth she remained inaccessible to any carnal corruption." Theodotus also provides the first surviving example of praise directed to her through "greetings" (*chairetismoi*): "Hail,

---

29. See Rubin, *Mother of God*, 23–28.

joy whom we have so long desired; Hail, brightness of the Church; Hail, spiritual fleece of salvation; Hail, stainless mother of holiness."[30]

The importance of devotion to the Theotokos for relations between the sexes can hardly be exaggerated. Men were not accustomed to looking up to a woman as someone holier, purer, and mightier than they. There were the pagan goddesses, to be sure, but like all the pagan deities they were essentially personifications of aspects of nature. The Virgin Mary was a historical person—one who, by receiving God in her womb, had been "burned pure" and is now forever with her son, where she intercedes for us. Soon tales began to accumulate of the power of her intercessions. Some were of historic significance, such as when she saved Constantinople from the siege of the Avars in 626. Unlike the power of the virgin goddesses Athena and Artemis, hers derived directly from her embrace of her femininity as a mother. She is at once Virgin, Mother, and Queen, one who embodies in herself everything that is both distinctly feminine and worthy of reverence.

It was in learning to revere the Theotokos that men learned to revere women. I cannot enter into this subject fully here, for to do so would require a discussion of courtly love and medieval romance, topics that are well beyond our present scope. Suffice to say that devotion to the Theotokos enabled men to see women, in all their femininity, not only as pleasure-mates or potential mothers, but as fountains of goodness and spiritual wisdom. That is what enabled the slow growth of the kind of love that we call romantic. And it is what has led us today to see in marriage, including its sexual dimension, not only the possibility of pleasure, offspring, and a secure life together, but that of heart-to-heart communion.

TOWARD RECONCILIATION

This is a powerful ideal. Yet because of its very power, it is also dangerous. We are all aware that to seek romance is to court disappointment, and that even when found, romance can wither and die. Western literature is full of tales of people like Madame Bovary and Anna Karenina who by seeking romance were led to disaster. The challenge has always been how to seek heart-to-heart communion, or at least something close to it, without undermining everything that the ancients rightly valued in marriage—its security, its stability, its fecundity, and, not least, its ethical and religious sanction.

30. Theodotus of Ancyra, "Homily 4," 113.

Orthodoxy and the Transformation of Marriage

It is at this point that the wisdom of the Church's devotion to the Theotokos becomes most apparent. In honoring the Theotokos, men not only learned to honor women; they also learned to honor chastity. By this I mean not simply the rule of no sex outside of marriage, but the beauty and holiness of one who is pure in body and spirit. As I have argued elsewhere, the traditional rites devoted to the Theotokos, such as the Akathist service sung during Lent, lead one to seek to be chaste and pure as she is—not out of conformity to a rule, but out of devotion to a person.[31] This is important, for it means that when the Church brought the possibility of romance into the world, it did so in a distinct ethical context. Romance is rooted in chastity. To seek romance without honoring chastity is as foolish as to seek to grow fruit in a desert. It is to become another Anna Karenina, one who by grasping at false and enticing goods ends with nothing.

From this standpoint we can understand, not only the power of the Christian ideal of marriage, but also why it is today so endangered. We have kept the high ideals that Christianity brought into the world—equality of the sexes, romantic love, the yearning for heart-to-heart communion—and removed them from the ascetic and devotional practices that enabled them to be realized. To realize them takes virtues like patience, humility, forgiveness, and chastity, and these can be learned only through the very practices that generated these ideals in the first place. Having abandoned these practices, we are left with the ideals alone apart from the underlying way of life that gave them harmony and integrity. What remains of sexual morality is widely perceived as merely a set of rules not to commit adultery, fornication, and so on. Such rules can be enough for people whose faith is strong and whose determination does not waver, but we should not be surprised that the rest of the world, not understanding their purpose, finds them arbitrary and oppressive.

The answer lies in the union of the two views that I distinguished at the outset. We must recover the ancient practices of asceticism and devotion that gave Christian sexual ethics its original power. And we must do so, if not for the purpose of saving marriage (which would be rather grandiose), at least with a realization of their transformative power. This means coming to see how the rich and humane form of marriage so well defended by Guroian depends upon the rigorous asceticism and devotion to chastity advocated by authors such as Behr. It is only within the unity of the Church that these can be recognized as different aspects of a single whole. Vigen

---

31. Bradshaw, "Orthodoxy and the Beauty of Chastity," 3–11.

Guroian has made an important contribution to this process, and for that he deserves our thanks and appreciation.

BIBLIOGRAPHY

Aristotle. *Politics*. Translated by C. D. C. Reeve. Indianapolis: Hackett, 1998.
Athanasius. "Life and Affairs of Our Holy Father Antony." In *The Life of Antony and the Letter to Marcellinus*, edited by Robert C. Gregg, 29–100. New York: Paulist, 1980.
Behr, John. "From Adam to Christ: From Male and Female to Being Human." In *Orthodox Tradition and Human Sexuality*, edited by Thomas Arentzen et al., 303–19. New York: Fordham University Press, 2022.
Bradshaw, David. "Orthodoxy and the Beauty of Chastity." In *Healing Humanity: Confronting Our Moral Crisis*, edited by Alexander Webster et al., 3–11. Jordanville, NY: Holy Trinity, 2020.
———. "Sexual Difference and the Difference It Makes: The Greek Fathers and Their Sources." In *The Reception of Greek Ethics in Late Antiquity and Byzantium*, edited by Sophia Xenophontos and Anna Marmodoro, 15–35. Cambridge: Cambridge University Press, 2021.
Brown, Peter. *The Body and Society*. New York: Columbia University Press, 1988.
Chadwick, Henry. *The Early Church*. 2nd ed. London: Penguin, 1993.
Demosthenes. "Against Neaera." In *Demosthenes: Orations*, 6:350–463. Translated by A. T. Murray. LCL 351. Cambridge: Harvard University Press, 1939.
Ferguson, Everett, ed. *Encyclopedia of Early Christianity*. 2nd ed. New York: Garland, 1997.
Ginn, Bernard, and John Meyendorff, eds. *Christian Spirituality: Origins to the Twelfth Century*. New York: Crossroad, 1997.
Guroian, Vigen. *Incarnate Love: Essays in Orthodox Ethics*. 2nd ed. Notre Dame: University of Notre Dame Press, 2002.
———. *The Orthodox Reality*. Grand Rapids: Baker Academic, 2018.
———. *Rallying the Really Human Things*. Wilmington, DE: ISI, 2005.
Guroian, Vigen, and William Wilson. "Sex and Danger at UVA." *First Things*, May 2015. https://www.firstthings.com/article/2015/05/sex-and-danger-at-uva.
Hunter, David G. *Marriage, Celibacy, and Heresy in Ancient Christianity: The Jovinianist Controversy*. Oxford: Oxford University Press, 2007.
Mitchell, Brian Patrick. *Origen's Revenge: The Greek and Hebrew Roots of Christian Thinking on Male and Female*. Eugene, OR: Pickwick Publications, 2021.
Rawson, Beryl. *The Family in Ancient Rome*. Ithaca, NY: Cornell University Press, 1987.
Rubin, Miri. *Mother of God: A History of the Virgin Mary*. New Haven: Yale University Press, 2009.
Russell, J. C. *Late Ancient and Medieval Population*. Philadelphia: American Philosophical Society, 1957.
Schaff, Philip, ed. *Nicene and Post-Nicene Fathers, Series 1* (NPNF[1]). 14 vols. Peabody, MA: Hendrickson, 1994.
Stark, Rodney. *The Rise of Christianity: A Sociologist Reconsiders History*. San Francisco: HarperCollins, 1997.

Talbot, Alice-Mary. "Women." In *The Byzantines*, edited by Guglielmo Cavallo, 117–43. Chicago: University of Chicago Press, 1997.

Theodotus of Ancyra. "Homily 4." In *Mary: A History of Doctrine and Devotion*, by Hilda C. Graef, 1:113. New York: Sheed & Ward, 1963.

Ware, Kallistos. "The Sacrament of Love: The Orthodox Understanding of Marriage and Its Breakdown." *Downside Review* 109 (1991) 79–93.

2

Eschatological Tension and Transfiguration
Guroian as an Exemplar of Orthodox Christian Ethics in America

Philip LeMasters

Vigen Guroian combines clear-eyed realism with theological integrity in a fashion both rare and needed today. One of the first Orthodox Christians to contribute to the scholarly discourse of "Christian Ethics in America," he is the first to have monographs published by mainstream presses such as the University of Notre Dame, William B. Eerdmans, and Baker Academic, as well as the first to publish a host of articles in first-rate journals in the field. His publications, together with his faculty positions at Loyola College and the University of Virginia, reflect Guroian's commitment to bringing Orthodox ethics into the mainstream of academic discussions about pursuing the moral life. His many books and articles have contributed to a remarkable growth of interest in the ethics of Orthodoxy in recent years. More than any other scholar, he has drawn the attention of colleagues of various ecclesiastical and theological traditions to engage the wisdom of the Eastern churches on what it means to lead a good life in relation to God and neighbor.

As an Armenian Orthodox and a doctoral student of Will Herberg with a thesis on Reinhold Niebuhr and Edmund Burke, Guroian was formed to draw deeply and broadly on diverse intellectual resources with broad application to a wide array of cultural, political, and ethical concerns. Having drunk deeply from such wells, it is not surprising that he has refused to relegate Orthodoxy to the intellectual equivalent of an ethnic ghetto or to a romanticized version of a long-distant past in which quotations from patristic figures easily answer all contemporary questions. Quite the contrary, Guroian's work provides a distinctive vision of how the vocation to share in the life of God demands that people discern how to respond virtuously to the seemingly mundane challenges of organizing their collective life in the world as we know it. That his work has drawn such significant attention is all the more remarkable because he writes in an American setting in which Orthodox Christians are a tiny minority whose theology and ethics were until recently almost entirely ignored by scholars of other communions; all the more had that been the case for Armenian and other *miaphysite* or non-Chalcedonian Orthodox.

As befits a student of sober-minded figures like Burke and Niebuhr, Guroian brings sharp critical insight to bear upon claims that would present any political or social order as an unambiguous instantiation of virtue, let alone those that would sacralize such an order as a straightforward manifestation of the Kingdom of God. Guroian applies his formidable critical skills to such naïve projects consistently and fairly. For example, he rejects the historic temptation of predominantly Orthodox realms to idealize their heritage in a way that equates an empire, nation, culture, or ethnicity with the Body of Christ. He also criticizes idealistic accounts of the quest for freedom that expect of western democratic institutions more than they can provide and overlook the necessity of prudent discernment of how to sustain the pursuit of virtue in the context of given cultures and societies. As Guroian writes, "There is no global narrative of freedom. But there certainly is an alternative to the ideology of democratism. It is a prudential politics that respects freedom but seriously takes into account the pluralism of culture and the discrete histories of nations."[1]

"Christian Ethics in America" began with proponents of the Social Gospel who came very close to identifying the growth of God's reign with the inevitable progress of western culture and the church with a civil society imbued by love and cooperation. Whether expressed by Orthodox,

---

1. Guroian, *Rallying the Really Human Things*, 200.

other Christian, or secular voices, Guroian's antennae are finely tuned to recognize illusory claims about the pretensions of political orders to embody, foreshadow, or otherwise stand in uncompromised harmony with the fullness of virtue and blessedness. These sensibilities lead Guroian to reject Orthodox adoption of the accommodationist stances almost universally embraced by churches in the United States. Instead of finding ways to present Orthodoxy as another flavor, albeit an exotic one, of American denominationalism built upon secular procedural assumptions about the proper division of the spheres of religion and public life, he calls upon the Orthodox Church to manifest the presence of God's kingdom in the world. That manifestation will inevitably result in tension as the Church forms people in Christlike virtue who do not embrace bifurcated lives that underwrite various forms of dualism, such as between the private and the public, that are contrary to Orthodox commitments. The point is not "to impose a new, presumably more just, ethic of power on the world. Rather, it is the calling of the people of God to demonstrate his love for the world through their obedient service to his Kingdom."[2]

In light of how Guroian appeals to foundational matters of ecclesiology, liturgy, and sacrament, he cannot accept the American separation of church and state "as normative for the life of the Church or indicative of the real relationship of church and world."[3] Acceptance of such an ontological dualism would deny "that the Church is the world as redeemed and reconciled, eschatologically stripped of the sin that sets the powers and principalities of this world against the reign of God." As such, the eschatological tension between them could perhaps be described as a type of ethical dualism the resolution of which is manifested, albeit imperfectly in its present state, in the life of the Body of Christ.[4] While Guroian does not deny that Orthodox may "on prudential and pragmatic grounds live with the American separation arrangement," he thinks that accepting it as essentially true amounts to endorsing "the secularist notion that the world really does not need the Church of God. It denies that there is a serious connection between religious practice and belief and the conduct or destiny of worldly affairs or even worldly justice."[5] To embrace such a dualism would require those who commune with Christ and one another in eucharistic

---

2. Guroian, *Incarnate Love*, 181.
3. Guroian, *Incarnate Love*, 179.
4. Guroian, *Incarnate Love*, 180.
5. Guroian, *Incarnate Love*, 179, 181.

celebration to pursue daily lives that deny the truth and reality of "the primary experience of Christian worship, that in and through the Church God heals the ruptured relationship between his creation and himself, reconciling all in Jesus Christ (2 Cor 5:17–21)."[6]

Guroian identifies an approach very different from, for example, expressing Orthodoxy's opposition to abortion through appeals to "the individual's rights to life, liberty, and the pursuit of happiness." Doing so amounts to an implicit acceptance "that the only criterion of truth is a procedural one, i.e., how best do we protect the rights of the individual without influencing the character of her life or that of her society, since any attempt at such influence would be an infraction of the individual's rights to private and self-determination?" Such approaches threaten to obscure the Church's "vocation as a community whose faith in an incarnate God, born of a human mother, who has called that community to be perfect in his divine-humanity."[7] Far from abstract pronouncements of philosophical platitudes, the Church's characteristic statements against abortion "are primarily exhortations directed to a specific community about what kind of a people it is and what behavior is or is not fitting with its identity as the bride of Christ and the sacrament of the Kingdom of trinitarian love open to all life."[8]

Guroian is certainly not an advocate of the Orthodox Church somehow becoming so successful in a culture war that it takes over administration of the institutions of American government or restricts the practices of other faith communities. He recognizes that secular accounts of rights may provide at most "a rough approximation of the righteousness and love of the kingdom of God. But this justice is, nevertheless real, because God is real . . . and because freedom and justice belong to God's eternal covenant with us."[9] His critique of the separation doctrine forces the issue of the challenges posed by uncritically embracing American cultural and political assumptions, especially those that would compromise the witness of the Church by insisting that the vocation of the Christian life concerns only matters of the spirituality of individuals or the quaint customs of private organizations. In either case, Christians would be required to leave the practice of their faith in their homes and church buildings as they live in

6. Guroian, *Incarnate Love*, 181.
7. Guroian, *Incarnate Love*, 149.
8. Guroian, *Incarnate Love*, 150.
9. Guroian, *Rallying the Really Human Things*, 230.

the public realm like other secular Americans. Instead of constructing an Orthodox social ethic on the basis of such dualism, his argument inspires creative discernment on how the Church may embody the blessedness of God's reign as a sign of the transformation of all things in Christ, including the dimensions of the collective life of humanity that remain in strong tension with the eschatological blessedness celebrated in the Divine Liturgy.

Political agendas associated with all points on the ideological compass in contemporary America routinely compromise the deep commitments of historic Christian faith to the demands of essentially secular projects. They easily become forms of religious secularism that use appeals to God to serve movements primarily oriented toward the accomplishment of certain political or cultural goals as ends in themselves. Guroian comments that, in such approaches, "The antinomy of Church and world is often replaced with an almost Manichaean dualism, whether it be capitalism against communism, or born-again Christians against secular humanists and other subverters of American Christendom."[10] When that happens, the prophetic edge of Christian social witness is dulled by accommodation to dynamics far different from the "eschatological tension" between God's reign and the corruption of human hearts and communities done by the "violence of the fallen powers and principalities of this world."[11] When Christians proclaim a gospel that is defined over against a particular cultural or political movement, it should not be surprising when they are characterized more by the virtues of cultural warriors than of the disciples of a Lord whose kingdom is not of this world. It should also not be surprising when those who view such temporal matters differently reject not only the political agenda preached by the culture warriors, but also the Christian faith itself. It is not surprising that, when the good news of Christ is presented within the confines of a conventional political ideology, people respond to it as such.

Instead of envisioning the Church's social engagement in such terms, Guroian goes to the heart of the matter by defining culture as "the cultivation of freedom, reason, conscience, and imagination . . . embodied in matters and mores . . . promoted by education: producing art, craft, music, poetry and literature, science and the like."[12] It "helps to form and shape human society, but it is not reducible to society," for it "manifests the human spirit, freedom, and self-transcendence more freshly and with greater

---

10. Guroian, *Incarnate Love*, 173.
11. Guroian, *Incarnate Love*, 173.
12. Guroian, *Orthodox Reality*, 6.

immediacy than society does."[13] He sees iconography as manifesting "the Orthodox ideal of culture. For just as Christ and the saints embody and confirm the biblical truth about human beings as having been created in the image of God, so human culture may be an expression of that divine image extended into the world. God intends the humanization of the world but also its divinization. God would have humanity imprint the *imago Dei* on the world through the culture it creates."[14] Essential to fulfilling such a vocation is "the Eucharist [which] renders human beings fit to make culture itself sign and image of the kingdom of heaven."[15] In its celebration, "God calls on human beings to act as priests of his creation, to recollect and return the entirety of it with whole heart and mind to God as matter and subject (Rev 5:13) of the 'eternal liturgy' (Heb 8:1–2) in which the old creation is translated into a new one."[16]

A calling with such eschatological gravity may not be reduced to any type of secular project that seeks to replace Christ's peace with a "plan for peace in this world," as though "by human effort alone perfection is possible and peace can be achieved." Regardless of the virtues affirmed by secular agendas, Guroian sees them as merely imitations of Christian virtue "stripped from the ascetical and spiritual disciplines that remind those who exercise them of their complete dependence on God and need to repent that they may become holy."[17] Regardless of political ideology, those who think that the basic mission of Christians is to engage the world as yet another interest group that supports this or that party, candidate, legislation, or social reform measure have missed the point. Those uses of religion are essentially secular, not being oriented toward hope for divinization through the Lord who "rendered to God, though his body and blood, all of creation as one holy oblation transformed into his resurrected body."[18] As Guroian quips, "Politics reforms; the Church transfigures."[19]

Guroian highlights a related form of accommodation among Orthodox jurisdictions as the Church, "having been rendered an instrument of ethnic and national aspirations" due to often tragic historical

13. Guroian, *Orthodox Reality*, 9.
14. Guroian, *Orthodox Reality*, 13.
15. Guroian, *Orthodox Reality*, 17.
16. Guroian, *Orthodox Reality*, 16.
17. Guroian, *Orthodox Reality*, 59.
18. Guroian, *Orthodox Reality*, 16.
19. Guroian, *Incarnate Love*, 25.

circumstances, "substitutes a secular religion of ethnicity for the catholic faith."[20] The Church then becomes an instrument for preserving the cultural identity of immigrant communities. "The liturgy itself becomes one instrument with which to legitimize the other more important activities that must take place." Focusing on ethnic foods, dances, bake sales, bingo games, and fundraising then becomes the primary practice of the community.[21] Such a misfocus calls the current generation of American Orthodox "who have abandoned the old ethnic and nationalistic goals to a new uncritical identification of their faith with the American Way, just as their parents and grandparents equated their Orthodox faith with Hellenism and Armenianism."[22]

While some Orthodox in America may be part of sociologically defined diasporas, Guroian denies that diaspora is a Christian theological term. His concern is that such usage underwrites the "powerful myth . . . that Orthodox religion in the diaspora is derivative and inferior to what it was in the old country." It also obscures the catholicity of a church "not restricted to a single holy place, city, or nation. Indeed, God commands the church to disperse and spread throughout the known world, to be a mission of salvation to all peoples. . . . The church is catholic and apostolic and its mission is to all humankind or it is not truly the church."[23] Guroian notes that, in the context of American denominationalism, Orthodoxy faces "the single greatest challenge . . . of coming to terms with its particularity." Ironically, the free church tradition of Protestantism may provide an instructive example of "practicing their particularity as discrete disciplined communities of faith" with a level of freedom over against the larger culture similar to that of monastic communities in earlier generations.[24] Even as monasticism began as a demanding lay movement that provided the witness of a life in sharp contrast to the easy identification of Church and world, maintaining both "its catholicity and . . . a truly evangelical presence in America may well" require such an Orthodox "lay movement that reaffirms the truths of the faith, the call to holiness, and the vision of Christ's Kingdom." Instead of seeking to meet "external standards" of what counts as engagement in public life, the Church provides in eucharistic worship "a taste of the unity of

20. Guroian, *Incarnate Love*, 195.
21. Guroian, *Incarnate Love*, 196.
22. Guroian, *Incarnate Love*, 183.
23. Guroian, *Orthodox Reality*, 72.
24. Guroian, *Incarnate Love*, 186–87.

life and peace which nations promise but are unable to deliver." Regardless of how insignificant that might seem by secular standards, the life of the eucharistic community will form people who bear witness to their distinctive vocation "by loving acts and by entering into just relations with others, by timely rebuke of economic and political evils, and by pioneering new forms of human association and human service."[25]

In order to resist the temptation to seek first any version of a kingdom of this world, Guroian insists that the Church must provide "an ongoing and living catechesis" which enables its members to articulate "what difference it makes to be an Orthodox Christian" in America.[26] Liturgical resources abound for shaping the distinctive "character and conviction" of Orthodox people, beginning with baptism. Far from a "liturgical revival" that amounts to "the esoteric interest of aesthetic savants addicted to ancient ritual and music," Guroian envisions people formed by liturgical practice and spiritual struggle entering into "active engagement with society" in sharp contrast with the all-too common example of parishes with "a life largely autonomous of and unrelated to the life of worship and prayer." Instead of a private club focused on raising funds to meet the religious and social needs of members of given ethnicities, the Church must become "a leavening agency of discipleship and Christian mission" for the salvation of the world.[27]

It is intriguing that Guroian sees the Protestant free church example as being instructive for the recovery of a monastic spirit in American Orthodoxy that may form people with a distinctive identity to engage the larger culture. The experience of centuries of identifying Orthodox Christianity with set national or ethnic identities has presented all Orthodox jurisdictions with the challenge of how to foster communities that form members prepared to pursue paths of discipleship that do not assume the sociological and religious-political dynamics of contexts as disparate as, for example, the Ottoman Empire or Czarist Russia. American culture is increasingly secular, prizes the rights of individuals to believe and live as they please, and promotes a consumeristic marketplace of spirituality. It cannot be assumed that present or future generations will identify with given religious or ethnic communities. If Orthodox parishes focus more on preserving an identity of little interest to those who embrace the American melting

---

25. Guroian, *Incarnate Love*, 187.
26. Guroian, *Incarnate Love*, 200.
27. Guroian, *Incarnate Love*, 201.

pot than on cultivating a true spiritual ethos that provides a sound basis for faithfully engaging contemporary challenges, the grandchildren of their founders will be elsewhere on Sunday mornings and live their lives accordingly.

In such a context, all churches are free churches that must fend for themselves in the midst of powerful cultural forces that would coopt, corrupt, or marginalize them. No one is forced by government authorities to affiliate with them; it is certainly possible for contemporary Americans to cultivate various types of spirituality, make business contacts, fulfill their social needs, celebrate their ethnic heritages, and rear their children without any religious affiliation at all. Churches function as purely voluntary organizations, which magnifies the necessity of attracting, forming, and retaining members for the pursuit of a vocation so worthwhile that it merits lifechanging devotion and commitment. Such communal praxis requires asceticism, strong communal support, and spiritual sustenance that stand in stark contrast to the emotionalism, entertainment, and politicization that are so widespread in American Christianity today. As Guroian has argued, these dynamics invite—indeed, they demand—that the Orthodox Church sustain an ethos grounded in substantive catechesis, spiritual formation, and eucharistic worship.

These are not the characteristics of an ecclesial body seeking to escape or ignore contemporary challenges; to the contrary, they are markers of a worshiping community that shines brightly amidst the darkness as a beacon of transformation. In order to do so, Guroian recognizes that communicants must develop the clarity to distinguish "between Christian ethics and the secular ethics around them," making only "selective use of the culture's idiom" in a fashion that rejects underlying secular assumptions. At times, they must affirm publicly "the christic and trinitarian basis" of their claims in ways that surely make them appear "countercultural and provoke the criticism of secular antagonists." The Church today needs "exemplars and catalysts of human flourishing," and not merely "agents and lobbyists for social change" who use religion to achieve some level of cultural improvement.[28]

There are positive signs for American Orthodoxy in this regard. Guroian observes that "an unprecedented trend of large numbers of converts to Orthodoxy is presenting a fresh opportunity to renew the sense of mission and evangelism in the church and to emphasize anew the need for unity." At

---

28. Guroian, *Ethics After Christendom*, 101.

the same time, those large numbers of converts present challenges for sustaining the catholicity of the Church, as they include "disaffected, disillusioned, or embittered Protestants and Roman Catholics . . . seeking retreat and cover in Orthodoxy." They present the potential danger of bringing to their parishes and dioceses "strong strands of voluntarism and an impulse . . . to transform their 'new' church into an enclave opposed to the secular culture." While such communities would no longer be characterized by a given ethnicity, they would risk becoming "either a sectarian refuge or a fortress" for waging "culture wars in the broader society." Such developments would amount to a terrible type of accommodation to American culture, for then Orthodoxy would become an "inverted" version of the churches from which the converts came, "a kind of religious lobby" the identity of which is taken from the dynamics of partisan politics and serves an ultimately secular agenda. Guroian also sees threats to the catholicity of the Church when converts bring the American tendency to create "entirely new break-off denominations" into jurisdictions with ethnic identities, as they might try to establish "their own independent dioceses cleansed of ethnic proclivities and laxities that inhibit serious Christian living and the will to combat the secular culture or to separate from it." The "monastic asceticism" admired by many converts as "an appropriate response to the moral laxity prevalent in our culture" could inspire a divisive faction that does see "how much it has accommodated itself to American realities and adopted habits that are just as compromising to the Orthodox Christian faith as was the old ethnocentrism."[29] Such risks speak to the pressing need identified by Guroian for catechesis, a point that he originally made with reference to Orthodox from ethnic backgrounds. In light of the influx of converts, who have often been formed by religious communities that embody troubling characteristics of American culture, the need for deep spiritual formation is all the more pressing.

Many converts come to Orthodoxy from churches engulfed in battles concerning sexuality in which lines are drawn according to those of fundamentally secular culture wars. Guroian has made a major contribution by placing such matters in genuinely ecclesiological and eucharistic contexts that transcend shallow partisan dynamics. Instead of viewing marriage within the context of legal contractual arrangements between individuals with a given set of rights, he sees "a 'natural' sacramentality in marriage even in its fallen condition." The healing of matrimony requires that "its

---

29. Guroian, *Orthodox Reality*, 77.

character and intentionality must change from selfishness, carnality, and possessiveness . . . [and] must be reconnected with the divine purpose through its full integration into the sacramental life of the Church, centered . . . in the renewing and nurturing actions of baptism and eucharistic assembly." Husband and wife are united in marriage such that they become "an ecclesial entity, one flesh, one body . . . and through the relationship to Christ image the triune life of the Godhead and express the great mystery of salvation in Christ's relationship to the Church."[30] Used as an image of the consummation of the eschatological reign in Revelation, marital union foreshadows the blessedness of the heavenly kingdom. Even as it serves as "a medicine that heals the ruptured relationship of men and women," matrimony offers spouses "the dispositions and virtues necessary for building up his Kingdom," not as a utilitarian social achievement but as a manifestation of the eschatological reign.[31] The holy mystery of marriage calls spouses to ongoing growth in "Christian catechesis and discipline," for "as their individual destinies become more intertwined, so should their marriage become identified increasingly with the mission and destiny of the Church."[32]

In this context, Guroian clarifies why a Gnostic-like heresy underlies proposals for same-sex marriage. The holy mysteries "belong to God's act of creation," healing and restoring them for the fulfillment of His gracious purposes for us. Consequently, "they must not be spiritualized so that they are removed from their grounding in creation, which includes 'natural' and biological needs and necessities (e.g., sexual attraction that leads to offspring)."[33] This is not merely a descriptive biological claim, but reflects the deep doctrinal affirmation that "God has inscribed the trinitarian structure of love on marriage and family." He points to the child as "born of the love of husband and wife, attendant on the sexual nature and generative powers of male and female." The family is a reflection of "the primordial three that mysteriously comprise the *imago Dei*," even as the command to "be fruitful and multiply" (Gen 1:17–28) follows immediately upon the creation of man and woman in the image of God. Guroian follows Chrysostom in recognizing that "the trinitarian character of their sexual and procreative

---

30. Guroian, *Incarnate Love*, 110.
31. Guroian, *Incarnate Love*, 114–15.
32. Guroian, *Incarnate Love*, 114–15.
33. Guroian, *Orthodox Reality*, 125.

union" requires "the love that draws persons into communion."[34] The marriage of man and woman serves as "sign and symbol of this unique spiritual and sacramental dimension of human sexual coupling. This is what makes marriage a sacrament; and male and female are the essential and nonsubstitutable elements of that sacrament."[35]

Bread and wine are "natural symbols" in which Christ becomes present such that communicants participate in him as one body. Guroian teaches that "Likewise, male and female are the exclusive elements and symbols of transformation in the sacrament of marriage." Matrimony provides the healing and restoration of "the rift and broken communion between male and female that the fall has brought about." It is not by accident or mere custom "that the male is groom and the female is bride," for Christ is the groom of his bride, the church. Here is the fulfillment of "the nuptial Adam-Eve humanity" as "the analogue of the heavenly nuptials of the marriage of the Lamb in the book of Revelation (19:7)." The creation of the primordial couple is nothing less than "an epiphany of the eternal humanity of God" and "a prophecy of the Church" in fulfilling creation "through its nuptial union with Christ." Guroian concludes that no amount of "human willing and choosing" can alter "marriage's essence or the symbolism that God has ordained for it."[36]

In response to the radical redefinition of marriage in light of the presumed legal, social, and ethical equality between homosexual and heterosexual unions, Guroian suggests that priests no longer serve as agents of the state in signing civil marriage certificates. Instead, legal and sacramental marriage should be separate in America, a state of affairs not unknown to Orthodox Christians living under Ottoman rule and still today in some Middle Eastern and other countries.[37] Regardless of whether Orthodox jurisdictions follow Guroian's suggestion, his account of the dissonance between the church's understanding of marriage and that of legally established revisionist accounts highlights the necessity of catechesis that forms communicants to pursue a distinctive marital and familial vocation that is very much at odds with dominant cultural sensibilities. His focus is not on what view of marriage and family best serves public morality or most

---

34. Guroian, *Orthodox Reality*, 113.

35. Guroian, *Orthodox Reality*, 132.

36. Guroian, *Orthodox Reality*, 135–36. See also Guroian, *Rallying the Really Human Things*, 127.

37. Guroian, *Rallying the Really Human Things*, 123.

fully respects the rights of individuals. Instead, Guroian's focus is truly theological, being deeply informed by the sacramental vision and eschatological hope of the Church. Instead of attempting to launch a culture war by conventional means, he sees the challenge as one to be met by parishioners who intentionally seek God's blessing for the transformation of their "conjugal union" that "does not depend merely on the consent of the parties," but which "heals and restores the unsullied and perfect communion of male and female that existed before the ancestral sin and fall brought alienation and discord between the sexes."[38] Marriage is not, then, simply about beautiful ceremonies or joyful receptions with a given religious or ethnic flavor. Instead, it provides "a sacramental sign of the union of Christ and the church," even an icon of "the triune life of God, the perfectly shared and communicated love of the Father, the Son, and the Holy Spirit."[39]

Throughout his many publications, Guroian wrestles with what it means for Orthodox Christians to fulfill their vocation to enter into the blessedness of the eschatological reign while living in a world that resists its healing. Having identified underlying and explicit points of disagreement between secular and Orthodox understandings of this and other topics, he calls for communicants to gain the spiritual strength and intellectual clarity to discern how to live in communion with the Holy Trinity in every dimension of their existence and to respond accordingly to the particular challenges that they face. His vision is not one of essential accommodation to any form of secularism, but neither does he simply condemn the world. Instead, the goal is nothing less than offering ourselves, and every aspect of our life in the world, for the transformation possible only by sharing in the life of God. With antennae finely tuned to facile attempts to overcome the inevitable tension between Church and world this side of the *eschaton*, Guroian's is a voice to which scholars, students, clergy, and laity should continue to pay close attention. Those of us who walk on the path that he has blazed for Orthodox Christian Ethics in America are greatly in his debt.

BIBLIOGRAPHY

Guroian, Vigen. *Ethics After Christendom: Toward an Ecclesial Christian Ethic*. 1994. Reprint, Eugene, OR: Wipf & Stock, 2004.

---

38. Guroian, *Rallying the Really Human Things*, 125–26.
39. Guroian, *Rallying the Really Human Things*, 127.

———. *Incarnate Love: Essays in Orthodox Ethics*. 2nd ed. Notre Dame: University of Notre Dame Press, 2002.
———. *The Orthodox Reality: Culture, Theology, and Ethics in the Modern World*. Grand Rapids: Baker Academic, 2018.
———. *Rallying the Really Human Things: The Moral Imagination in Politics, Literature, and Everyday Life*. Wilmington, DE: ISI, 2005.

3

Notes Toward an Eastern Orthodox Disability Ethic

Katherine Karam McCray

When Vigen Guroian first published his "Notes Toward an Eastern Orthodox Ethic" in 1981, Eastern Orthodox diasporic communities in North America were not significant epistemic locations for ethical scholarship. In response to this minoritization, Guroian scaffolds the architecture of Eastern Orthodox moral theology using conditional language, shaping his observations as notes toward constructing an Eastern Orthodox ethic. However, his use of future progressive tense should not intimate that Eastern Orthodoxy lacks a robust ethical tradition, but instead that the sense of eschatological unfolding common to all branches of Orthodox theology influences Guroian to portray ethical models as always arriving and always unfolding. In this way, Guroian uses aspects of virtue ethics and applied ethics not to create an Eastern Orthodox ethic, but instead to describe it. To this end, Guroian begins by establishing a relationship between the liturgical or sacramental and the ethical. An Orthodox social ethic must, somewhat straightforwardly, derive from the social practices, customs, and beliefs of Eastern Orthodox communities in motion. As Guroian states plainly, because "Orthodoxy has not made a formal distinction between theology and ethics," it follows that "the distinctiveness of an Orthodox ethic is derived from Orthodox theology."[1]

This chapter highlights the distinctive features of Vigen Guroian's work that could enliven discourse about disabled embodiment. Because Guroian questions Western representations of human nature, his critiques offer a framework for habilitating an Eastern Orthodox disability ethic by decentering rationality and other performative abilities as core to the representation of the image of God in the human being. By instead introducing iconographic representations of the human being, Guroian emphasizes the non-fixed and participatory subject, who depends on trusted others to facilitate moral flourishment. In this participatory ecosystem, *theosis* represents not only the transformation of persons in community, but also the transformation of social systems. A just society constantly facilitates the ongoing moral development of the person, puncturing the border between the individual and the social community that facilitates the moral subject. Guroian's description of *theosis* is participatory on personal and social levels, meaning the person is facilitated by the community and in turn acts upon the community to strengthen and transform its moral goals.

Guroian emphasizes that personal transformation is facilitated by a community in an ethic of love. The social environment is what provides access to moral choice and personal progress in virtue. I argue that Guroian's description of *theosis* as social transformation dovetails with the social model of disability, which in turn could provide a theological account for accessibility supports. The social model of disability emphasizes the socially facilitated community that either provides access or creates barriers. Guroian's model for personhood, like the social model for disability, focuses on community responsibility, how social environments collectively produce barriers to access. Rather than centering on the individual's responsibility in a vacuum to access moral or material goods, Guroian's model for Eastern Orthodox virtue ethics emphasizes the community's responsibility to constantly evaluate the structures it builds—how it participates in social transformation. This focus on community facilitation can provide the foundation for examining how virtue ethics itself can be made more equitable and can, in turn, expand into how an interdependent sense of habituation into virtue might enact more equitable spaces for people with disabilities.

---

1. Guroian, "Notes," 240.

Part One: Ethics and Reality

A NON-RATIONALIST VIRTUE ETHIC

Prior to activist movements, disability was largely defined by what Michael Oliver terms the medical model. The medical model compares individuals to a universal standard for health that associates ability with wellbeing and disability with disease or pathology.[2] Other theorists describe the medical model as the individual model, emphasizing that the pathologizing of disability isolates the individual from others, rendering the person with a disability as a single anomaly to correct rather than a member of the community with shared needs and experiences.[3] Tobin Siebers describes how an individualist model enacts individualist solutions rather than systemic change: "A local street sign may designate the presence of a Deaf child in the neighborhood, supposedly protecting the child but also eliminating the need to develop universal forms of accessibility."[4]

In contrast to the individualized, medicalized definition of disability as a lack of ability or lack of wellbeing, Oliver constructs a social model for disability, which has become a catalyst for legal reform in the UK and North America. Oliver's social model unpacks how disablement occurs, the process through which a society fails to structure its buildings, social supports, and medical or legal systems around complex bodies. Disablement occurs when a social environment fails to facilitate access and instead minoritizes disabled experiences through a system of barriers. Nancy Eiesland, speaking from the social model, explains that the Church has often been complicit in justifying social and material barriers, becoming a space where people with disabilities cannot feel at home. The church exists like "a city on a hill, physically inaccessible and socially inhospitable."[5] Eiesland emphasizes the Christian tradition's reliance on rationality, individualism, and perfection when she surveys the historical Church. Rationality has so often been tied up with self-sufficiency and self-reliance that the only alternative Eiesland sees in historic Christianity is what she calls "segregationist charity" movements. Because Christian traditions have emphasized rationality and individual agency as qualities that define human nature, Eiesland explains, persons who have variable needs or depend on family members,

---

2. Oliver, *Politics of Disablement*, 78.

3. Oliver's early work, *Politics of Disablement*, also uses the terminology of the individual model.

4. Siebers, *Disability Theory*, 46.

5. Eiesland, *Disabled God*, 20.

caregivers, ambulatory devices, or medical care fall outside the Christian definition of being human.

Rationality often functions in Western virtue ethics as the quality that defines personhood. The *imago Dei* is taken to be rational capacity, the quality of the human being that distinguishes it from mere animality. Two major theological camps describe the image of God in the human being, which Molly Haslam describes as substantialist or relational. The substantialist account views the image of God as "some quality, capacity, or characteristic inherent in [the human being's] creaturely substance that renders it similar to God."[6] Depending on the distinguishing quality, a variety of scholars regard a particular capacity as the image of God in the person, especially as it delineates between human beings and non-rational or non-relational animals. Through comparison, Haslam highlights how such constructions can both devalue non-human animals and justify poor ecological practices in the name of human dominion.[7]

In contrast to the substantialist model, instead of determining the particle or substance in each human being that distinguishes us from the animals, the relational model for the *imago Dei* focuses on one's relationship with God. Haslam emphasizes that for this model, "the *imago Dei* does not indicate possessing something, but rather being or doing something."[8] Martin Luther's *imago* typifies the relational model where the goal of the Christian life is to restore the fractured and fallen relationship between the human being and the divine. Haslam observes that while some scholars, like Paul Ramsey, might want a stronger distinction between substantialist and relational models for the image of God, rationality is a significant feature in both systems, both emphasizing individual human capacities as essential. Even in the relational model, "the substantialist tendency remains, since the requisite participation in relationship with God requires the intellectual ability to believe."[9]

Rationality is the essential quality in a system which prizes knowledge of God in order to obey divine law, pursue virtue, and restore the divine-human relationship. Major figures in the so-called Western virtue tradition have held either substantialist or relational positions on the image of God in the human being. Thomas Aquinas, for example, views the image of

---

6. Haslam, *Constructive Theology*, 93.
7. Haslam, *Constructive Theology*, 94.
8. Haslam, *Constructive Theology*, 94–95.
9. Haslam, *Constructive Theology*, 95.

God as a scale of gradation with intellect—the more intellectual, the more fully a being embodies the image—and Haslam details how he imagines various intellectual capacities as necessary to be "proper image-bearers."[10] As Haslam traces similar constructions through other major figures, one conclusion remains steadfast, that persons with intellectual disabilities are tangibly other, outside either the knowledge based relationship or the rational capacities required to bear the image of God, rendering a group of human beings outside the definition of being human.

In both models, the association between rationality and personhood is so profound that the link between cognitive or rational faculties and human nature becomes the major theme against which disability theologians struggle, asking what other qualities of the human being could be swapped out for rationality—certainly human beings are relational, interdependent, social in a way that other animal species are not. Molly Haslam argues that our relationality is the image of God;[11] Tom Reynolds argues that it is our hospitality;[12] Hans Reinders argues that it is our bond of friendship;[13] Nancy Eiesland argues that it is our shared solidarity with Christ through suffering.[14] Defining the image of God inside the human being as a single quality that delineates us from other species links together each of these arguments.

Whether it is rationality, which dominates Western virtue discourse, or another quality of human behavior, the structure and logic of this anthropology is that there is a quality inside the human being that sets us apart, connects us with the divine, and marks us for a special type of moral development. Where rationality might become less central to the *imago Dei* constructions of disability theologians, Haslam points out that rationality still provides the moral infrastructure for these other image types because rationality is the primary way human beings are shaped as moral choosers, and all other constructions serve as caveats, preferential options for persons with disabilities but not the primary construction of human nature.[15] She contends that because of such orientation, even disability hospitable models for the image of God prioritize rationality as the primary quality

10. Haslam, *Constructive Theology*, 98.
11. Haslam, *Constructive Theology*, 98.
12. Reynolds, *Vulnerable Communion*, 177.
13. Reinders, *Gift of Friendship*, 223.
14. Eiesland, *Disabled God*, 67.
15. Haslam, *Constructive Theology*, 13.

through which God is known, experienced, obeyed, and proclaimed—and as such, this excludes persons with cognitive or intellectual disabilities from being fully human.

However, Guroian's vision of virtue ethics takes the Aristotelian construction of human nature to task on two points, its focus on rationality and its individualistic moral agent, arguing that unlike Western models, an "Eastern Orthodox ethic is a virtue ethic, but not a rationalistic one."[16] Substantialist and relational models for the image of God in the human being rely on the individual's abilities to know God through personal discernment and consequently portray the human being as a knower. Through individual capacity, the human being, unlike other animals, recognizes God through cognitive processes and relates to God through progressive knowledge, through rationality. In contrast, Guroian does not describe the image of God as a particular quality inside the human being, but instead offers an iconographic model for the *imago Dei*.[17] Rather than serving as a quality contained inside human knowledge, the image of God in an Orthodox framework is a person, the only full human being and the second person of the Trinity, Christ himself.

The image of God is not a quality that sets the human being apart, an emblem of human capacity or a trait that could be lost or diminished. Instead, Guroian restates, with the Letter to the Colossians, that "Christ is the image of the invisible God, the firstborn of all creation" (Col 1:15). In an iconographic representation, the icon portrays the archetype in a dependent relationship. The icon is not an emblem or merely an alternative term for the word "image." An icon has a reflexive and derivative relationship to the archetype, the original image, in an active and mediated sense. Christ is the archetype of humanity, the firstborn of all creation, and as icons human beings actively reflect and participate in Christ's human nature. For this reason, Guroian describes ethics and morality as dealing with "the restoration of the image of God in [humanity]."[18] It is not inside rationality or intellect alone that moral progress occurs, because "conscience is strictly speaking neither a faculty of mind nor limited to practical reason; rather it is a movement of the whole person in . . . intellect, will, and emotions toward the perfection of [the person's] nature."[19] The entire person, inclusive

16. Guroian, "Notes," 228.
17. Guroian, "Notes," 233.
18. Guroian, "Notes," 230.
19. Guroian, "Notes," 230.

of all variabilities and not merely one fixed quality, is relationally participating in the representation of Christ's humanity.

This relationality moves past rationality-centric models that require human beings to primarily be knowers, and instead highlights the revelatory relationship between icon and archetype. The image of God is not contained inside the human being in one aspect or displayed in one characteristic that one might be able to microscopically analyze a person's capacities and discover the one trait that makes human beings fully human. Instead, Christ is the image of the invisible God, and human beings, by being taken up into his incarnation and resurrection, reflect Christ together through our variable embodiment. The image of God in Eastern Orthodox anthropology, or in Guroian's reshaping of its ethical potential, is not an aspect of the person, a particle to be found underneath brokenness as a capacity or a quality that proves one's humanity or else be rendered as an animal. Rather, the image of God is the second person of the Trinity, the cornerstone laid before the foundation of the world, the new Adam.[20] Christ is the firstborn of creation and the archetype for humanity, meaning that the human attributes of Christ reveal the ontology of the human being, our composition. Where we see Christ dependent on food, subject to the environment, where Christ describes his own iconographic representation in the hungry, the orphan, those in prison, there we see the representation of human nature (Matt 25:31–40).

In the iconographic representation of human nature, the human being references Christ in a dependent way. The icon draws meaning from the image, reflecting and revealing a relationship between archetype and icon.[21] The substance of the human being is revealed through this relationship, combining aspects of the two *imago* models while also expanding them. Guroian explains that right reason is "not sufficient for [humanity] to achieve the full theandric potentiality of [human] nature."[22] The iconographic relationship between God and humanity transforms human experience into revelation, meaning that disability or variable embodiment is not ancillary to the spiritual life but instead revelatory. Christ as *Logos*, as rationality itself, serves as Guroian's model for right reason. Through communal participation in Christ, humanity becomes reasoned. In Guroian's social ethic, then, rationality is not a particle or trait that the individual

20. Guroian, "Notes," 230.
21. Guroian, "Notes," 230.
22. Guroian, "Notes," 229.

displays as a proof of essential humanity. Rationality is not an individual quality, but instead is a participatory relationship with the *Logos* through community and communion. Rationality becomes defined through an intimate relationship with the divine that is lived out through interdependency, introducing a relational model for rationality which can include variable cognitive and intellectual capacities inside the human community. This relational interdependency allows for a more capacious image of human nature, one which does not require an individual type of performative rationality to prove one's own worthiness or full humanity. Instead, rationality in Guroian's relational model is defined by participation and community contribution to the flourishing of the moral subject.

THE PARTICIPATORY BODY

Individualist models for autonomy and moral action have long been leveraged against people with disabilities. Shaping ability as natural creates a binary between abled and disabled, where persons with disabilities are unnatural, fallen, or lesser. If the human being naturally possesses an independent will and the agency to carry out free choices, then persons who lack freedom, intellect, or individual agency become, by necessity of a binary, persons with diminished capacity. When persons with disabilities are compared to individualist standards for health that expect fixity or a certain aggregate of qualities, disability is shaped as a deficit or a pathology to be cured. In healthcare models, individual autonomy is the goal for medical decision-making, which shapes persons who need facilitation toward making choices as edging toward diminished agency.[23] People who use communication aides, ambulatory devices, or depend on a variety of caregiving relationships often fear that their everyday lives might be seen as less valuable, especially as it relates to the potential of medical need. During the height of the COVID crisis, many disability communities expressed this fear as potentially life threatening, where doctors might consider disabled lives as permanently unhealthy and not intervene with lifesaving procedures.[24] People with disabilities face disproportionate medical bias, all because they are compared to a version of individual autonomy which many critique as an unattainable, often mythic standard.[25]

23. Beauchamp and Childress, *Principles of Biomedical Ethics*, 57–99.
24. Robin Wright, "Who Is 'Worthy'?"
25. Fineman, *Autonomy Myth*, 13.

However, in Guroian's social ethic, the person is not an atomized subject, but instead a dynamic member of a community which facilitates action and produces moral movements. The human being constitutes thousands of constituent parts, elements of other people's participation in one's development over the lifecycle. While able to differentiate the individual, Guroian uses a Chalcedonian formulation to specify that each person, made in Christ's image, is separate but undivided.[26] The individual's borders can be dotted and outlined, but never made to be so distinct as to be separated from the human community which facilitates moral action. Who we are is knitted from the participation of trusted others, often in unseen and unacknowledged ways. Like St. Maximus the Confessor suggests, the person is a microcosm of the universe,[27] individuated but not isolated, a collection of thousands of other unseen saints who have made the social, spiritual, and material environments in which we live and grow. In this socially facilitative community, one of the key elements of Guroian's anthropology comes alive—*theosis*, which functions both as personal or intercommunal transformation and social transformation. The spiritual transformation of the person inside an interdependent community forms the cornerstone to Guroian's imagination of a just society.

This is a participatory model for transformation, not an individualistic or isolated orientation but rather a tapestry of influence. Trusted others facilitate the social and material environments for personal transformation, meaning that the actions of others contribute to moral wellbeing and flourishment of the individual—whom Guroian describes as individuated but not isolated—who then in turn participates in the facilitation of others in the community. This participatory environment alters the moral subject in Guroian's social ethic. He explains that when autonomy begins with ego—as *auto nomos* or self-governed—it trends toward isolation and unsociability.[28] When self-sufficiency is assumed of the moral subject, the human being is described as autonomous, individual, self-secured, and self-directed. In such a model, the individual will is expected to secure social and material goods for the self or else be unnatural, behaving in ways that are dependent rather than independent.

However, Guroian challenges individual autonomy as a core trait of human nature. Unlike an atomistic type of autonomy, *individuated* rather

---

26. Guroian, "Notes," 233.
27. Maximus the Confessor, "Ambiguum 41," 105.
28. Guroian, "Notes," 233.

than individual personhood functions for Guroian as both distinctive and communal.[29] Guroian uses the Trinitarian relationship to describe communal love.[30] In a relationship defined by divine love, the individual's needs cannot become collapsed in the collective. Likewise, the individuated subject cannot arise without the constant facilitation of the community, even where such facilitation might be concealed or less visible through distance. We may not be aware of all the layers of production that go into food systems, for example, but the person who is ignorant is no less reliant on healthy food than the person who is aware of her deep dependency. Both the person who is aware of one's dependent subjectivity and the one who believes themselves to be individually autonomous and self-reliant are dependent on social factors beyond their individual control or production. As St. Basil describes, social contingency impacts a wide range of unseen disciplines, industries that provide food, shelter, clothing, and safety. Each human being is reliant upon the farmer for food, the textile worker for clothing, the lawmaker for social safety, and the physician for physical health. Each of these disciplines are icons of dependency, that the wellbeing and flourishment of the human being relies upon the work of others, though often unacknowledged. In turn these dependencies figure our dependency on God, St. Basil explains, because each aspect of material and social facilitation is "vouchsafed by God."[31]

That we are embodied introduces variable needs. Human wellbeing is contingent on a myriad of factors: access to clean water, nutritious food, education, medical care. Access, however, is itself contingent upon a social community that facilitates a diverse range of physical and intellectual capacities across the lifecycle. In this way, the human being is not fixed but instead contingent on physical and social needs, meaning that the moral subject is variable, dependent on others for access to material goods, and reliant on social supports. Each of us has what Tobin Siebers calls a variable body.[32] Guroian positions this type of variability and social contingency as central to human relationships. Interdependency is human nature, and Guroian explains that Orthodox theology asserts that "division of our common nature into selves which assert themselves over and against other

---

29. Guroian, "Notes," 233.
30. Guroian, "Notes," 233.
31. Basil of Caesarea, "Long Rules," 330–36.
32. Siebers, *Disability Theory*, 184.

selves represents the deprivation of love, the loss of genuine freedom, and the disintegration of personality."[33]

The human being acts in full freedom when in cooperation with others. The trusted community facilitates individuation and the full realization of personality and distinctiveness. Here Guroian amplifies his application of the Chalcedonian formulation further, describing the human being as both highly participatory and yet distinctive, individuated but undivided. Human nature is both contingent on the participation of others and fully realized when being nurtured in distinctiveness through love. Failing to recognize our shared contingency and reliance on one another, for Guroian, amounts to a denial and deprivation of love wherein the human community fractures and each member operates in isolation and competition instead of in communion—"a deprivation of love accounts for humanity's attraction to the polar extremes of either an anarchy of competing autonomous 'selves' or a totalitarian order in which the person is diminished to a mere individual and part of the social 'organism.'"[34] In contrast to the isolation of broken communion, love ought to unify but not consume, unite individuated members without subsuming them—"love unites persons, it does not reduce them to parts of a whole."[35]

For this reason, Guroian concludes that "love is freedom, but also the negation of autonomy. Love is the very 'energy' or movement . . . whereby the 'self' is renounced and a communion of persons who are of one nature and will is realized."[36] In Guroian's vision of the community, united through divine love, there is one human nature, not many. Because his ethic is non-rationalistic and non-individualistic, Guroian resists the configuration of human nature around many disparate capacities and thereby undermines constructions of the human person which would valorize the individual, autonomous body as natural, and castigate variability and disability as unnatural or less human. If there is one human nature, united in love with Christ, then all persons in the community are united in love under one human nature. The participatory body reveals to us that all of us participate in the mediation and facilitation of the community, however in distinctive and individuated ways. This means a person with intellectual disabilities participates in the mediation and facilitation of the community differently

33. Guroian, "Notes," 233.
34. Guroian, "Notes," 233.
35. Guroian, "Notes," 233.
36. Guroian, "Notes," 233.

than a person without disabilities, but both are equally included in human nature as they live out their interdependencies. Both are facilitated, yet in different and distinctive ways. It is not that a person with disabilities is facilitated and a person without disabilities is not facilitated, but instead that the distinctiveness of the individuated person makes a specific moral claim on the community according to one's own variability. We are not a community of independent selves and dependent selves, abled and disabled, but instead a community of equally contingent and reliant persons who are all variable in different ways.

THEOSIS AS SOCIAL TRANSFORMATION

Guroian's description of *theosis* has a vulnerable subject with a variable body in mind. By challenging individual autonomy as essential to human nature, Guroian recenters an Orthodox social ethic around love, augmenting the participatory and facilitative community as key to personal wellbeing. Love includes dynamism, sensitivity, specificity, and responsiveness. Love sacrifices for another's benefit, prioritizes togetherness, and remains open. Guroian describes a love ethic as self-sacrificial and kenotic but only in the context of *theosis*, only in completion, not as if self-emptying is a complete act alone. Many disability theologies emphasize the suffering of isolation and disability, that disabled persons face disproportionate judgment and hardship through social and environmental barriers.[37] The model of the suffering servant, for example, often provides the theological justification for ignoring the ways in which suffering for people with disabilities stems from injustice rather than from disability itself.[38]

Kenosis by and large has not been a theme which empowers persons with disabilities, but instead provides a dangerous theological justification for social humiliation. Disabled people face stigmatization and exclusion, and *kenosis* or self-emptying justifies such injustices as opportunities for transcendence with the right personal outlook. In this way, *kenosis*-forward theologies may obscure the experiences of discrimination, as though such isolation comes packaged with disability itself rather than produced through social harms.[39] Theologies of self-emptying often communicate little difference between the experiences of suffering that come with being human,

---

37. Eiesland, *Disabled God*, 39.
38. Eiesland, *Disabled God*, 20.
39. Eiesland, *Disabled God*, 39.

like chronic pain or susceptibility to injury, and the types of suffering that are derived from the sins of others—the injustices of judgment, isolation, and bias that historically segregate and exclude people with disabilities from full participation in legal, medical, social and religious spaces. *Kenosis* often does more to justify suffering as a general experience than to identify specific injustices, hampering meaningful solidarity toward social change.

However, Guroian does not describe *kenosis* as a mere self-emptying. He argues that an Eastern Orthodox ethic must shape love through social transformation. Self-sacrifice is not in itself a complete moral action: "*Agape* is a love which descends in order to elevate, unite, and transfigure. And it is self-emptying love in order to fill all things with the divine life."[40] In this way, a love which iconographically figures both the Trinitarian qualities of distinction and unity does more than self-sacrifice, it elevates. Christ's love enters into human existence and is brought low to in turn elevate and restore humanity through love. *Kenosis* is incomplete without *theosis*. *Theosis* involves transformation through both movements of love—through the *kenosis* involved in entering into another's experience of being brought low, and through *theosis* involved in the transformative elevation of the person. Both movements of love are essential. Love which empties must also elevate, and when applied to an Eastern Orthodox disability ethic, this example of love must recognize the distinctiveness of each person with disabilities while also elevating the dignity of the person made in Christ's image, requiring the community to act upon social injustice and material inaccessibility. Love must not only require self-sacrifice but also elevation, not only *kenosis* but *theosis*, self-sacrifice made perfect through communion, self-sacrifice toward social transformation.

The experiences of persons with disabilities need to be seen by the community, their needs met by the community, voices of generations heard by the community—because it is the community's moral obligation in an ethic of love to partner with the *kenosis* of persons with disabilities to facilitate *theosis*. The community, as the moral facilitator, has social obligations to persons with disabilities to provide the material and spiritual environments required for their flourishing, such that we would see how persons with disabilities have experienced injustice and been brought low because of social harms and we would correspondingly recognize that such injustices need to be transformed. That Christ entered into states of degradation to show solidarity with us does not justify injustice or valorize suffering.

40. Guroian, "Notes," 232.

Instead, it proves to the community that the purpose of entering into another's experience of injustice is not merely self-sacrifice but also to elevate, not merely to empty oneself or divest of one's security but to complete this act with love. *Kenosis* is incomplete without *theosis*, without recognizing how certain moral obligations are woven throughout a social ethic of love.

CONCLUSION

Guroian's vision of *theosis* includes transforming our social systems and recognizing a communal sense of moral responsibility. This more global and community focus in moral facilitation, when applied to disability, makes material and social accessibility for persons with disabilities a moral imperative. Often when we consider accessibility, we imagine buildings, perhaps building ramps where stairs currently exist, but not creating accessible theologies. Guroian's sense of Eastern Orthodox social ethics unfolding gives the community the foundation for considering how to restructure more than the material spaces we create, but also the belief systems which produce them. If we have an independent, autonomous, and self-sufficient moral actor in mind when we speak about community responsibility, then the variable and changing body becomes an anomaly, rather than common to human embodiment.

By uprooting these atomistic definitions of human nature, Guroian introduces alternative constructions of self-sacrifice and transformation which revolve around the non-fixed moral subject who is always changing, being acted upon, depending on others, and in turn transforming interdependent relationships in participatory love. A non-rationalistic virtue ethic means eschewing performative rationality and constructions of the human being which seek to prove some persons as non-human. Guroian's ethic of love pushes the moral community beyond conversations of whether or not the human being meets the standards for what it means to be human and asks instead how communion operates in responsiveness to the needs of the individuated subject. By challenging individualistic and rationalistic constructions of the human person, Guroian's vision of Eastern Orthodox social ethics gives the framework for the development of an applied disability ethic that recognizes the diversity of disabled persons and the innate worth of disabled experiences.

BIBLIOGRAPHY

Basil of Caesarea. "The Long Rules, Q. 55." In *Ascetical Works*, edited by M. Monica Wagner, 330–36. Fathers of the Church 9. Washington, DC: Catholic University of America Press, 2010.

Beauchamp, Tom L., and James F. Childress. *Principles of Biomedical Ethics*. 6th ed. New York: Oxford University Press, 2009.

Eiesland, Nancy L. *The Disabled God: Toward a Liberatory Theology of Disability*. Nashville: Abingdon, 1994.

Fineman, Martha Albertson. *The Autonomy Myth: A Theory of Dependency*. New York: New Press, 2005.

Guroian, Vigen. "Notes Toward an Eastern Orthodox Ethic." *Journal of Religious Ethics* 9.2 (1981) 228–44.

Haslam, Molly C. *A Constructive Theology of Intellectual Disability: Human Being as Mutuality and Response*. New York: Fordham University Press, 2011.

Maximus the Confessor. "Ambiguum 41." In *On Difficulties in the Church Fathers*, edited by Nicholas Constas, 2:102–21. Cambridge: Harvard University Press, 2014.

Oliver, Michael. *The Politics of Disablement*. Basingstoke: Macmillan, 1990.

Reynolds, Thomas E. *Vulnerable Communion a Theology of Disability and Hospitality*. Grand Rapids: Brazos, 2008.

Reinders, Hans S. *Receiving the Gift of Friendship: Profound Disability, Theological Anthropology, and Ethics*. Grand Rapids: Eerdmans, 2008.

Siebers, Tobin. *Disability Theory*. Ann Arbor: University of Michigan Press, 2008.

Wright, Robin. "Who Is 'Worthy'? Deaf-Blind People Fear That Doctors Won't Save Them from the Coronavirus." *New Yorker*, April 28, 2020.

Part Two

Inheriting Paradise

4

The Wondrous Garden in Early Christian Imagining

John Anthony McGuckin

There is a tendency in gardens that runs away, if it can, into wildness: an entropy of landscape. The priest-poet Gerard Manley Hopkins famously lauded that *energeia* of the natural world, which refuses to be tamed, in his poem "Inversnaid." This celebrates a little tumbling stream that runs through wild heather and bracken and falls like a thread of silver from a height into Loch Lomond below. The final verse ends with: "What would the world be, once bereft / Of wet and of wildness? Let them be left . . . / Long live the weeds and the wilderness yet."[1] It is a sentiment I fully share: but only by the shores of Loch Lomond; decidedly not in my garden: which strangely enough (though I did not know it at the time we bought the house) is sandwiched between "Orchard Road," and "Eden Lane": thus giving me some claim, however slight, to have inherited the horticulture of the Garden of Eden.

Vigen Guroian has taught me, as well as countless others, to think of the garden as a theological symbol and proving ground. He is the θεολόγος του κῆπου; the theologian of the garden grove; in a similar way to how

1. Hopkins, "Inversnaid."

Hermann Hesse stands as its *Magus*.[2] He has brought back into the theological imagination a long overdue corrective to the profoundly depressed way in which many parts of ancient Christian literature approached the concept of the garden: lamenting its paradisial loss (before quite understanding its paradisial significance) and elevating the story of the garden as a threnody to explain why life in the cold[3] and barren wilderness[4] into which Adam and Eve were banished (namely this lush and radiantly beautiful world) is a harsh punishment that brought us, as a species, to sorrow and death. Subsequent Christian imagination, has often thrilled to push this sorrowful lamentation[5] to the forefront of its mind,[6] sometimes even to the point of overwhelming the evident fact of the natural world's immense and sacred beauty, as well as the even more luminous faith the church has now been given in the power of the Resurrection of its Lord: the *Anastasis* as redemptive grace illumining and transfiguring the Cosmos.

Were there no other readings apart from the threnody of being cast out of the paradisial garden: that is, the garden as a locked gate, with us on the wrong side: in the lane, in the dust, weeping for the lost sights and perfumes, and gracious conversation we might have enjoyed there? Well let's see.

In antiquity a garden was not a common thing. Even the Genesis account wishes to stress the unusual features of the Paradise[7] Garden by

---

2. Hesse, *Hours in the Garden*.

3. Needing divinely-fashioned skins to warm our chilled flesh. "And the Lord God made vestiment out of animal skins for Adam and his wife, and so he vestured them" (Gen 3:21, all scripture translations in this article are my own versions).

4. Needing sorrowful work to make anything grow. "Because of what you have done, the earth will be under a curse. You will have to work hard all your life to make it produce enough food for you. It will produce weeds and thorns, and you will be forced to eat wild plants. You will have to work hard and sweat to make the earth produce anything, until you go back to the earth from which you were formed. From dirt you were made, and to dirt you shall return" (Gen 3:17–19).

5. The lamenting mind-scape of a gardener exiled into the sandy wilderness of Iraq.

6. As, for example, in Augustine's desire to forefront the view of all humanity as *massa damnata et damnabilis* as a result of Adam's sin (Augustine, *To Simplicianus* 27). The idea runs strongly in much of Latin theology, though not all, and thus proved to be a very pessimistic ingredient of the Radical Reformed movement. The *Easter Exultet* (c. 500–700), however, offered a more fitting footnote to it with its verse: "*O felix culpa quae talem ac tantum meruit habere Redemptorem* [O happy fault that merited such and so great a Redeemer!]."

7. The word in Greek (παραδέισος) means an enclosed grove; from the Medean-Persian *paridaiza* (enclosed yard). After Origen, the term Paradise sometimes meant

dwelling on its abundant water and numerous fruit trees clustered around the sacred Tree of Life, and its closeness to the land of Havilah which offered the prospect of gold, perfumes and precious stones (Gen 2:8–12). The Genesis narrative suggests that the human being was created precisely in order to enjoy this garden of God, but specifically as its cultivator and guardian: it was Man's fundamental purpose, that is, to be a steward, a gardener, a keeper of the wondrous place where God himself wished to walk (as master of the house) in his own garden in the evenings (Gen 2:8, 15). And this is, perhaps, the first thing that a more hopeful reading of "gardens" might tell us: that this beautiful Earth is not the property of Humankind. It remains God's own garden. It is a holy thing. Humankind stands within it, among animals and plants and seeds, but stands there in order to keep it sacral: to prevent the profane. For if the garden is profaned, the Genesis story warns of the cessation of the desire of the deity to converse with his steward in the evenings under the trees. Perhaps this anti-profane aspect integral to a garden is why so many gardeners still testify that they feel the sacralizing effect of being in its embrace and being glad to work the earth: for something is sensed as being made whole again and it entices God to walk once more alongside his good gardeners. Was it not the Christ who even called the Father his own good gardener?[8]

No being in ancient times could ever have thought that human keepers, however incompetent or lazy they might be, could ever damage the structure of the garden *per se*. There simply weren't enough human beings and, despite the recurrent theme in Genesis of Man having "dominion," the earth was simply too big, and humanity far too small to do more than passing damage. Today it is different. We have not just mismanaged the entirety of the Earth, we have, as guardians, still carried on sleeping while more alert voices have been crying in alarm that the very walls of the garden are falling down and the greenhouse [effect] is no longer a nursery of life but, by our own lack of foresight, a harbinger of destruction. And yet, even so, we should remember Hopkins once more: who, having lamented the squalid besmirching of the natural world caused by Victorian era industrialization, ends with the day-dawn note of hope: "There lives the dearest freshness deep down things"; calling that which is "deep down" in the very structure

---

the post-death training ground for righteous souls to prepare them for their ascent, once purified, to Heaven. See Origen, *First Principles* 2.11.6–7; 3.6.8–9.

8. "ὁ πατήρ μου ὁ γεωργός ἐστιν [My Father is the one who works the earth]" (John 15:1).

of the natural order: the Holy Ghost, who "over the bent world broods with warm breast and ah! bright wings."[9] A similarly hopeful thought is brought to me each time the divine liturgy is served and the veils of the chalice and diskos are being censed in the Prothesis service to the accompaniment of the prayer: "The Lord has clothed and girded himself with power. He has established the world and it shall not be shaken."[10]

The Genesis scribe,[11] with the sadness of an exile's heart, wishes to make us sad with the feeling of being locked out of the garden. It is certainly sad to feel locked out of anything. Even if we never wanted to join a club, it is sad that they never invited us in. Groucho Marx famously resigned membership of the Hollywood Delaney club with a telegram saying: "Please accept my resignation. I don't want to belong to any club that will accept me as a member." But his humor in that instance masked the fact that the antisemitic snub of an existing member there had taken away his delight to belong to that class of people.

Yet, gardens, in the antique world were exclusive in the main; largely about private space keeping people out, not letting them walk round free of charge. The ancient Greek literature about gardens suggests (chiefly because they were a very rare thing in antique urban societies that had little time for, and no great range of, flowers) that they are a half legendary (certainly imaginary) thing; a fantastic luxury of idleness. Such were the gardens of Alcinoüs[12] with their fruit trees and fountains and multiple types of flora; or those of the Hesperides.[13] When the Greeks did actually encounter the concept of a real garden it was in the form of the *paradizai* of the Persian Satraps,[14] which the British Victorian scholar Philip Smith notes, in a rather flat manner, "resembled our parks."[15] He means, I am sure, a large space of lawns and trees and a few flower beds, as in the parks of London; though I was first drawn, on reading that, to think of my own municipal park, as a child; adjacent to gasworks, shipyards, and a coke burning factory, but with

---

9. Hopkins, "God's Grandeur."

10. *Proskomedia* from John Chrysostom, "Liturgy of St. John Chrysostom." Prayer of the censing of the Veils; cf. Ps 104:5.

11. Likely to be writing in or just after the time of Babylonian captivity (for the book is a late one in the canon despite its traditional placement). He surely laments the loss of his own fertile land and imprisonment in the arid deserts surrounding Babylon.

12. See Homer, *Odyssey* 7.112–130.

13. Hesiod, *Theogony* 25.

14. Xenophon, *Anabasis* 1.2, 7; *Oeconomicus* 4.26–27; Plutarch, *Alcibiades* 24.

15. Smith, *Dictionary of Greek and Roman Antiquities*, 618–19.

The Wondrous Garden in Early Christian Imagining

a climbing frame, yellowed patchy grass, and a few militarily ordered flower beds, as well as a very grumpy resident park-keeper. There were residual memories of Eden, nevertheless, in the numerous "Keep Off" signs that were placed everywhere.

The exception to this ancient paucity of gardens was the Greek "sacred groves" which seem to have especially cultivated vines and olives[16] and scented flowers such as violets and roses, which may have been employed for the making of ritual artifacts such as garlands.[17] So even for the pagans, scented gardens were associated with divine presence. While setting about finding sets of exemplary morals about reconciling adversities, Plutarch refers his readers to the good gardening practice of interspersing rows of roses and violets with leeks and onions;[18] which sounds odd at first. But then if you reconsidered rows of Roses and Violet with intervening Allium and Agave it would all be quite nicely balanced: with the benefit falling to the Greeks that they could, at least, eat half the produce in the Fall.

Rich Romans had a more pronounced taste for formal garden layouts where walks could be taken (*ambulatoria*). Their range of flowers was more extensive than the Greeks, a taste they seemed to have learned from Ptolemaic Egypt.[19] Longus, in his *Pastoral Romance* describes an idealized Egyptian "all-year" garden: "In spring, with roses, lilies, hyacinths, and violets. In summer, with poppies, pears and all manner of fruit. In autumn, vines and figs, pomegranates and myrtles."[20] But the run of the mill élite Roman garden[21] seems to have been more of a flat terrace divided up by formalized box hedges with set places for strolling, in between, and shaped topiary scattered about to give height and effect. Indeed the standard Latin word for a gardener (as distinct from a farmer) is *topiarius*. After the time of Martial and Pliny, who are the first to mention them, some of the gardens of the very rich even had hot-houses to bring on exotic plants and late season fruit; and almost every Roman garden had a special area set aside for vegetables (*olera*).[22] At Pompei, where space was at a premium, at least one of the villas inside the town had a small walled garden where the external

16. Sophocles, *Oedipus at Colonus* 16; Xenophon, *Anabasis* 5.3.12.
17. Aristophanes, *Birds* 5.1066.
18. Plutarch, *De capienda ex inimicis utilitate* 10.
19. Smith, *Dictionary of Greek and Roman Antiquities*, 618.
20. Longus, *Pastoralia* 2.
21. Pliny the Younger gives a full account of his own in *Epistle* 5.6.
22. Smith, *Dictionary of Greek and Roman Antiquities*, 619.

walls depicted an even larger garden in *trompe l'oeil* fresco, and where the owner had set pots of flowers against the walls to increase the illusion: an example illustrated in Sir William Gell's *Pompeiana*.[23]

Among the later Christian fathers who clearly find delight in the notion of the garden, were the many who had taken Origen's warning to heart that the text of the scriptures, especially Genesis's cosmogonic narrative, was not to be taken woodenly and literally. The garden is meant to be a symbol more than a fact even when it is being used as a sad lament. Severian the bishop of Gabala in Syria, who became a popular preacher in Constantinople in the early fifth century, feels he needs to make the point "scientifically" to his readers. He made careful note of the fact that the relatively small size of the garden as recorded in Genesis proves that it cannot be identified with God's paradise.[24] But Severian[25] was a "naïve and unscientific" exegete, as Quasten describes him,[26] excessively literalist even to the point of vociferously defending the flat earth theory too. He uses the term κηποῦριν to signify that he is talking here specifically about the garden of Eden.

St. Gregory of Nyssa, a writer whose Epistle 15 *To Adelphius* demonstrates how greatly he appreciated a well laid out garden, mixing fine architecture with vines and fruit trees and water features with fish ponds, develops the imagery of a garden to explain, in his major treatise *On the Making of Man*, how it is that God develops a variety of things (bones, cartilage, veins and so on) out of a common substrate of the human body. He takes the notion of a well irrigated garden to show, by analogy, that the single substance of water flowing in all parts of the soil can become bitter in wormwood, poison in the hemlock, but completely other in saffron balsam and poppies where it is, by turn, hot and cold and moderately flavored. The same water becomes scent in the laurel and mastic trees, sugar in the fig and pear, juice for making wine in the case of the vine. The selfsame water is red in the rose, radiant white in the lily, blue in the violet and purple in the hyacinth.[27] As with his enthusiasm over Adelphius's garden estate, Gregory demonstrates here his eye for beautiful symmetry like other classical authors, but also underscores the immense variety that God has

---

23. Gell, *Pompeiana*, 2:4.
24. Severian, *Orations On the Making of the World* (PG 56:478).
25. See Gennadius, *De Viris Illustribu*, 21.
26. Quasten, *Golden Age*, 484.
27. Gregory of Nyssa, *De Opificio Hominis* 27 (PG 44:252).

put into the created synthesis of life. Elsewhere he applies the metaphor of the garden (κῆπος) to describe the church.[28] He takes the text of the Bride calling upon the wind (πνευμα) to blow gently through her garden to be the Church of Christ which perpetually enjoys the inspirations of the Holy Spirit (Πνευμα). The image, lifted from the *Song of Songs*[29] is also an evocation of how the lost garden of delight has now been restored in Christ's living community.

Other fathers move from this use of *Canticles* to using the symbol to refer to the Blessed Virgin as a personal summation of creation once again made perfect and radiant, like a scented garden, in the Redemption. Epiphanius of Salamis says: "She is that enclosed garden" of delightful spices and pleasant breezes "that the prophet cries out about."[30] The emphasis on "enclosed" is taken patristically as a symbol of her virginity, but they also know, quite exactly that "enclosed garden" is the very definition of the word paradise: and this is how they extract the double-sense of the theology of Mary's spiritual radiance as being the icon *par-excellence* of Paradise restored. St. Theodore the Studite hymns her, saying: "Rejoice Thou Garden Enclosed."[31] Proklos of Constantinople offers us one of the finest examples of such *Chairetismoi* (acclamational) hymns of the Blessed Virgin where he piles on title on title, but surely alluding to the *Song of Songs*, where the "enclosed" garden and "sealed" spring are ciphers for her Virginity: "Mary: that Servant, Mother, Virgin, and Paradise. The only bridge from God to humankind," he says.[32] Chrysippus of Jerusalem acclaims her as the: "Very garden of the Father Himself."[33]

While knowing this Marian tradition, Gregory of Nyssa wishes to make the point in his *Homilies on the Song of Songs* that this divine acclamation of being the scented garden and the Bride of Christ, actually refers to the divine calling which God gives to all true disciples. All believers are called to the restoration of beauty and intimacy with God (like Mary

---

28. Gregory of Nyssa, *Homily on the Canticles* 10 (PG 44:985).

29. "Awake, North wind; Come, south wind. Breathe on my garden and spread the fragrance of its spices. Let my Beloved come into his garden and taste its choicest fruits" (Song 4:16).

30. "My sister bride is an enclosed garden; a garden enclosed, a fountain sealed" (Song 4:12); cf. "The garden is closed, my sister, my bride: Ah, the garden is closed, the spring is sealed" (Epiphanius, *Homiliae in laudes Mariae deiparae* [PG 43:492]).

31. Theodore, *In Nativitatem Beatae Virginis Mariae* 7 (PG 96:692C).

32. Proclus, *Chairetismoi Theotokou* (PG 65:681).

33. Chrysippus of Jerusalem, *Encomium Mariae deiparae* 7 (336).

herself) that the concept of garden evokes. Gregory teaches: "Where the Bridegroom says 'My bride is an enclosed garden,' we learn how one can become the Lord's sister and spouse. If, then, someone is so changed as to become bride because he has been joined to the Lord (cf. Eph 5:31), and sister because she has done his will as the Gospel says (cf. Mark 3:35), let her thus become a thriving garden that contains the splendor of all the plants: the sweet fig tree with the fruitful olive, the lofty-headed date palm, and the flourishing vine; and no thorn or briar, but instead cypress and myrtle."[34]

Shortly after this passage he identifies this same mystery of the soul becoming a wondrous garden as a veritable synonym of the deification of the believer through the transformative grace of the Redemption: "For the goal of the entire life of virtue is participation in God, and it is surely Godhead which the reference to frankincense[35] signifies. Yet the soul that is ever being led by the Word toward something more sublime does not come to a halt even here, but after her fragrance has become similar to that of frankincense, she becomes a garden after the likeness of the paradise; and no garden untended or unguarded, as among the first human beings, but rather a garden walled on every side by recollection of the commandment."[36]

So we can see that, after all, we do have in all of this a veritable tradition that lauds the beauty of the garden rather than lamenting our sad loss through its motif. But there is one garden, with which we shall end, that is both a beauty and a sorrow at the same time: a place of radiant glory and simultaneously of deep tragedy. It is the anvil of our salvation in many ways: the garden of Gethsemane.

This garden was, from before Jesus's time, an olive grove (the name comes from *gat shemanim*, or "olive press"). It lies at the foot of the slope of the Mount of Olives in Jerusalem, on a low eastern ridge parallel to the ancient city walls. There can hardly be a Christian that does not know this garden, and the story attached to it; and yet, perhaps, few have thought about it from the perspective of what it meant to be in a garden very late at night. Why this garden; here at this place; at this particular and unusual moment? So, let me tell the story in a way Emily Dickinson would have

---

34. Gregory of Nyssa, *On the Song of Songs*, Homily 9. Both the flowers and black berries of the Myrtle are highly scented, like Eucalyptus. The Cypress has a delicate sandalwood scent.

35. He refers to the various scents of the garden as mentioned in the Song of Songs.

36. Gregory of Nyssa, *On the Song of Songs*, Homily 9.

approved: "Tell all the truth but tell it slant—Success in Circuit lies / Too bright for our infirm Delight / The Truth's superb surprise."[37]

The old city where Jesus and his disciples held the Last, or Mystical, Supper together was in a narrow maze of buildings not far away from the now excavated site of Caiaphas's residence. The latter was possessed of dungeon cells as it was also the headquarters of the much feared personal police force of Caiaphas who had charge of all security arrangements relating to the city as a religious pilgrimage centre. The Gospels tell us that the High Priest's police were already on the lookout to arrest Jesus, especially after his causing of a particular fracas in the money changing area of the Temple.

Animals for sacrifice entered the Temple precincts by the west side of the Southern Court, between the present Barclay gate and the Royal Stoa. Here, adjacent to the animal corrals, were the changing tables so that foreign/secular money could be exchanged for Temple shekels before ritual animals were purchased. It was in this area that Jesus overturned the coin dealers' tables: partly in a protest against the trafficking of sacrificial animals, and partly in protest against the venality of the merchants and priests.[38] From that moment onward, politically speaking, Jesus and his disciples were reckoned as guilty of sacrilege and were "wanted" by the police. The Gospels, recounting Jesus's last meal with his followers in the old city, therefore, are telling us of an immense risk that he was taking. Caiaphas's police were stationed all over the city and the rooms where they were eating (not the so-called Upper Room which was a Crusader-era invention without historical support) were probably close to the ancient stairway (itself near to the house of Caiaphas, close by Kaiser Wilhelm's modern church of the Dormition of the Blessed Virgin) which can still be seen running down the hill into the Kidron valley below, and exiting near the so-called "tombs of the prophets."

In the Gospel accounts much is made of the fact that Judas "betrays" Jesus at the meal and walks out of the room. What was this betrayal other than his decision to go across the street a few hundred yards and enter the house of Caiaphas to tell them one particular thing: and that was the place where Jesus and his disciples were lodging that same night. As all good totalitarian police forces know, arrests of groups of dissidents are best made between three and four in the morning when all the household will be fast asleep and the whole crowd can be seized and bound before they

---

37. See Dickinson, "Tell All the Truth."
38. Further McGuckin, "Sacrifice and Atonement."

can muster resistance. What the police needed to hear was exactly *where* Jesus and friends would all be at three that morning: and the answer Judas supplied to them was: Bethany, (modern Al Eizariya) just over two miles to the south of the ancient city.

After the Supper, burned in Christian memory now, of course, because of the institution of the eucharist celebrated there, Jesus would have left the upper room cautiously, but not seeing any police presence would have known that the expected trouble would come much later. The disciples exited the festal occasion, having drunk abundantly one presumes, but happily singing the *Hodayot* (Thanksgiving) psalms appointed for the occasion. Passing down the ancient stairway (still visible today) Jesus would have turned left at the empty and imposing Mausolea in the west of the Kidron valley (reminding him doubtless of his own prophetic words how Jerusalem preferred to kill prophets and build memorials for them afterwards).

These "whitewashed sepulchres" gleamed pallid marble in the full moon of that evening (we know this, for it was Passover time) and loomed over them all as the disciples cheerfully walked up the valley eastward to Gethsemane, while Jesus became more and more thoughtful and anxious. And here, at this precise spot, he stopped. As it tells us in the texts: "For here was a garden." It was also, as may be less well known, the major crossroads out of Jerusalem. One road led into the wilderness of the Judaean desert (where no police force could ever find them in the dark: and Jesus was already skilled in evading the police of Antipas we remember); another of those roads led up the coastal path to Tyre (perhaps back to Capernaum where they had started?); yet another led over the brow of the hill at Gethsemane on to the short road back to Bethany where they were supposed to be staying the night. The disciples were surely eager now to get on to Bethany and a good sleep after a heavy festive dinner. Bethany for them was safety, and home. For Jesus it was arrest and death; probably fatal for all of them, for he now knew the police were planning to act that very night. And this is why he commanded the disciples to set a watch. This has been so often interpreted piously as "keep watch (i.e., pray) with me" that it has obscured the fact that he meant it so as to "keep watch for me, while I pray."

The reason for this was that Jesus needed urgently to confer with the Father in prayer about whether he could avoid this disaster that loomed, or whether that fatal outcome was what his Father intended. And so he prayed, for hour after hour, in a torment of agony. As long as the others kept watch however, they could not be surprised. Anyone looking down the length of the Kidron valley from the raised vantage point of Gethsemane's garden could see all the foot traffic that was coming their way for at least half a mile. As planned, the police force of Caiaphas, with Judas in tow, came clattering down the Kidron valley, with torches flaring and not a care for any stealth: only thinking they needed to be quiet and under cover of darkness after they had walked the further two miles to Bethany. By this time of night, after so many hours had passed since the Jesus group had been noted to have left the city, they thought they must surely have been in bed asleep for hours.

But one person, of course, was awake in that garden: one person had prevented the group from moving on over the hill and had heard the police chatter coming; one person saw their torches moving towards him even before they came to the garden gate. And looking to see why his disciples had not warned him a long time earlier, Jesus saw that they were all in various states of sleep. In that same instant he knew he had no choice: no choice unless he was to shout a warning and they could all wake up as fast as they could and run—but in that, risk the capture of several, and their possible deaths, and the even worse prospect of abandoning them to save himself. In that instant, he knew he had no other choice but to shout that warning and then walk resolutely down the road through the garden gate, thus blocking it, to call out to the police, greet them and identify himself. In that chaos of surprise that followed, it is no accident at all that Jesus alone was arrested. Every one of the disciples had time to wake up, see for themselves exactly what was transpiring and do the instinctive thing: run away into the darkness and escape.

It was only afterwards, surely, that reflecting on that chaotic moment they must have realized that if there was any single moment (though it was a lifetime of process not a single moment) when Jesus could have been said to have freely delivered himself over to death for their sake—it was that instant when he chose to protect his loved ones and walk through the garden gate into the hands of his enemies: precisely so that they could go free.

This is what fills my mind, when I think of our last garden, the olive grove of Gethsemane: a moonlit garden where immense courage and profound love and loyalty temper the tragedy of betrayal, brutality and carelessness that surrounded him that night. This was a garden of love, nonetheless: a love that with its brightness and courage is remembered as our *Soteria*, our safety and salvation through and beyond all the guilt and shame attendant on it. And that is why it can serve very well as our last scene of a garden. It has some of the pain of the Genesis garden: much of the tragedy of loss that accompanies that archetypal narrative. But it is also a garden of love and light, like the other gardens that our tradition speaks of, where they stand as images of loving hopefulness in our Redemption. Though the night was full of moonlight on that Passover in Gethsemane, it was a garden lit up by a loyalty and protectiveness of the Saviour that dwarfed the moonlight and in so doing became a beacon of salvation for countless generations to come: *O felix culpa quae talem ac tantum meruit habere Redemptorem.*

BIBLIOGRAPHY

Chrysippus of Jerusalem. *Encomium Mariae deiparae.* In *Patrologia Orientalis*, edited by M. Jugie, 19:336–43. Paris: Firmin-Didot, 1925.

Dickinson, Emily. "Tell All the Truth but Tell It Slant—(1263)." In *The Poems of Emily Dickinson: Reading Edition*, edited by R. W. Franklin. Cambridge: Belknap, 1998. https://www.poetryfoundation.org/poems/56824/tell-all-the-truth-but-tell-it-slant-1263.

Gell, William. *Pompeiana: The Topography Edifices and Ornaments of Pompei: The Result of Excavations Since 1819.* London: Lewis & Lewis, 1835.

Hesse, Hermann. *Hours in the Garden and Other Poems.* Translated by Rika Lesser. New York: Farrar Straus & Giroux, 1979.

Hopkins, Gerard Manley. "God's Grandeur." *Poetry Foundation*. https://www.poetryfoundation.org.

———. "Inversnaid." *International Hopkins Association*. https://hopkinspoetry.com/poem/inversnaid.

John Chrysostom. "Liturgy of St. John Chrysostom." *Greek Orthodox Archdiocese of America*, December 10, 2024. https://dcs.goarch.org/goa_2024_0912/dcs/p/s/2024/12/10/li/en/se.m12.d10.li.pdf.

McGuckin, John A. "Sacrifice and Atonement: An Investigation into the Attitude of Jesus of Nazareth Toward Cultic Sacrifice." In *Remembering for the Future: Working Papers and Addenda*, edited by Yehuda Bauer et al., 1:648–61. Oxford: Pergamon, 1989.

———. "Sacrifice and Atonement: An Investigation into the Attitude of Jesus of Nazareth Towards Cultic Sacrifice." In *Witnessing the Kingdom: Studies in New Testament and History and Theology*, 51–88. New York: St. Vladimir's Seminary, 2017.

Migne, Jacques-Paul, ed. *Patrologia Graeca* [PG]. 162 vols. Paris: Garnieri Fratres, 1857–1886.

Quasten, Johannes. *The Golden Age of Greek Patristic Literature.* Vol. 3 of *Patrology*. Utrecht-Antwerp: Spectrum, 1975.

Smith, William, ed. *A Dictionary of Greek and Roman Antiquities.* London: Murray, 1875

United States Conference of Catholic Bishops (USCCB). "The Exsultet: The Proclamation of Easter." 2010. https://www.usccb.org/prayer-worship/liturgical-year/easter/easter-proclamation-exsultet.

5

Love God, Love Thy Neighbor, Love the Trees
Ecological Justice in Orthodox Christianity

PERRY HAMALIS

FOR FAR TOO LONG, much Christian theology around the world was pursued and taught without a significant connection to ecology. While theologians traditionally provided some account of the origin of the cosmos, and of God as the Creator, there was little discussion of the organic relationship between ecology, the study of the relationships among living organisms, and theology, the study of the divine and of religious beliefs.[1] Thus, when the destruction of the environment became a matter of wide-spread concern in the twentieth century, Christian theology was perceived as being irrelevant or, worse, as the cause of environmental destruction. Thinkers like Lynn White placed the blame for environmental destruction largely upon Christianity because of:

1. Its sharp distinction between Creator and Creation, which emphasized God's transcendence;

---

1. See Pihkala, "Early Twentieth-Century Ecotheology," 268–85.

2. Its account of creation, which placed human beings hierarchically above the rest of the natural world and seemed to sanction humanity's domination and unrestricted use of nature; and

3. Its prioritization of saving souls and reaching a heavenly kingdom beyond this world over material and earthly concerns.[2]

Thankfully, in recent decades, good work has been done across many denominations to correct false interpretations of Christianity and many scholars have advanced our understanding of the intimate relationship between ecology and Christian theology, as well as the potential for Christian thought to contribute positively to the protection and care of the natural world, a field sometimes referred to as "ecotheology."

Similarly, for far too long, much Christian theology around the world was pursued and taught without a significant connection to liberating oppressed and enslaved persons from dehumanizing conditions. While care for the poor remained a central theme in most Christian communities, critiquing the laws and other social structures that sustain inequality and undermine the full dignity of so many human beings was not, for many theologians, a major focus. Once slavery became illegal in nations around the world during the nineteenth and early twentieth centuries, too many Christian thinkers either assumed, falsely, that slavery had in fact ended or they accepted the equally false belief that the poor are poor because they are sinful, undisciplined, or lazy. However, especially over the past fifty years, many theologians have refocused upon the central message of liberation within Judaism and Christianity. They have drawn from the Exodus story and from Jesus' recitation of Isaiah 61, recorded in the Gospel of Luke, "*The Spirit of the Lord is upon me, because he has anointed me to bring good news to the poor. He has sent me to proclaim release to the captives and recovery of sight to the blind, to let the oppressed go free, to proclaim the year of the Lord's favor*" (Luke 4:18–19 NRSV). They have identified and critiqued not only the reality of human suffering but also the social structures and cultural attitudes that promote and perpetuate such neglect, exploitation, and abuse. These Christian thinkers, sometimes referred to as "liberation theologians," have focused on the connection between theology and human dignity, between God's love and the liberation of those human beings who are treated unjustly—and even enslaved—because of their poverty, their race, their

---

2. White, "Historical Roots," 1203–7.

nationality, their gender, their disability, their refugee status, or some other characteristic beyond their control.

While connections are being rediscovered between theology and ecology, on the one hand, and between theology and human dignity on the other, *the integration of all three areas of reflection has been slow*. Christian theologians who embraced ecology often did not pay attention to the ways that harming the natural world affects those who are poor and oppressed disproportionately more than it affects those who are wealthy and free. In other words, they did not connect "human dignity" to their reflection on ecology and theology. Similarly, theologians who examined the deep interconnectedness between theology and human dignity typically did not pay attention to the ways that modern slavery—the horrifying reality of forced labor, sex trafficking, child soldiering, exploitation of migrants and refugees, and other violations of basic human dignity and liberty—are inescapably tied to the environmental crisis. In other words, they failed to connect "ecology" to their reflection on human dignity and theology.

However, current thinkers have been discerning and directing our attention to the mutuality between *ecology* and *human dignity*—between the abuse of the environment and the abuse of human beings, spurring Christian theologians and ethicists to search for normative resources that illuminate the triple intersection of theology, ecology, and human dignity. Orthodox Christian ethics, the focus of Vigen Guroian's scholarly work, can help us respond to some of today's greatest social and global challenges, precisely because ecology, human dignity, and theology are inseparably interrelated and integrated within Orthodoxy's worldview and ecclesial life, a point that several pillars of contemporary Orthodox thought—including Ecumenical Patriarch Bartholomew, Metropolitan John Zizioulas, Paulos Mar Gregorios, John Chryssavgis, and Guroian himself—help us to grasp.

In *Encountering the Mystery*, His All-Holiness Ecumenical Patriarch Bartholomew provides a concise overview of Orthodoxy's integrated theological-ethical vision:

> Orthodox theology . . . recognizes the natural creation as inseparable from the identity and destiny of humanity, because every human action leaves a lasting imprint on the body of the earth. Human attitudes and behavior toward creation directly impact on and reflect human attitudes and behavior toward other people. . . . Scientists estimate that those most hurt by global warming in years to come will be those who can least afford it. Therefore, the ecological problem of pollution is invariably connected to

the social problem of poverty; and so all ecological activity is ultimately measured and properly judged by its impact and effect upon the poor (see Matt 25).[3]

Similarly in his opening address at the Ecumenical forum on modern slavery, His All-Holiness stated:

> We are convinced that responding to the problem of modern slavery is directly and inseparably linked to creation care.... The entire world is the body of Christ; just as human beings are the very body of Christ. The whole planet bears the traces of God, just as every person is created in the image of God. The way we respect creation reflects the way we respond to our fellow human beings. The scars we inflict on our environment reveal our willingness to exploit our brother and sister.[4]

For His All-Holiness, and for Orthodox Christianity more broadly, theology, ecology, and human dignity are intertwined and interdependent. Guroian underscores the importance of holding together all three when he writes:

> From an Orthodox perspective, ecclesiology and concern for the global ecology are virtually the same thing. We *must* keep both church and household better. Nothing short of this will do sufficient honor to the name of the One in whom alone there is hope for all God's creatures of liberation "from bondage to decay" and of the freedom "of the children of God" (Rom 8:21).[5]

Below, I will first offer two concrete examples that highlight the interconnectedness between ecology and human dignity. After this, I will explore two of Orthodox Christianity's teachings that highlight the Church's integrated worldview.

TWO EXAMPLES: ENVIRONMENTAL RACISM AND MODERN SLAVERY

In the City of Chicago, where my family and I are now living, ecologists recently published a study analyzing the distribution of environmental risks and benefits. The report included a map that showed all the city's

---

3. Bartholomew I, *Encountering the Mystery*, 94–95.
4. Bartholomew I, "Opening Address."
5. Guroian, *Ethics After Christendom*, 174.

various sections and color-coded the quality of environmental health in each section based upon a large set of factors, including levels of air and water toxins, quantities of heavy metals in the soil, and proximity to industrial factories and waste treatment centers. Neighborhoods that were colored blue or blue-green on the map had the lowest levels of pollution and the healthiest overall environment. *None* of these "blue" neighborhoods included facilities that produced or processed large-scale industrial waste. In contrast, neighborhoods that were colored red or red-orange on the map had the highest levels of pollution and the most dangerous overall environment. Often these "red" neighborhoods included *multiple* factories or waste disposal sites.

Who lives in the "blue" neighborhoods? Primarily wealthy Chicagoans who are almost exclusively white/Caucasian. And who lives in the "red" neighborhoods? Chicago's economically poor, who are primarily racial minorities—African-Americans, Latinos, recent immigrants, and refugees. The study also showed that public schools in the "red" zones are often located very close to major pollution sources, which puts children in these neighborhoods at even higher risk for exposure to neuro-toxins linked to learning disabilities.[6] And on top of this, because they are viewed as a financial risk, "red zone" neighborhoods are likely to have *no* local supermarkets that offer fresh fruits, vegetables, and other healthy food options. It is a grim and offensive picture: some human beings are breathing clean air, drinking safe water, enjoying easy access to healthy foods, and attending schools far from industrial sites, while other human beings—*living in the same city*—experience the opposite reality.

This social reality is an example of what scholars call "environmental racism," a prominent form of environmental injustice. It provides us with a picture of the interconnection between polluting the environment and oppressing human beings; between abuse of the natural world and abuse of persons; between ecological harm and loss of human dignity. Citizens of Chicago who live in "red zones" carry a disproportionate amount of the environmental risk because they are less wealthy, less educated, and less connected to the politicians who determine where high-polluting businesses can be located. In short, the poor are trapped, and any effort to move elsewhere presents different obstacles and injustices. Simultaneously,

---

6. For the color-coded map, see Geertsma, "New Map Shows Chicago Needs." For a study on the proximity of schools to sources of pollution, see Grineski and Collins, "Geographic and Social Disparities," 580–87.

those living in "blue zones" confront minimal environmental risks yet gain maximum benefits—from better health, to increased property values, to excellent schools, to profits from investing in companies that dump their waste in red zones. Ecology and human dignity are inseparably connected, for good and for ill.

While environment injustice in Chicago grows out of decades of racism and segregated housing, other parts of the world confront similar challenges. Recent studies on Environmental Justice in the Republic of Korea, for example, consider the "Toxic Release Inventory (TRI)" and show that distribution of environmental risks and benefits are not evenly balanced across different sociopolitical groups on the peninsula.[7] In addition, the study suggests, as more foreigners migrate to Korea and settle in low-income urban neighborhoods, these immigrant-concentrated neighborhoods tend to be targeted as locations for new factories and waste management facilities, which further concentrates environmental harms among the most vulnerable and powerless members of society.

A second example, modern slavery, further demonstrates the connection between ecology and human dignity in today's world. In *Blood and Earth*, Kevin Bales details the vicious cycle of "ecocide" and "modern slavery" through a series of examples from around the globe. One example Bales develops relates to massive shrimp farms along the coasts of Bangladesh, Southern India, and Indonesia.[8]

The abusive cycle begins with increasing demand for inexpensive shrimp in countries like the United States. To meet this demand (and generate huge profits) miles of mangrove trees growing in shoreline swamps are cut down to give shrimp farmers clear access to the water. The destruction of the mangrove trees itself does extraordinary ecological harm. Not only are the trees killed and the creatures living in and among them displaced, there are at least two additional consequences. First, mangrove trees are "carbon sinks"; like other trees, they pull CO_2 out of the air and generate fresh oxygen but, unlike other trees, mangroves are able to lock away carbon by depositing it into the ocean, a process called "sequestration," which has an exponential benefit in reducing global warming. Their destruction, therefore, carries an exponential loss. And second, mangrove trees growing miles deep along the coast of countries like Bangladesh and Indonesia have

---

7. See Yoon et al., "Environmental Inequity in South Korea," 1886; Choi et al., "Assessment of Environmental Injustice in Korea," 28–37.

8. Bales, *Blood and Earth*, 71–97.

historically provided a natural barrier during cyclones and tsunamis. Now that shrimp farmers have removed more than 80 percent of the mangroves in some regions, the scale of deaths and damage during such storms has skyrocketed.

Yet even worse than the ecological effects of shrimp farming is the assault on human dignity that the industry fuels. The demand for inexpensive seafood increases the need for laborers. Recruiters visit poor villages promising good paying jobs and offering small salary advances to families, only to then enslave children and adults in forced labor at the shrimp farms. Recruits often work for 24- or 48-hour shifts without rest, sufficient food, housing, or basic medical care, all while surrounded by the stench of shrimp heads and shells. In addition, girls, boys, and adult female workers are frequently sexually assaulted by their bosses, while other recruits never even make it to the shrimp farm because they are immediately sold to sex traffickers.

Big profits provide the incentive for those in power to expand operations—to clear more mangrove forests and build larger farms... which further harms local and global ecologies... which accelerates climate change and increases natural disasters... which destroys towns and increases poverty... which provides willing "recruits" for slave-based businesses. The cycle is complete. While this example centers on shrimp, similar vicious cycles exist around diamonds, gold, beef, sugar, steel, and the minerals necessary for cell phones and flat-screen TVs. As Bayles puts it, "environmental change is part of the engine of slavery [and] the sharp end of environmental change... comes first to the poor."[9] We again see that Ecology and human dignity are inseparably connected, for good and for ill. The examples of environmental racism and modern slavery pierce the heart and unsettle the conscience, prompting both critique and action. Furthermore, as Guroian reminds his readers:

> Certainly, the Church is summoned to voice prophetic criticisms of collective injustices, calling the world back to its divinely ordained end. Within its sacramental life the Church proclaims and pursues this vocation. It must not forget that the world, including its political life, is truly the "matter" of its sacraments.[10]

---

9. Bales, *Blood and Earth*, 8–9.
10. Guroian, *Incarnate Love*, 26.

The Christian community has a special responsibility not only to critique collective injustices but to draw deeply from Christianity's theological, ethical, and ecclesial tradition, releasing the tradition's vibrancy in today's world.

TWO TEACHINGS FROM THE THEOLOGICAL-ETHICAL TRADITION OF ORTHODOX CHRISTIANITY

Despite the heart-breaking reality of environmental racism and modern slavery, the Christian community trusts that we "may abound in hope, by the power of the Holy Spirit" (Rom 15:13 NRSV). There is a relentless hopefulness within Orthodox Christianity, which is grounded in Christ's Incarnation, Life, Death, Resurrection, Ascension and sending of the Holy Spirit; this hope is cultivated by the beauty and mystery of liturgy and prayer, and it is confirmed by the reality of saints across history. For those who are searching, or who are skeptical, the Orthodox Church invites you to "Come and see" (John 1:39 NRSV).

How, then, might Orthodoxy help us as we strive to protect both human dignity and the environment? There are no quick, easy, or automatic solutions. The brokenness and corruption we find around us, and within us, stems from passions that trace all the way back to the two most ancient of trees (Gen 2:9), and to humanity's most ancient act of rebellion against the God who created us (Gen 3). Nonetheless, I repeat my earlier claim, *part of the promise that Orthodox Christianity holds lies precisely in the way that ecology, human dignity, and theology are inseparably connected and integrated within an Orthodox worldview*. Two threads within the Orthodox tradition that highlight this claim are icons and the expansion of the greatest commandment.

A Way of Seeing: Icons

Icons are perhaps the most distinctive characteristic of Orthodox Churches. People who enter an Orthodox Church for the first time are struck—and sometimes overwhelmed—by the presence of icons throughout the church. There are small icons when one enters the narthex, large icons painted on the walls and ceiling of the nave, and a screen of icons between the nave and the holy altar. Within Orthodox Christianity, the meaning and purpose of icons is multi-layered. One function of icons is to engage us visually, to capture and hold our attention, and to lead us to a reality beyond what we usually see. Icons are surfaces that take us into the depth, windows into a mystery. They reveal to our eyes a world that we typically do not see.

The basis, or foundation, for icons is Jesus Christ. In his Letter to the Colossians, St. Paul writes that Christ "*is the image of the invisible God, the firstborn of all creation; for in him all things in heaven and on earth were created, visible and invisible*" (Col 1:15–16 NRSV). Notice, first, that St. Paul describes Christ as "the image of the invisible God." Christ, who is God incarnate, the "Word made flesh" (cf. John 1:14), is the *visible* presence that reveals the *invisible* God. Furthermore, in the original Greek text, the word that Paul uses for "image" is "icon"; thus, Christ is the "image/icon of the invisible God (εἰκὼν τοῦ Θεοῦ τοῦ ἀοράτου)." Christ Himself is the *first* and the *ultimate* icon, in whom one sees the face of God.

While the term icon applies to Jesus Christ Himself, it also applies to all that was created by Christ, "in heaven and on earth," "visible and invisible," as St. Paul stated. All of creation is iconic, because all of creation points beyond itself to a depth, to the God who brought all things into being. This is stated directly in the Genesis creation account, where God says, "*Let us make humankind in our image, according to our likeness*" (Gen 1:26 NRSV). In the ancient Greek (Septuagint) translation of "image" and "likeness," the word for image is, again, "icon" ("Κατ' εἰκόνα και καθ' ὁμοίωσιν"). Thus, since every human being is created in the image of God, every human being is an icon, a perceivable presence that reveals God. Christ's words in the Gospel of Matthew confirm this iconic quality, this connection between visible creation and invisible Creator, "just as you did it (or did not do it) to one of the least of these, you did it (or did not do it) to me" (Matt 25:40, 45 NRSV).

In the Orthodox theological-ethical tradition, non-human creation is also iconic. This was certainly true for Moses when he stood reverently before the burning bush and encountered the living God (Exod 3), but it is also true in our relationship to the natural world more broadly. The eighth-century saint John of Damascus, one of the greatest defenders of Christianity's use of icons, draws a connection between Christ as icon and the natural world as icon when he writes, "Because of the Incarnation, I gaze upon all of material creation with reverence."[11]

Much more can be said about icons and their significance for seeing the inseparable relationship between ecology, theology, and human dignity, but

---

11. John of Damascus, *First Apology* 16.

I offer just one further comment. The icons one sees in Orthodox Churches themselves play a vital role in cultivating an iconic way of seeing and experiencing God, neighbor, and the natural world. For as one gazes reverently upon a painted or mosaic icon, one is drawn into the depth's mystery; the depth's mystery works on the viewer; it heals the viewer; and the viewer is reminded—given "another" mind—by the icon. In other words, icons promote repentance, a literal "change of mindset" (μετάνοια). Thus the icon's connection to the Creator, to the Incarnate God, helps to heal the one who encounters it, correcting one's vision so that one may see God both in "the least of these," one's neighbors, and in the most vulnerable of all God's creatures, the voiceless animals, rocks, waters, and trees.

A Way of Acting: The Greatest Commandment—Expanded

A second teaching from the Orthodox tradition shifts us from a way of seeing to a way of acting, from icons to commandments. War and foreign occupation generate not only human death, suffering, and multiple forms of slavery, but also environmental destruction. When my family and I spent a year in South Korea through the Fulbright Scholars Program, we noticed the great care that Koreans show toward trees. It was explained to us that during the Japanese occupation (1910–1945), and then during the Korea War (1950–1953), many trees were destroyed and, when the Republic of Korea began its miraculous recovery, there was a strong emphasis placed on planting and protecting trees. Trees, therefore, became a sign of freedom and hope for Koreans. Similarly, during the eighteenth century, when Greece was occupied by the Ottoman Turks, St. Kosmas the Aetolian (1714–1779) traveled around Greece teaching the Orthodox faith in villages. As he journeyed, his practice was to plant trees. St. Kosmas famously said, "People will remain poor because they have no love for trees."[12] Notice the direct connection St. Kosmas makes between neglecting the environment and poverty, between ecology and human dignity. To escape poverty—which, in his context, included slavery—the faithful must "love the trees." Seeing trees as icons leads to acting toward them with loving care.

Having "love for trees" is not merely a sentimental statement within Orthodoxy, it is an affirmation of the Church's integrated worldview. This point becomes especially clear when we consider the example of one of Orthodoxy's most recently canonized saints, Amphilochios of Patmos

12. Gkiolas, *O Kosmas Aitolos*, 93.

(1889–1970). For St. Amphilochios, caring for creation was not an option for Christians—it was a divine command. Along these lines, the saint once made a very bold claim: "Do you know that God gave us one more commandment," he said, "which is not recorded in Scripture? It is the commandment *'love the trees.'*"[13] In addition, when St. Amphilochios would hear the confessions of local faithful, he would frequently give them an unusual penance: he would tell them that, to complete their repentance, they now needed to plant and take care of a tree. Reflecting on this bold teaching, one should notice, first, that St. Amphilochios does not simply say, "We should love the trees"; instead, he says *God has commanded us* to do so. All Christians are familiar with the greatest commandment, *"You shall love the Lord your God with all your heart, and with all your soul, and with all your mind,"* and with the second greatest, *"You shall love your neighbor as yourself"* (Matt 22:37, 39 NRSV), but St. Amphilochios expresses the deep spirit of Orthodox Christianity when he adds as a third, *"You shall love the trees."* Love God; love thy neighbor; love the trees—theology, philanthropy, and ecology are integrated into one iconic vision for love-centered action.

In addition, St. Amphilochios's practice of asking people to plant and care for a tree after confession carries profound significance: it connects reconciliation between the person and God, and between the person and their neighbor, to reconciliation between the person and the environment. Thus, if I confess that I hurt my family member, or neglect the needs of a refugee, being instructed to plant a tree expands my vision—it teaches me that how I act toward my neighbor affects *all* of creation. Similarly, the saint's practice communicates that the way one treats non-human creation affects the way we treat our fellow human beings. Planting and caring for a new tree is good in itself, but it is also good because it teaches one to be more caring in one's relationships with others. This is an integrated worldview, wherein the spiritual healing of the human person, through God's mercy and love, leads to the healing of nature. Ecology, theology, and human dignity are connected in a single, Orthodox Christian vision.

In 2020, a groundbreaking Orthodox social ethics text, *For the Life of the World: Toward a Social Ethos of the Orthodox Church*, was published with the endorsement of His All-Holiness Ecumenical Patriarch Bartholomew and the Holy Synod of the Ecumenical Patriarchate. Among the text's many striking normative claims is the following:

---

13. See Ware, "Through Creation to the Creator," 86.

None of us exists in isolation from the whole of humanity, or from the totality of creation. We are dependent creatures, creatures ever in communion, and hence we are also morally responsible not only for ourselves or for those whom we immediately influence or affect, but for the whole of the created order—the whole city of the cosmos, so to speak. In our own time, especially, we must understand that serving our neighbor and preserving the natural environment are intimately and inseparably connected. There is a close and indissoluble bond between our care of creation and our service to the body of Christ, just as there is between the economic conditions of the poor and the ecological conditions of the planet.[14]

An Orthodox Christian worldview is promising for ecological justice, in part, because it goes beyond mere secular responses, beyond mere eco-theology, and beyond mere liberation theology. It is a worldview that speaks both to environmental racism and to modern slavery; one that seeks justice here and now, without losing sight of the "age to come." It is an integrated worldview that is liberating, iconic, and centered upon Eucharistic thanksgiving and love for God, neighbor, the trees, and all of creation.

BIBLIOGRAPHY

Bales, Kevin. *Blood and Earth: Modern Slavery, Ecocide, and the Secret to Saving the World*. New York: Spiegel & Grau, 2016.

Bartholomew I. *Encountering the Mystery: Understanding Orthodox Christianity Today*. New York: Doubleday, 2008.

———. "Opening Address." Speech delievered at Sins Before Our Eyes: A Forum on Modern Slavery, Istanbul, Turkey, February 7, 2017.

Choi, G., et al. "Assessment of Environmental Injustice in Korea Using Synthetic Air Quality Index and Multiple Indicators of Socioeconomic Status: A Cross-Sectional Study." *Journal of the Air & Waste Management Association* 66 (2016) 28–37.

Geertsma, Meleah. "New Map Shows Chicago Needs Environmental Justice Reforms." *Natural Resources Defense Council*, October 25, 2018. https://www.nrdc.org/experts/meleah-geertsma/new-map-shows-chicago-needs-environmental-justice-reforms.

Gkiolas, Markos A. *O Kosmas Aitolos kai I epochi tou*. Athens: Ekdosis Tymphrēstos, 1972.

Grineski, S., and T. Collins. "Geographic and Social Disparities in Exposure to Air Neurotoxicants at US Public Schools." *Environmental Research* 161 (2018) 580–87.

Guroian, Vigen. *Ethics After Christendom: Toward an Ecclesial Christian Ethic*. 1994. Reprint, Eugene, OR: Wipf & Stock, 2004.

Hart, David Bentley, and John Chryssavgis, eds. *For the Life of the World: Toward a Social Ethos of the Orthodox Church*. Brookline, MA: Holy Cross Orthodox, 2020.

---

14. Hart and Chryssavgis, *For the Life of the World* §76.

John of Damascus. *On the Divine Images: Three Apologies Against Those Who Attack the Divine Images*. Translated by David Anderson. Crestwood, NY: St. Vladimir's Seminary, 1980.

Pihkala, Panu. "Rediscovery of Early Twentieth-Century Ecotheology." *Open Theology* 2 (2016) 268–85.

Ware, Metropolitan Kallistos. "Through Creation to the Creator." In *Toward an Ecology of Transfiguration: Orthodox Christian Perspectives on Environment, Nature, and Creation*, edited by John Chryssavgis and Bruce Foltz, 86–105. New York: Fordham University Press, 2013.

White, Lynn. "The Historical Roots of our Ecological Crisis." *Science* 155 (1967) 1203–7.

Yoon, D. K., et al. "Exploring Environmental Inequity in South Korea: An Analysis of the Distribution of Toxic Release Inventory (TRI) Facilities and Toxic Releases." *Sustainability* 9 (2017) 1886.

6

A Garden Grows Around Him

WINN COLLIER

WHEN I READ MARILYN Robinson describe "great theology [as] always a kind of giant and intricate poetry, like epic or saga," her words pierced, a hot iron poker into my soul's cold embers.[1] In all my years of theological study (a Bible major in college and ThM in seminary: amassing close to 150 credit hours in systematics, Biblical languages, and an exegetical tour through every book of the Bible), no one had ever kindled my imagination with such a rousing vision. In those educational years, little touched the ache I carried but could not yet name, my yearning for the One who "is before all things and in [whom] all things hold together" (Col 1:17 NRSV). I longed for the consuming delight and holy wonder—the trembling *terror*—that ought (surely) to thread through every pursuit of the ineffable God. But (and maybe it was me, too young or self-absorbed to receive the good on offer) I mostly received brittle doctrinal schemes and hackneyed indoctrination into small-minded cul-de-sacs.

Something was amiss. If doing theology is how we tinkering humans ponder and seek after the Almighty, then theology should rattle our bones.

---

1. Robinson, *Death of Adam*, 117.

A Garden Grows Around Him

It should spark fire. Entering the classroom, "we should," as Annie Dillard warned, "all be wearing crash helmets."[2]

But I needed a teacher to show the way. I needed a teacher to walk with me into the vast labyrinth of Scripture and Christian tradition. I needed a guide freed from that tired rationalism that promises so much but inevitably drains all the heat and blood. I needed a teacher with the lilt of a poet, the grit of a novelist, the attention of a gardener. I needed a teacher aflame with grace, who knew something about the sacred illumination reflected in every good human endeavor. I needed to hear how novels and poetry and gardens—like carpentry, physics, homemaking, and every noble vocation—make up this world "charged with the grandeur of God."[3]

I needed Vigen Guroian. I'd always loved C. S. Lewis's stories of his tutor William T. Kirkpatrick, affectionately dubbed "The Great Knock." I always wished I'd had a teacher whom I held with such gratitude and affection. Then, at the University of Virginia, I encountered Professor Guroian. And through Vigen's teaching, through his manner and way, God's haunting, glimmering world opened before me, within me. While Vigen and The Great Knock are (thankfully) worlds apart in both philosophy and disposition, I gladly borrow Lewis's words about his teacher as my own for Vigen: "My debt to him is very great, my reverence to this day undiminished."[4]

In every class I took with him (and I signed up for as many as the registrar allowed), Vigen typically arrived slightly disheveled, bushy silver hair askew, carrying his scuffed leather satchel, his black Starbucks coffee, and a pastry (usually a scone or blueberry muffin). Khakis, bow tie, and (so long as it wasn't roasting hot) a tweed jacket. And over the next couple hours, we'd roam. Gregory of Nyssa, Bulgakov, and Boethius. Bach, Barth, and Andrea Wulf. Philip Sherard, Wendell Berry, and T. S. Eliot. Poetry. Movies. Symphonies.

Usually, you could count on at least one moment when Vigen's eyes would dance, and he would slap the desk or let out that full-bellied laugh, signals that you were about to detour into one of his raucous stories. He reminisced about college-day shenanigans: living in his frat house (I seem to remember one story about a balcony—*and were the police involved?*—the details are fuzzy) or hitchhiking weekend rides to Sweet Brier, the all-women's college fifty miles away, to meet new girls.

---

2. Dillard, *Teaching a Stone to Talk*, 40–41.
3. Hopkins, "God's Grandeur."
4. Lewis, *Surprised by Joy*, 82.

These diversions were part of Vigen's magic. His classes were so human. The space he cultivated taught us, without ever saying as much, how laughter and sorrow and memory were all part of a whole life lived toward God. Once, when talking about his weekend chores, he shared his conviction that "leisure is an essential part of gardening." It was obvious that he believed leisure was an essential part of teaching too. In his class, we had space to breath, room to roam and ponder. You never felt pressured to pump out an answer or use big words to make a mediocre idea sound erudite. We could be ourselves. "When I'm rushing around in the garden, frantic" Vigen said, "something is breaking down." In his classroom, we didn't rush. We meandered, on purpose. We followed our noses.

We didn't rush, but sometimes there were fireworks. Vigen might vent his agitation over a university policy or some happening in the popular zeitgeist. If he got especially amped, his voice ratcheted, and his face went splotchy red. I loved it when Vigen got fiery, even if I disagreed with him. In an age of suffocating cynicism and tightly scripted opinions, it's marvelous when someone cares enough about the truth, about humanity and life and God, to toss a little dynamite.

Michael Fishbane's description of Abraham Heschel works just as well for Vigen. His "passion was promethean—no fire of the spirit was alien to him."[5] Things tweaked Vigen, not because he was crusty or inflexible (though sometimes he could be grumpy and sometimes his ire was predictable), but because he *believed* strongly and *loved* deeply. Vigen knew that ideas have consequences. Beauty can be, and often is, marred. The glory woven into each human can be blunted, wounded, and muddied. Vigen's energy piqued because he "was imbued . . . with a 'radical reverence' for the holy possibilities of life and for the divine face hidden in all things."[6]

This God-saturated life evokes Vigen's reverence, and he intends to guard and nurture this awe, in spite of every trite, desacralizing force. Like Heschel, Vigen is temperamentally unable to abide "people who are never embarrassed at their own pettiness, prejudices, envy, and conceit, never embarrassed at the profanation of life." He laments how a "world full of grandeur has been converted into a carnival."[7] So, Vigen's belligerent, cheerful response has been to write, teach, and live as if it's actually true that we hallowed creatures are immersed in a hallowed creation.

5. Fishbane, "Foreword," xiii.
6. Fishbane, "Foreword," xiii.
7. Heschel, *Who Is Man?*, 114.

On the first day of the first class I had with Vigen, we read bits from St. Ephraim the Syrian. Ephraim delivered most of his theological discourse via hymns, hundreds and hundreds of hymns overflowing with lyrical lines and poetic imagery, each singing a luminous song to the Holy. You can't easily categorize or distill Ephraim's theology; you must simply sing it. You can't (if you want to hear Ephraim on his own terms) dissect the text with critical detachment; you must let the music wash over you.

Vigen knew what he was up to. He was unsettling our too-easy assumptions about God and the words we use to talk about God. "If we try to over-describe too much of our faith," Vigen said, "we will veer into heresy." My heart stirred, as if awakened from a long slumber. I began to furiously scratch Vigen's words in my black Moleskine notebook: "Let the mystery be. Hymn it. Praise it. And you will eventually find the truth in the mirror of your soul."

If we say too much, we'll veer into heresy—I can't imagine a more fitting line for a PhD student situated in a world class religion department. I can't imagine a more fitting line for a young pastor aching for that "giant and intricate poetry." This was no bland appeal to a vaguely spiritual "mystery," but a summons into a shattering, cataclysmic encounter with the God revealed in the Incarnation, Cross, Resurrection, and Ascension. Here was an invitation to take off our shoes before the God who burns in a bush, to kneel before the Spirit who hovered over creations' waters and who hovers still.

Vigen's class that day, and every day following, were a baptism into the cosmic reality weighted with (to borrow once more from Fishbane) "the urgent messages and the dying words" of a story that "has a claim on us."[8] Vigen taught with the conviction that the God we were discussing is the true Lord of the universe and the only sane object of our loyalty and our affections. It was madness to be aloof or disinterested. We were engaging in the ultimate concern, a matter of living and dying.

Theology, then, was the word we used to name our best but always inadequate efforts to grapple with God. Theology was how we would humbly, doxologically, seek the God who fills us with divine breath, the God who carries us with a tender grip. Theology was how we would lean toward the God who speaks our name, how we would muster some response to the God who is himself (whether or not we recognized this yet) our truest

---

8. Fishbane, "Foreword," xiii.

desire. "The denial of Christ," Vigen said, "is our denial of our deepest longing."

It was subversive act, right at the start, to have us dive into St. Ephraim's hymns. Following Ephraim's ancient cue, Vigen insisted that "good theology has to be sung. If you can't sing it, it's bad theology." In other words, any genuine conversation about God will resonate at a frequency deeper than words alone. His conviction grew out of a lifelong immersion in Eastern theology, a way of being that carries a peculiar tone and tenor, a harmony that held together by threads stronger than linear arguments. We students may have sought mastery and methods, but Vigen wanted to give us the music. Too often, academic theology tries to squeeze the pieces into the puzzle. "But instead," Vigen would say, "just be dizzied by the metaphors."

We shouldn't miss how Vigen titled his introduction to Orthodox theology *The Melody of Faith*. Music happens to you. Music is grace. Music demands our closest attention, but then the music takes us on a journey out of our control. And God, Vigen knew, is the soul's deepest music.

I once visited Vigen and his wife June when she was in the hospital suffering from the lung disease that would eventually take her life. He asked me to make a pastoral visit, though I was neither their priest nor Orthodox. I prayed over June. I offered a blessing. Later, Vigen and I sat in the sterile hospital dining hall, sipping weak coffee from paper cups. I heard Vigen's sorrow, his frustration with the industrial medical apparatus, his sadness over how he would too soon enter a life without his beloved wife and friend. But amid all the grief, I could still hear the song. Vigen clung, like a man amid a ship's wreckage, to his hope in the God who has already entered the valley of shadows and come out the other side. Here, in the country of death, talk about God was no abstract concept, no ethical principle or speculative inquiry. Here, God was the song of resurrection and life.

Anyone who knows Vigen knows that one of his purest joys is bound to this annual rhythm of death-turned-resurrection. Gardening, which he says is "nearer to godliness than theology," is where Vigen has for decades marveled over how the flowers and the vegetables die every winter, only to rise again come Spring.[9] Knees pressed into black humus, Vigen has allowed the garden to be his teacher. Good theology must be sung, but maybe good theology must be gardened too.

I believe the first thing I ever heard about Vigen, before I ever met him, was tales of this professor and his garden. Students traveled north on

---

9. Guroian, *Inheriting Paradise*, 3.

US Route 29 to his and June's Culpepper farm. Everyone loved being with Vigen, pulling weeds and planting seeds. After an afternoon's work, Vigen grilled burgers and regaled the undergrads with stories.

And just as the talk of music was never only about *music*, the garden was never only about the *garden*. One student, Daniel Garner, told me that being with Vigen made him realize how he'd never really seen the ground. "Vigen had a way of teaching that made you realize you needed to touch dirt." Daniel remembers Vigen teaching *Snow White*, "transforming the boring first paragraph into one of the greatest examples of prose I ever encountered." Literature and the garden—they were intertwined. "He taught me not to read over words but to work with them like soil." We touch words, and they touch us. "And suddenly *Snow White* was a sacrament."

Vigen's calloused hands bore testimony to how gardening wasn't something you talked about but something you *did*. And in the classroom, it was the same. Theology wasn't merely something to muse over, but a reality you entered, a song you sang, a garden you tilled, a prayer you prayed. Theology was a story that lays a claim on you. Because God lays a claim on you.

Daniel described walking with Vigen across UVA's grounds. Down the outdoor stairs of South Lawn. Across the grass. Down the sidewalk. Daniel remembers Vigen's aura, remembers recognizing how in Vigen he was seeing up close a well-lived life: a life that alters the atmosphere, the soil, around him. A life spent tending to corn stalks as they push through dewy soil. A life spent nurturing minds and hearts as they pursue goodness and beauty. "A garden was always growing around him," Daniel said.

"Every gardener is an imitator of Mary's Son," Vigen wrote, "every gardener is an apprentice of the good Gardener of creation."[10] Though he'd wave off me turning his words back toward him, it's unmistakable how Vigen has tended so many gardens in so many places. For his whole life, Vigen has imitated the generative, beauty-making presence of the God who fills all things, heals all things, the one who will make all barren patches new.

A garden really does grow around him.

BIBLIOGRAPHY

Dillard, Annie. *Teaching a Stone to Talk: Expeditions and Encounters*. New York: Harper & Row, 1982.

10. Guroian, *Inheriting Paradise*, 61.

Part Two: Inheriting Paradise

Fishbane, Michael. "Forword." In *Holiness in Words: Abraham Joshua Heschel's Poetics of Piety*, by Edward K. Kaplan, xiii–xiv. SUNY Series in Judaica. Albany, NY: State University of New York Press, 1996.
Guroian, Vigen. *Inheriting Paradise: Meditations on Gardening*. Grand Rapids: Eerdmans, 1999.
Heschel, Abraham. *Who Is Man?* Stanford, CA: Stanford University Press, 1965.
Hopkins, Gerard Manley. "God's Grandeur." *Poetry Foundation*. https://www.poetryfoundation.org.
Lewis, C. S. *Surprised by Joy: The Shape of My Early Life*. London: Bles, 1955.
Robinson, Marilynne. *The Death of Adam: Essays on Modern Thought*. New York: Picador, 2005.

7

Return to the Garden
Vigen Guroian's Christian Ecological Ethics

Jonathan Elliott

CREATION

THERE ARE FEW THINGS that I enjoy more than standing in a lush pasture watching, hearing, and smelling our livestock graze. There is an abundance of sights, sounds, and smells to delight the senses. But just as a great symphony cannot be deeply enjoyed by untrained ears (such as my own), creation's beauty requires not only attentive and attuned senses but also a certain understanding to be fully appreciated for what it is. Certainly, one can stand in awe of a mountain view or a vivid sunset independent of one's beliefs. But knowing what creation is at its most fundamental level opens up the possibility of a much deeper appreciation. When I arrived at the University of Virginia as an undergraduate student, I came, like almost all of my classmates, steeped in a materialist view of nature and for all intents and purposes numb to its abundant beauty. It was through Vigen Guroian's teaching, writing, and then friendship that I began to escape the straight-jacket of that materialist perspective and, over time, replace it with a Christian one.

In *The Melody of Faith*, Vigen writes, "Creation, the immense diversity of the universe, is God's ecstatic recapitulation of the plenitude of his Triune Being."[1] Creation is of course not a word that describes a divine action that took place however many years ago. It is the always-present activity of God by which "all things hold together in him" (Col 1:17 RSV) and "live and move and have their being" (Acts 17:28). All creation exists only by participating, in a created manner, in God's uncreated Being. Creation exists not because of any kind of necessity on God's part (creation adds nothing to God) but because "God loves Creation into existence perfectly freely, for perfect love is perfect freedom."[2]

If creation is the ecstatic recapitulation of the plenitude of God's Triune Being and an expression of God's perfect love, how is this manifested by creation? St. Thomas Aquinas provides a helpful answer:

> He brought things into being in order that His goodness might be communicated to creatures, and be represented by them; and because His goodness could not be adequately represented by one creature alone, He produced many and diverse creatures, that what was wanting to one in the representation of the divine goodness might be supplied by another. For goodness, which in God is simple and uniform, in creatures is manifold and divided and hence the whole universe together participates the divine goodness more perfectly, and represents it better than any single creature whatever.[3]

The seemingly infinite multitude of creatures, ourselves included, manifests God's infinite goodness. The great diversity of being in the universe shows forth all the endless ways in which God's being can be participated. What's more, the harmonious ways in which the great diversity of beings relate to one another reveal God as Goodness and Beauty itself.

Creation not only manifests God's divine attributes, particularly his infinity and goodness, which all three persons of the Trinity "possess" in perfect unity, but it also manifests something of God's Trinitarian character. The Father, Son, and Holy Spirit are distinguished from each other not by anything they possess (for then God would not be truly Triune) but by the relations to one another. And the character of these relations is reflected in

---

1. Guroian, *Melody of Faith*, 13.
2. Guroian, *Melody of Faith*, 12.
3. Aquinas, *Summa Theologica* 1.47.1.

creation, albeit in a rather hidden and mysterious way. St. Thomas writes of each created being:

> Therefore as it is a created substance, it represents the cause and principle; and so in that manner it shows the Person of the Father, Who is the "principle from no principle." According as it has a form and species, it represents the Word as the form of the thing made by art is from the conception of the craftsman. According as it has relation of order, it represents the Holy Ghost, inasmuch as He is love, because the order of the effect to something else is from the will of the Creator.[4]

The Father does not proceed from the Son or the Spirit, and so every creature considered as a subject in and of itself, represents the Father. The Word (or the Son) is the procession of God's complete and perfect knowledge from the Father. And so every creature considered as the *kind* of thing it is, reflects the Son as the source of its form. Finally, because every creature necessarily stands in relationship to other creatures, it reflects the Holy Spirit because the Holy Spirit is the procession of God's complete and perfect love and love is always in relationship to another.

From the Christian perspective then, Goodness, Love, and Wisdom are the source of and reason for creation. This perspective fundamentally stands in contrast to materialism. The materialist view sees chance, competition, and randomness as the sources of creation and finds no fundamental reason for creation. Beauty, on the Christian view, is at the heart of creation. From a materialist view beauty does not really exist in things, it is really just a description of a mental state. Vigen puts the difference poetically:

> In June I step into the cottage garden where the peonies grow. They surprise me with enormous rose blossoms. Where did the come from? Just a month ago they were under the earth. Oh, I know that I planted them three years ago and that I fed them with bonemeal in March after the last snow. But these flowers are sheer gift.[5]

ETHICS

Just as Vigen opened my eyes to an alternative view of creation, he also made me aware of different ways of understanding the nature of ethics.

4. Aquinas, *Summa Theologiae* 1.45.7.
5. Guroian, *Inheriting Paradise*, 41.

When I first read his book *Incarnate Love* before my senior year of college I struggled to make sense of the book. I had, to that point, simply absorbed from popular discourse the idea that ethics is essentially about a set of rules or a list of dos and don'ts. Vigen's approach to ethics simply didn't fit within that paradigm: what do the liturgy or the Trinity have to do with ethics, I wondered.

What I came to understand was that Christianity had traditionally understood ethics to be more or less synonymous with the idea of divinization or sanctification. Christian thinkers, inspired by their meditations on the Scriptures, began not with the question of what makes an action right or wrong, good or bad. Rather, they began from the premise that the purpose of every human life is to grow in holiness, to become more and more an image of God. As Vigen puts it, "morality has to do, ultimately, with the restoration of the image of God in humankind."[6] As such, "ethical striving or *askesis* has one end only, deification and union with God."[7]

Our union with God is, of course, perfected only after this life. But a very real, though imperfect, union is possible now through grace. The theological virtues of faith, hope, and charity are theological not only because they are gifts *from* God, virtues that we are incapable of developing ourselves, but also because they direct our minds and our wills towards and into God. Where all creatures faintly reflect the Trinitarian relations, human beings can radiate the Trinity through faith, hope, and charity. These virtues are our human participation in divine life and an anticipation of our eschatological union with God.

Relatedly, the many moral virtues, including prudence, justice, temperance, and fortitude, enable us to live lives of genuine friendship with other people in a way that anticipates the perfect friendship we will enjoy in the life to come. Ethics then is not fundamentally concerned with right and wrong actions (though the rightness or wrongness of our actions is certainly an aspect of ethics), but with the growth of friendship with God and with our neighbors. As Vigen puts it, ethics is "concerned primarily with the realization of love, righteousness, and divine similitude in persons and social institutions."[8]

When I finally understood that, the liturgy's central place in Vigen's ethical thinking made supreme sense. In the regular course of the Christian

---

6. Guroian, *Incarnate Love*, 15.
7. Guroian, *Incarnate Love*, 17.
8. Guroian, *Incarnate Love*, 27.

life the liturgy is the closest we come to the experience of heaven. Not only do the prayers of the Church orient and guide us towards union with God, but through communal worship and reception of the Eucharist we can experience a particularly intense friendship with God and with each other. In other words, the liturgy is both an essential source for understanding how we are to live our lives and is itself the pattern of ethical living. As Vigen puts it, "at heart Christian ethics is an invitation to the great banquet"[9]

ECOLOGICAL ETHICS

Vigen's writing would hold a preeminent place in the contemporary theological landscape simply for its role in recovering the Christian tradition's understanding of creation and ethics. Of course, there have been a number of other recent and contemporary philosophers and theologians that have contributed to that effort, albeit with somewhat different approaches than Vigen's. But in Vigen's writings I found the resources for the explication of an ecological ethics in a way that no other single author, that I have read at least, has made available.

Within Vigen's books *Ethics After Christendom*, *Inheriting Paradise*, *The Fragrance of God*, and *The Melody of Faith*, there is much material to draw on regarding ecological ethics. I will try to hone in a just a few points. First, that non-human creation is intrinsically good and would be so even if God had not created human beings. Second, that creation is indeed ordered to our human good but in a way that does nothing to diminish its intrinsic goodness. Third, that our perfection as men and women, our growth in holiness, includes our working for the good of all creation. I may not articulate all this in quite the same way Vigen does, but I think my presentation is true to his thinking.

As I tried to articulate earlier, Vigen understands creation to be the pouring out of God's infinite goodness. As such, all creation is good in and of itself, regardless of its relationship to us. As Vigen writes, "the worth of God's creatures consists is more than just their utility to humanity. As part of an ecological system, all life is of inestimable and inherent value to the Life-giver himself."[10] Not only do all creatures exist through a participation in God's Being, they also give praise to their creator. Simply through being themselves, all creatures express an aspect of God's infinite goodness.

9. Guroian, *Incarnate Love*, 93.
10. Guroian, *Ethics After Christendom*, 169.

One important way in which all creatures show forth God's splendor is through their relationship to other beings. All creatures are only fully what they are in terms of their relationship to other creatures. Plants would not truly be plants if not for their relationship to the multitude of soil organisms. And cattle would not be cattle if not for their relationship to the plants they graze. The same I believe can be said of all created beings. So we find in creation a faint reflection of the Trinity, for God is only who He is because of the eternal relations of Father, Son, and Holy Spirit.

But creatures are not only good in and of themselves, they are also ordered to our good in a variety of ways. Most obviously, an uncountable number of other creatures are ordered to our sustenance. If we think even just about those that provide our food, the number is beyond our comprehension: protozoa, bacteria, fungi, nematodes, arthropods, insects, plants, and animals all play essential roles in our health. Of course, physical well-being is only one aspect of what it means to be human, and certainly not the most definitive. All of creation is also there for us to know it, to marvel at its beauty, to praise God for its existence, and to care for it.

Just as creation exists for us (and for itself and for God), we exist for creation. Explicating the first chapter of Genesis, Vigen says:

> Christian tradition holds that human beings are created in the image and likeness of God. For this reason alone, humanity is bestowed with an exceptional power over creation. This power entails both a special vocation and a special responsibility. Humanity must mediate God's presence and God's care to the rest of creation. As human beings, we are called out by the very act through which God creates us to be priests and stewards of creation.[11]

In this passage Vigen touches on two of the central and complementary understandings of the phrase "image and likeness" within the patristic and medieval tradition. First, our "exceptional power over creation" is rooted in our capacities to know and to love in ways that no other creature can. Our ability to know and love is the image and likeness of God because the Trinitarian relations are relations of knowledge and love. Second, our vocation to mediate God's presence and care is what it means, what necessarily follows from, being created in God's image and likeness. In the historical context in which Genesis was written, a king's image and likeness was used

---

11. Guroian, *Ethics After Christendom*, 159.

to represent his authority over a region. Humanity then is to be "God's vice regent, the embodiment of his authority here on earth."[12]

We can see then how the pieces of Vigen's ecological and ethical thought fit together: the Trinitarian image in us is perfected through our bringing the Trinitarian reality in all creatures to greater perfection. I think Vigen's approach could rightly be called a Trinitarian ecological ethics. Recall that for Vigen ethics is "concerned primarily with the realization of love." The gift of charity, that participation in Divine Love, impels us to love not only our neighbor but all of creation. The more we love God, the more we should love His creation and the more we should desire to assist in its flourishing.

ECOLOGICAL ETHICS IN ACTION

Assuming I have offered an accurate-enough account of Vigen's ecological ethics, what would this all look like in practice? There are many ways to answer that question, but there are three answers that Vigen gives that I would like to focus on: consumerism as the anti-ethic, gardening in a theological mode, and the eschatological orientation of ethics.

In *Ethics After Christendom* Vigen quotes the great Orthodox theologian Alexander Schmeman:

> The fall of man is the rejection by him of his priestly calling, his refusal to be priest. The original sin consists in man's choice of a non-priestly relationship with God and the world. And perhaps no word better expresses the ssence of this new, fallen, non-priestly way of life than the one which in our time has had an amazingly successful career, has truly become the symbol of our culture. It is the word *"consumer."* . . . But the truth is, of course, that the "consumer" was not born in the twentieth century. The first consumer was Adam hiself. He chose not to be priest but to approach the world as consumer: to "eat" of it, to use and to dominate it for hiself, to benefit from it but not to offer, not to sacrifice, not to have it for God and in God.[13]

Schmeman is making the claim that consumerism is antithetical to the mission of the Church. If he is right, then it is certainly the case that consumerism contradicts Vigen's Christian ecological ethics. Consumerism

---

12. Martin, *Sacred Scripture*, 196–97.
13. Schmeman, *Of Water and the Spirit*, 96.

disconnects us from ecology, surrounding us instead with products that are entirely abstracted from their natural context: you needn't know anything about how to grow, harvest, and process cotton to buy a t-shirt or how to husband and shear a sheep to purchase a sweater. Consumerism likewise separates us from the people who produce the goods we buy. As far as ecological ethics is concerned, the absence of a relationship between producer and consumer means the consumer never need attend in thought or deed to the ecological context in which the products they purchase are produced. Finally, consumerism also encourages a "throw away culture" to borrow a phrase from Pope Francis. Rather than attend to the things we own in order to maintain and repair them, we simply replace them.

Consumerism is the air we breathe and it is all but impossible to escape it entirely. Nonetheless, we can all reduce our consumerist habits by producing more of the things we use. That can take many forms, be it work on our homes, gardening, cooking, making or repairing clothes, farming, etc. These kinds of tasks open us to the possibility of correctly seeing creation as a marvelous gift, capable of providing in abundance for all our needs. It provides an opportunity to rightly recognize ourselves as co-creators rather than just consumers.

I mentioned gardening as a way to reduce our consumerist habits. Vigen has written more extensively on gardening than perhaps any other contemporary theologian. A visit to his home in Culpeper, Virginia, leaves no room for doubt that his reflections on gardening are the fruit of countless hours tending to his own garden. The beautiful and impressive landscape of flowers, native grasses, fruit and ornamental trees, and many delicious vegetables leaves one wondering how "one man" did all of that.

In *Inheriting Paradise* Vigen organizes his reflections by liturgical season, exploring how the work in the garden and the fruits of that work relate to the mysteries commemorated by the Church at that time of year. Drawing connections between one's experiences weeding, harvesting, or simply marveling in the beauty of a rose bush relate to Christian revelation and the spiritual life could be taken as a somewhat arbitrary interpretation. What I think it reveals, however, is the deeply Trinitarian reading of reality that Vigen has. If the Trinity is truly at the heart of all reality, then seeing Christian revelation reflected in creation is anything but arbitrary. All things were created through the Word, who took on our human nature to reveal Himself to us, to reconcile us to Himself, and we become fully human only through our participation in Christ. Reading revelation with the Church Fathers, Vigen understands that the mystery of Christ has not only human significance but a cosmic significance as well. From that perspective, finding the Resurrection in the bursting forth of life in a garden bed is eminently fitting and genuinely logical. We find in Vigen's writings, which draw from life-long experience, a model of encountering and engaging creation in a theological mode.

There is one final question I'd like to address to help round out this explication of Vigen's ecological ethics. I hope that all of the above provides something of clear picture of why Vigen's thought is truly a Christian ecological ethic. Nonetheless, I think further clarity might come from asking how living out this ethic practically looks any different from living out the broadly utilitarian ecological ethic that dominates our cultural imagination and public policy debates.

There are at least two features of Vigen's thought that make his ethic a genuine alternative to utilitarianism, rather than a post-Christian flavor of it. First, by reminding us that love of God and love of neighbor is at the heart of ethics, Vigen encourages us to evaluate our actions in terms of our concrete relationships. How can I create a beautiful garden for my family and friends? How can the food I prepare nourish our guests? How can I avoid polluting the soil, air, and water on which my neighbors depend? How can I acquire the things I need without exploiting the dignity of those that produce those things? These are different kinds of questions than those that seek to create the greatest good, or happiness, or pleasure for the greatest number. As such, they will lead to a different self-narrative and a different set of actions.

The utilitarian perspective is concerned largely with questions of policy, for it is only with questions of policy that one can make any plausible claim to be able to effect the greatest good (or happiness, or pleasure) for the greatest number.[14] It quickly becomes clear that for your typical citizen, it is all but irrelevant to ask how one's day-to-day actions can results in the greatest good. In other words, only bureaucrats and the bureaucrat-adjacent can be practicing utilitarians. By contrast, a Christian ecological ethic is interested in the development of virtues, both as they are practiced by individuals *and* shape society. It is as universal as the call to union with God.

14. We will set aside the question of whether or not the greatest good, happiness, or pleasure for the greatest number is something that is *per se* impossible to determine. For an extended argument against utilitarian determinations, see MacIntyre, *After Virtue*, 91–107.

Second, and perhaps more importantly, Vigen's ecological ethics, like his broader ethical framework, is eschatological in nature. That is to say, it understands the ultimate significance and value, or lack thereof, of our actions in light of our perfect union with God and perfect relationship to one another. There is a tension there, in that we should always be striving to make present God's kingdom here and now while recognizing that we will always fall radically short of the reality of heaven. But this tension is ultimately a source of hope because it is the love of God and neighbor with which we pursue the perfection of creation that is of ultimate significance.

Our contemporary debates about ecology and climate immanentize and thus distort the eschatological character of ecological ethics. The success or failure of our environmental efforts is what is of ultimate significance, and success or failure must be determined by quantifiable metrics. Success might be achieved then without love of either God or neighbor. From the Christian perspective, this is incoherent. It is essentially to say that we can succeed as human beings by failing at what it means most fundamentally to be human. For, as Vigen has so forcefully and eloquently articulated across his many works, love is at the heart of all Christian ethics and the heart of what it means to be a human being.

BIBLIOGRAPHY

Guroian, Vigen. *Ethics After Christendom: Toward an Ecclesial Christian Ethic.* 1994. Reprint, Eugene, OR: Wipf & Stock, 2004.
———. *The Fragrance of God.* Grand Rapids: Eerdmans, 2006.
———. *Incarnate Love: Essays in Orthodox Ethics.* 2nd ed. Notre Dame: University of Notre Dame Press, 2002.
———. *Inheriting Paradise: Meditations on Gardening.* Grand Rapids: Eerdmans, 1999.
———. *Melody of Faith: Theology in an Orthodox Key.* Grand Rapids: Eerdmans, 2010.
MacIntyre, Alasdair. *After Virtue: A Study In Moral Theory.* 3rd ed. South Bend, IN: University of Notre Dame Press, 2007.
Martin, Francis. *Sacred Scripture: The Disclosure of the Word.* Naples, FL: Sapientia, 2006.
Schmeman, Alexander. *Of Water and the Spirit.* Crestwood, NY: St. Vladimir's Seminary, 1974.
Thomas Aquinas. *Summa Theologiae. Prima Pars 1–49.* Lander, WY: Aquinas Institute for the Study of Sacred Doctrine, 2012.

Part Three

Tending the Heart

8

A Wardrobe of Images
Children's Stories and the Moral Imagination

Daniel B. Coupland and Rebecca Schwartz

"What then is the end, object, or purpose of humane letters? Why, the expression of the moral imagination; or, to put this truth in a more familiar phrase, the end of great books is ethical—to teach us what it means to be genuinely human."
—Russell Kirk[1]

In *Tending the Heart of Virtue: How Classic Stories Awaken a Child's Moral Imagination*, Vigen Guroian takes part in a literary conversation— upheld by mainstays of the Western literary tradition such as Plato, Aristotle, and Shakespeare—largely concerned with the formation of the person in relation to perennial truths about human nature and reality itself. And, like all significant works tend to do, *Tending the Heart of Virtue* continues to inspire new streams within that larger conversation. Of course, this great, abstract conversation operates much like everyday exchanges, with the same dynamic potential: a seemingly simple chat can suddenly transform

1. Kirk, *Redeeming the Time*, 73.

into a life-altering encounter that shapes not only a certain period of a participant's thinking, but the whole of his or her intellectual life. *This* is the sort of book that not only enters into conversation with its readers, acting as a meeting point between perennial truths and particular, everyday moments (such as the moment when a parent picks up a storybook to read at bedtime), but also encourages the reader to encounter other books, other instances of the conversation, and to carry that conversation forward just as *Tending the Heart of Virtue* has done.

Given this emphasis upon the way a conversation can be passed on from one participant to another like an inheritance of letters, it comes as no surprise that the interests animating this book were largely Guroian's own interests in shaping the hearts of children. Guroian's journey with literature, in some ways, began in earnest when he started reading to his own children.[2] In the fall of 1983, Guroian sought the advice of Russell Kirk, acclaimed author, American political theorist, and Edmund Burke scholar—or simply, as Guroian calls Kirk, "a man of letters"—regarding the kinds of stories he ought to be reading to his own children. Kirk suggested a few of his favorite stories: George MacDonald's *The Princess and the Goblin*, Carlo Collodi's *Pinocchio*, C. S. Lewis's *Chronicles of Narnia*, John Ruskin's *The King of the Golden River*, Oscar Wilde's "The Selfish Giant," and the fairy tales of the Grimm Brothers and Hans Christian Anderson.[3] Kirk's recommendations were so influential to Guroian, personally, that the stories Kirk suggested eventually came to comprise the basis of a college course entitled Religion in Children's Literature that Guroian taught for twenty-five years.[4] These stories richly described the human condition: worlds defined by moral boundaries, characters facing moral dilemmas fraught with the promise of consequences, and perhaps most importantly, the breathless longing for a hero and magic to step in and *save* despite all seeming hopeless and lost. As Guroian continued to teach this course, he found that there was very little for parents and teachers that discussed how children's literature could inform, shape, and nurture children to inhabit a moral universe. Thus, it is for the explicit benefit of parents and teachers that *Tending the Heart of Virtue* was born. It is, at its essential heart, a book for people who have concerns about "raising children to be ethical persons"

---

2. Guroian, *Tending the Heart of Virtue*, 4.
3. Guroian, *Tending the Heart of Virtue*, 4.
4. Guroian, *Tending the Heart of Virtue*, 4.

through a rich inheritance of great literature and thereby bringing them into the fullness of humanity.[5]

The two authors of this chapter, Dan Coupland and Rebecca Schwartz, are inheritors of this great tradition of children's literature by means of Guroian's profound book. Coupland, a professor of education and dean of the Graduate School of Classical Education at Hillsdale College, read *Tending the Heart of Virtue* in the fall of 2008, when he, like Guroian himself, became concerned with the kinds of stories he ought to be reading to his own children. *Tending the Heart of Virtue* provided him with a set of insights so illuminating that they not only affected this father of three young children but also fundamentally altered the choices that he was making as an educator. At Hillsdale College, Coupland reshaped an existing children's literature course around the guiding principle of Guroian's "moral imagination," believing that this view of children's literature was, bar none, the best one that he could share with classrooms full of future parents and teachers. In the fall of 2017, Rebecca was one such student: a future teacher sitting in Dr. Coupland's Children's Literature course. Listening to lectures that had been shaped by Guroian's book, she came to understand the moral imagination as the key to all moral formation—a realization that simultaneously illuminated her own favorite childhood stories as well as instilled in her a desire to help cultivate the moral imagination in her own students. And, when she graduated from Hillsdale College in 2018, Rebecca began teaching to young students the same stories that were taught to her. Students from the sixth to twelfth grades were learning the stories that had been passed down, person-to-person, through a literary inheritance that—in this context, in this time—so often hinges upon Vigen Guroian's *Tending the Heart of Virtue*. Someday, Rebecca and her husband, David, hope to further practice this tradition by reading the same stories to their own children (when they arrive).

In *Tending the Heart of Virtue*, Guroian writes, "The moral imagination is not a thing, not even so much a faculty of the mind, as *the very process by which the self makes metaphors out of images that memory supplies*. It then employs these metaphors *to suppose correspondences* in experience and *to make moral judgments*."[6] The moral imagination that Guroian describes, whereby a person might actually make serious moral decisions on the basis of metaphors, provides a means of understanding the real

---

5. Guroian, *Tending the Heart of Virtue*, 4.
6. Guroian, *Tending the Heart of Virtue*, 24.

importance of literature. If it is indeed possible for a person's discernment (both of the world and his respective relation to it) to rest upon his or her remembrance of certain stories, then it is of the utmost importance that those stories should be Good, True, and Beautiful. If we are to be educators at all, then we take upon our shoulders the responsibility of ensuring that—whatever equations, whatever data, whatever philosophizing our students take up—their moral imaginations are "fed" with good literature, literature that is capable of illuminating the ordered, unmoving truths of life in the world. If we are not tending to the hearts of virtue within children, as Guroian suggests, then we are not teaching them anything worthwhile.

"THE SHAPE OF OUR WORLD": THE MUSES AND PLATO'S FORMS

In the first chapter of *Tending the Heart of Virtue*, Vigen Guroian writes, "Narrative supplies the imagination with important symbolic information about the *shape of our world* and appropriate responses to its inhabitants."[7] While the real object of our interest is how narrative, as Guroian writes, "supplies the imagination" with "symbolic information," we want to begin this inquiry by examining a different phrase in the quotation above: "the *shape of our world*." Guroian's use of this phrase aligns him not only with towering figures of antiquity such as Plato and Socrates, but also with a much broader classical configuration of the world and reality itself: a configuration that underlies the entire tradition of Western thought. Thinkers in classical antiquity went so far as to link the very concept of "story" to the divine, and this link can be examined through the example of the Muses.

The Muses were not merely a poetic device; these mythological Greek goddesses were actually regarded as the source of all stories. Through the exercise of their divine knowledge, the Muses precluded the possibility of sole authorship—solely human authorship—and the existence of a story that had not been, in some way, *touched* by the gods and thereby imbued with a measure of divine truth.[8] And, by reminding audiences that the Muses provide inspiration for all stories, the Greek poets of antiquity also reminded audiences that there is an *eternal realm* that exists in dialogue

---

7. Guroian, *Tending the Heart of Virtue*, 14 (emphasis added).

8. The Muses truly cover an astonishingly large amount of content: history, music, comedy and pastoral poetry, tragedy, dance, love and lyric poetry, hymns, astronomy, and epic poetry. See Woodard, "Hesiod and Greek Myth," 83–165.

with the corporeal, veiled realm of everyday life. In addition to "guaranteeing" the truth value of the stories that they themselves inspired, the Muses also provided a purview for storytelling that encompassed, according to the poet Hesiod's *Theogony*, "What is, and what is to be, / and what was before now,"[9] which only the divine could possibly know. In other words, because of the Muses' existence, all events comprising the fabric of reality were made teleological within a fixed, ordered, created, and re-creatable reality. These events were, in some way, the subject matter of *all* stories.

While belief in the Muses and their divine ability to inspire poetry, of course, waned over time, the relationship between the poet and truth that they helped to describe has remained firmly ingrained in the Western tradition. The purview of poetry, the fixed nature of reality, the beauty of created order, and the beautiful order of creation, first described in Western thought by the form of the Muses, have continued to inspire not only our ideas about storytelling but our ideas about reality, as well. We might even say, as Guroian does, that there is a distinct *"shape of our world,"* and that stories have a unique ability to furnish our imaginations with images of this shape, this world, and our place within it.

Like divinely-inspired storytelling, the kind of navigation of "symbolic information" is also a process long known and quite indispensable to the Western tradition. In Plato's *Republic*, for example, Socrates (in)famously bans poetry—in context, another word for stories—from the ideal state primarily because poetry is not "true." In other words, the shape of the world described by poetry is a false impression of the real thing. While Socrates's indictment of poetry might, at first brush, seem untenably draconian, it is actually a more nuanced assertion.[10] Many of these misreadings arise from a failure to recognize the semantic disagreement between *factual truth* and *normative truth*, which is the difference between truths about concrete, factual things and truths about the *shape of our world*, to quote Guroian. Socrates only banishes poetry that is *normatively* false from the republic. Poetry is, therefore, only unconscionable when it deceives its audience in regards to the truth of the Forms, which constitute the purest, most perfect, most complete form of reality for the ancient Greeks. Stories that are normatively true and, as such, reflect the actual shape of our world are allowed to remain in the republic even if they are factually false (as in

---

9. Hesiod, "Theogony," 125.

10. I owe the concept of factual vs. normative truth (as seen in Plato's *Republic*) to Battin's excellent article, "Plato on True and False Poetry."

the case of fiction).[11] And yet the weight of Socrates's indictment against normatively false stories remains heavy enough to echo across the span of two millenia. The importance of discernment—of consciously tending an affection for those stories that, even through fiction, supply the moral imagination with "symbolic information" describing the true, the beautiful, and the good—has been a fixture of Western thought for as long as stories have been recognized for their capacity to furnish the mind with images of our created world.

Plato's conception of the Forms as the source of all paradigmatic truth has been translated into the more general conception of an ordered cosmos: a conception that has since come to both underlie and characterize Western thought. The concept of an ordered cosmos brings with it several implications: firstly, that reality is both fixed and complete; secondly, that the existence of a Creator can either be presupposed (as in the Christian conception) or detected as a self-evident fact (as in the Greek conception); and, thirdly, that it is possible and necessary for humans to find their place within this created order. Importantly, these three claims lay certain responsibilities upon stories, which function as our primary means of comprehending both the world and ourselves. For example, John Henry Newman writes that literature is "a study of human nature," which presents an illustration of how man *is* and not how he *ought* to be. Newman, therefore argues that literature can provide a truthful, realistic image of man's perennial nature.[12] Josef Pieper, taking up the outward-looking potential of storytelling, calls the Western cosmos a "domain of eternal archetypes"[13] wherein we humans might find *and* place ourselves.

This tenacious belief in truth makes it possible for humanity to answer the great imperative underlying Western ideas about storytelling all the way from the poet Hesiod to Guroian: not only to tell the truth, but to both receive the truth when it is told and allow it to shape one's affections. Toward this, Pope Benedict XVI writes, "When a man conforms to the measure of the universe, his freedom is not diminished but expanded to a new horizon."[14] And this relationship to reality necessitates, as it did with

11. Consider the fiction of Socrates's Noble Lie: in Book 3, Socrates encourages a myth about the origin of the three social classes in order to maintain social harmony within the republic.

12. Newman, *Idea of a University*, 174.

13. Pieper, *Only the Lover Sings*, 23.

14. Pope Benedict XVI's words are quoted in the introduction to Caldecott, *Beauty for Truth's Sake*, 15.

Hesiod, that one must *submit* in order to *know*—that, whatever truths there are, they must be elevated above the will of the individual if they are to, in any sense, liberate the individual.

Here at last we make an explicit return to teaching and the importance of stories to the practice of training a student's affections or, to quote Guroian once more, "tending the heart of virtue." The seven liberal arts were codified in late Roman antiquity in order to *liberate* free men to pursue virtue and excellence, but, as Socrates makes clear with his indictment of normatively false poetry, all this liberation will be undone if a student has no clear sense of the shape of our world. In order to experience liberation, one must first become attuned to normative truths about the world into which he will be liberated. And, while literature is not one of the seven liberal arts, we might nonetheless argue that stories therefore underlie every liberatory act achieved through the practice of these arts: man can only be *truly* virtuous and excellent if he has learned to perceive correctly the fixed nature of reality and his own relationship to it. In a Christian context, this means becoming attuned to the character of God Himself, in whom all order exists and upon whom all order rests.

"THE WARDROBE" OF EXPERIENCES:[15] CHILDREN'S STORIES

If the *shape of our world* is, indeed, a fixed and created reality toward which we must conform ourselves if we are to experience real liberation, virtue, and excellence, then the ways in which we encounter this world must be considered of the utmost importance. If, as Guroian writes, "The moral imagination is not a thing, not even so much a faculty of the mind, as *the very process by which the self makes metaphors out of images that memory supplies*" and that the moral imagination "employs these metaphors *to suppose correspondences* in experience and *to make moral judgments*,"[16] then we must conclude that stories are the vital points of connection between every individual and the world that stands waiting, demanding from him some moral action. And because being in the world is a lifelong experience, this imperative—to learn the beautiful, created order of the world—must be met with a lifelong effort to tend one's heart and train one's loves. This

---

15. Guroian borrows the term "the wardrobe of a moral imagination" from Edmund Burke's *Reflections on the Revolution in France* (1790).

16. Guroian, *Tending the Heart of Virtue*, 20 (emphasis added).

prompts us to take children's literature as seriously as Socrates takes poetry in the *Republic*: to recognize, in other words, that the seeds of virtue are sown every time a child reads or hears a *normatively* true story, and, in some respects, the moral imagination begins with the first stories that children learn.

As Guroian suggests in *Tending the Heart of Virtue*, the formation of a child's character requires much more than "mere instruction in morality,"[17] as is supposed by more didactic and positivistic approaches to inculcation. Guroian calls such attempts at moral instruction "heavily exhortative," and remarks that they often leave "the pupil feel[ing] coerced"[18] instead of "crowned and mitered over himself," as Virgil leaves Dante in the last lines of the *Purgatorio*.[19] Rather than emblems of truth, beauty, and goodness (or, in a worst case scenario, some smattering of ideas about how to get along in society), Guroian argues that students need a "compelling vision of the goodness of goodness itself"—a vision of goodness that is "attractive and stirs up the imagination" in the unique way that stories do.[20]

Simply put, the difference between the kind of didacticism that Guroian rejects and the moral imagination that he proposes is the difference between an education interested in making automata and an education interested in cultivating virtuous discernment. The latter approach to education should train students not to memorize and regurgitate certain edicts but, rather, to develop a sensitivity to goodness—an ability, indeed, to *recognize* goodness as if it were an old friend who might appear in any crowd at any time and needed only to be caught and greeted. Toward this end, Guroian posits that children's stories, and fairy tales in particular, should be considered the primary means by which a child's discernment and character are formed. Characterized by their "vivid descriptions of the struggle between good and evil" and "difficult choices between right and wrong,"[21] fairy tales exist in a world that presents moral realities without the ostentatious overtness that characterizes didacticism. Instead, children are given stories that they can easily interpret, situations that they can imagine themselves experiencing, and a truthful depiction of the rewards and consequences that come with certain choices. Such stories are, as Josef

---

17. Guroian, *Tending the Heart of Virtue*, 16.
18. Guroian, *Tending the Heart of Virtue*, 16.
19. Dante Alighieri, *Divine Comedy*, 524.
20. Guroian, *Tending the Heart of Virtue*, 16.
21. Guroian, *Tending the Heart of Virtue*, 14.

Pieper writes, in "harmony with the fundamental realities"[22] and render these realities intelligible to children so that later, when real goodness and real evil appear, they will not be difficult to recognize. Between the story and the world a sense of *harmony*—some kind of connection or mediation—thereby brings the individual human soul in line with the "shape of our world."

The moral imagination, as Guroian proposes, is, in some ways, a great faculty of connection and interpretation by which living stories become similarly living maps of the created world; in other ways, it is a microcosmic picture of life in the fallen world, always feeling the acute sensation that there *should be* some goodness that *is not*. Faced with this, it becomes necessary to recall that neither Socrates nor Guroian believe that stories should contain goodness, truth, and beauty *exclusively*. Instead, the imperative of normative truth demands that a story should truthfully reflect the *shape of our world*—a world that is profoundly troubled and regularly cruel beyond the capacity of words to describe. But here darkness and light exist in one place. Ours is a fallen world that is nonetheless created, ordered, and, beneath it all, imbued with the deep goodness of its Creator. The Greeks, similarly, held no suspicion that the realm of the Forms was really the realm of everyday life; the world of Western tradition is a good world in spite of the fact that it is also a bad world. "We find it difficult," J. R. R. Tolkien claims, "to conceive of evil and beauty together,"[23] but time and again—certainly in modernity—we see that the world is exactly as Tolkien describes it. So, if we are to meet the standards of storytelling that we have set forth so far, this conception of reality must be reflected in our stories, even our stories for children.

While this conception of the world might tempt us to say that Guroian's desire for children to see a "compelling vision of the goodness of goodness itself" is impossible to fulfill in "earthly" storytelling, the unique properties of normatively true literature shine through once more in answer to Guroian's desire. Tolkien, for instance, emphasizes that despite their factual falseness, fairy stories possess a unique quality of reflecting reality more clearly through the more dramatic (and, in this way, more readily discernible) portrayals of evil and beauty that are unique to narrative fiction. The "sudden and miraculous grace" that occurs near the end of a fairy tale

---

22. Pieper, *Only the Lover Sings*, 27.
23. Tolkien, *On Fairy Stories*.

in spite of the seeming futility of hope mimics the ultimate reality of God's overwhelming goodness. Toward this point, he writes:

> Probably every writer making a secondary world, a fantasy, a sub-creator, wishes in some measure to be a real maker, or hopes that he is drawing on reality . . . It is difficult to conceive how this can be, if the work does not in some way partake of reality. The peculiar quality of the "joy" in successful Fantasy can thus be explained *as a sudden glimpse of the underlying reality or truth*. It is not only a "consolation" for the sorrow of this world, but a satisfaction, and an answer to that question, "Is it true?" The answer to this question that I gave at first was (quite rightly): "If you have built your little world well, yes: it is true in that world . . . But in the 'eucatastrophe' we see in a brief vision that the answer may be great—it may be a far-off gleam or echo of *evangelium* in the real world."[24]

Tolkien assumes that reality is undergirded by a principle of grace and that the fabric of reality is just as tightly woven with joy as it is with darkness. And any story that is inherently meaningful will reflect the existence of grace, which is, as Josef Pieper writes, a "primordial archetype"[25] essential to any normatively true story about the world. Goodness, grace, joy—these things triumph, and when Goodness triumphs it is not triumphing over some sterile version of its own non-existence: it triumphs over evil. And, in our children's stories, defeated evil should be as recognizable as goodness triumphant.

We might say that the function of children's stories is to provide children with clear, true, interesting, and intelligible encounters with the created order—an encounter upon which they might base their deepest structures of virtue-recognition. That said, it is difficult to imagine any one impression of goodness or virtue adequately preparing a person for the variety of moral quandaries that arise with life in the world. This is where the moral imagination comes in most powerfully—specifically, a conception of the moral imagination that Guroian draws from Edmund Burke's *Reflections on the Revolution in France*, wherein Burke describes the iconic image of a wardrobe. Describing this wardrobe and the moral imagination, Jon Fennell writes as follows:

> The notion of "wardrobe"—a place where valuable things are kept (and also, I would say, a word standing for those things

---

24. Tolkien, *On Fairy Stories*.
25. Pieper, *Only the Lover Sings*, 64.

themselves)—seems to me apt because the role of imagination is to capture or represent the world to an individual in a certain way. The wardrobe is a stock of concepts—that is, ideals, principles, meanings, and possibilities—in terms of which the world is clothed and we thereby understand it. Actions and events, if noticed at all, are seen as an instance, consequence, or harbinger of something. The contents of the wardrobe are what allow us to see in one way or another. In the words of Michael Ward, imagination is "the organ of meaning." The individual, due to his moral imagination, will be disposed to see in a particular way. If moral imagination is well formed, the individual will see in a salutary way.[26]

In other words, just as the individual articles of clothing in a normal wardrobe are uniquely suited to various bodies, seasons, occasions, outfits, and so on, lessons contained in the well-stocked "wardrobe" of a moral imagination are uniquely suited to a wide variety of complex situations—situations that demand virtuous action.

In the words of Russell Kirk, the purpose of all literature is "to teach us what it means to be genuinely human." This kind of humane education necessarily instills in students a sense of intellectual heritage in tandem with a *moral* heritage, which prompts in students a desire to *live out* the virtues contained within the literature that they are reading. And, while all great works of literature are capable of teaching us "what it means to be genuinely human," Guroian points out in *Tending the Heart of Virtue* that it is children's literature, specifically, that acts as the vital, beating heart of humane education, as children's literature is perhaps the most reliable way to align the student's affections with that which is Good, True, and Beautiful. The act of "tending a heart" or of aligning a student's affections is the act of teaching a young person how to love the best things—things that can, as Guroian writes, describe the true "shape of the world." In other words, this alignment cultivates a real means of understanding the moral shape of the universe in which we live by encouraging and furnishing the "moral imagination." By acknowledging and describing these time-honored truths, *Tending the Heart of Virtue* inspired a generation of classical educators and parents to read great stories to the children in their lives in the hope that these stories will help cultivate a robust moral imagination and ultimately help them to be more "genuinely human."

---

26. Fennell, "What Is the Moral Imagination?"

BIBLIOGRAPHY

Alighieri, Dante. *The Divine Comedy: The Inferno, the Purgatorio, and the Paradiso*. Translated by John Ciardi. New York: New American, 2003.

Battin, M. Pabst. "Plato on True and False Poetry." *Journal of Aesthetics and Art Criticism* 36.2 (1977) 163–74. https://doi.org/10.2307/429756.

Caldecott, Stratford. *Beauty for Truth's Sake*. Grand Rapids: Brazos, 2009.

Fennell, Jon M. "What Is the Moral Imagination?" *Imaginative Conservative*, April 11, 2016. https://theimaginativeconservative.org/2016/04/what-is-the-moral-imagination.html.

Guroian, Vigen. *Tending the Heart of Virtue: How Classic Stories Awaken a Child's Moral Imagination*. 2nd ed. New York: Oxford University Press, 2023.

Hesiod. "Theogony." In *Hesiod*, edited by Richmond Lattimore, 119–86. Ann Arbor: University of Michigan Press, 1959.

Kirk, Russell. *Redeeming the Time*. Wilmington, DE: ISI, 1996.

Newman, John Henry. *The Idea of a University*. Edited by Martin J. Svaglic. Notre Dame: University of Notre Dame Press, 1982.

Pieper, Josef. *Only the Lover Sings: Art and Contemplation*. San Francisco: Ignatius, 1990.

Tolkien, J. R. R. *On Fairy Stories*. Oxford: Oxford University Press, 1947.

Woodard, Roger D. "Hesiod and Greek Myth." In *The Cambridge Companion to Greek Mythology*, edited by Roger D. Woodard, 83–165. Cambridge Companions to Literature. New York: Cambridge University Press, 2007.

9

Spontaneous Grace
Vigen Guroian as Teacher and Friend

WILLIAM M. WILSON

I MET VIGEN GUROIAN in 1968 in my very first college class. I sat in the back row which seemed appropriate for a freshman (or "first-year" as we were taught to call ourselves at the University of Virginia), and also because I had no solid idea why I had signed up for this class or even what it would be about. A faculty advisor had suggested that if I had even a barely conscious interest in a given field of study I should go ahead and try it out.

Vigen sat in the front row directly in front of the podium, and even before the professor entered the room he was holding court. The front rowers, all obviously old friends, began throwing around names like Malinowski, Durkheim, Marx, and Feuerbach; I had no idea what they were discussing, but whatever it was Vigen had the last word. The only one of those odd sounding names that I recognized was Marx, who goes down in my thanks for supplying the very first sentence in the class reading that I completely understood. It was, "Religion is the opium of the people." Now I began to feel that I belonged.

When the professor entered the room Vigen cocked his head to the left (which he still does when things get underway) and flashed all around a big "bring it on" grin. This, anyway, is my memory of my first class in college. You must understand that I did not know the name of this fellow. He was simply "that guy" in the front row. I remember nothing else about the rest of the semester, only the first day, but "that guy" is always there in my memory.

It is easy to fall into sentimentality in praising one who has distinguished his profession. This is especially so in the case of a scholar and teacher as so much of his influence lies in the personal exchanges he has had with waves of students down the years. Fortunately, on this occasion to "praise famous men" I have my own relationship to take as an example. He has been a treasured friend and stalwart teacher in good times and in bad, for over five decades. To know his praiseworthiness you need to know him in both of these virtues.

"That guy" graduated at the end of the year, and as I got deeper into the study of religion and theology, I forgot about him. I went on to earn a MDiv at Harvard Divinity School, returning to Virginia to enroll in its brand new PhD program. At the beginning of my fifth semester there a new young faculty member came on board with a three-year non-tenure track appointment and a knack for befriending all of the nervous graduate students who were completely unsure what this new program would bring to bear upon them. He was entirely in his element, exuberant and spontaneous, and if he had any anxiety about winning a tenure-track post at another school he never showed it. To us, he was our source of enthusiasm, friendship, and hope that we would complete the degree in fine style and go on to a great career. Then one day it hit me quite out of the blue that this man we called Vigen was "that guy" in the front row holding court. I must emphasize that there was no reason for me to make this connection; there was no more reason for it than there was for me to have walked into *that* first-year college class. It was not possible for me *not* to recognize the hand of providence working out a plan. The recognition made me understand that it was time for me to meet and join up with a true first-rower who in his own way was inviting me to participate in the joy of this profession.

A well-known mid-twentieth-century New Testament scholar, C. H. Dodd, once translated the Greek word for "grace" as "spontaneous," a rather odd rendering but it fit Vigen's grace to a tee. I said above that he was in his own element as a young professor, and oftentimes what was *peculiar* to him (to use that word correctly) was simply "peculiar" to us (to use it as it is commonly used). For instance, he and I once went to a conference and arrived before the event opened. There was a span of old oaks and poplars below the conference building, and Vigen motioned for me to follow him down there. He strolled deep into the woods, stared down a gigantic poplar, then turned and grinned at me. He then embraced the tree with arms outstretched, held his head back and laughed hysterically. He thereby confessed to the world that he was a *bona fide* Tree Hugger, a term used for allegedly over enthusiastic environmentalists. "Look at this big thing just growing out of the ground," he shouted in utter amazement.

This was a side of Vigen I had never seen. I was to see many more such "spontaneous" behaviors, most of which did not even have a context (e.g., environmentalism) as did this first one. For instance, he was given to entering class walking on his hands (he was a gymnast in college) and spending most of the lecture, thus, upside down, lecture notes on the floor. If asked why he did this you got the tree hugger historical laugh. Nor did he explain lying on his stomach with arms outstretched for the entirety of the class. I believe he was demonstrating how a sect of Orthodox monks prayed, but who knows for sure?

This next example of spontaneity helped me figure out at least some of his MO, but grace can never be fully understood if understood at all. It happened at the start of a school year when some faculty must endure a "training session" orchestrated by administrators to prepare them to be good advisors. Vigen was chosen to participate, and to start the story off, what a red rag is to a bull, so a training session is to Vigen. It got off to a very bad start. Then the worst happened.

We had both left Virginia and joined the Theology Department at Loyola College (now University), so this happened in a Catholic setting. A young and very green priest stood up and gave a short speech about the office of Campus Ministries and all it had to offer incoming students. He urged the advisors-in-training to send their students to the office and get acquainted with it. Then he said this: "Come on down yourselves. We aren't a bunch of Holy Rollers. We are into stuff like Psychology." I turned to Vigen and whispered "don't do it. *Please do not do it!*" But I was too late. He had already stood up, and he had the "bring it on grin" locked and loaded. He said, interrupting the session, "my name is Vigen Guroian from the Theology Department, and if any of you all need to see a Holy Roller you can always come see me." The standard coffee and doughnuts were then served a whole lot earlier than planned.

Soon thereafter I returned to Virginia and Vigen followed along a little later. I have told the Holy Roller story (Vigen loves it) to those who love Vigen and it always gets a great laugh. Down the years it has come to shed light, and great light at that, on our beloved friend. Vigen's great joy in life and vocation is a result of having looked into the abyss. He took Faulkner's advice and "wept over universal bones." As an Armenian he lives daily knowing that people tried to exterminate his people, made a good job of it, and very few people know about it (as Hitler predicted) and the US Government makes no comment about it. Turkey, after all, offers a nice landing zone in the Middle East. I am one of the handful of students and friends who know of his terrible temper and how it has driven him into the arms of the Armenian Orthodoxy. Each aspect of the faith is a deep and salvific mystery. He will not make a specimen of it. Its history must not be seen as a "religious" history, one among many that is; rather it must be seen as its own thing, something *peculiar*. You know it when you know there is nothing else like it, as if it can only be properly presented by walking on your hands or likened to a "huge thing that just grew out of the ground."

Accordingly, it must never, never be reduced to something else. It is *not* a specimen of psychology, or a kind of drug (Marx's opium). In fact I now know that that whole first class at Virginia was a pitched battle for Vigen, placing him in the front row with lieutenants. The "strange" names I mentioned at the outset of this remembrance all said that religion is a specimen of something else, for instance "society worshiping itself," or "humanity worshiping itself," or the opium of the State. Dostoevsky, Eliot, Auden, Picasso, and other great artists found the joy of modern life by scouting out our unique forms of evil. Vigen taught their works brilliantly, as he did the stories and fables that haunt, terrify, and then delight children.

Those who learned of Vigen's great worth as a friend and teacher saw that he took us down to the pits (as Dante called the depths of Hell) and brought us up laughing, mirroring truth to be like nothing else with his own peculiarity. When one of my children took his first communion, Vigen looked down and asked him, "How did it taste?" It is now my great privilege to honor a distinguished teacher and friend.

10

Tiller of Significant Soil
Vigen Guroian as Teacher, Mentor, Gardener, Friend

Brian Martin Lapsa

Τοὔνεκά με προέηκε διδασκέμεναι τάδε πάντα
μύθων τε ῥητῆρ᾽ ἔμεναι πρηκτῆρά τε ἔργων.

For this reason he sent me, to instruct you in all these things:
To be both a speaker of words and a doer of deeds.

—Homer, *Iliad* 9.442–443

THE SKY WAS OVERCAST the day we started drilling the last row of postholes. The Professor was grimly determined to leave his vegetable garden walled against the ravages of the cloven-footed beasts he bitterly dubbed his "deer-ly beloveds." In anticipation of antlers deployed like siege weapons, and of the inevitable onset of rot, we were to plant the fenceposts of "Fort Guroian" in several feet of concrete. But the thick red clay of Culpeper, Virginia, makes for tough digging. So the Professor had rented a two-man, gas-powered earth auger for the job. With a drill bit about a foot in diameter, a big orange motor box, and four long handles sprouting out of the top like the blades of a propeller, the post-hole digger resembled less a garden tool than it did an alien drone. It certainly took some wrangling. But with perseverance we got the better of it, and even managed to sink a few holes without amputating any limbs.

It was April 2011, the week before graduation. Jonny, Joseph, and I had decided to spend the week at Professor Guroian's Arcadian homestead. In reality we auxiliaries were two, since Joseph, famed for what we called his "academic constitution," was doubly incapacitated: first by his propensity for engaging the Professor in interminable debates about political philosophy, to the great detriment of the digging, and secondly by levels of melanin scarcely in excess of the threshold for clinical albinism. It was, alas, very sunny the day he arrived. After a particularly spirited discussion of Burkean thought on that first afternoon, Joseph retired early and awoke the next morning as red as a lobster, scarcely able to move from his bed. He spent the remainder of his stay being nursed back to health by the solicitous attention of our gracious hostess, Mrs. June Guroian.

We had bored perhaps half of the post-holes we needed—it would have been some twenty in all, I think—when we felt the first rain drops. Before long it was a downpour, and the hill was running with rivulets of red clay mud. We kept at it. "Ah-*ha!*" came the Professor's cry over the roar of the engine, the whipping of the wind, and the rumble of thunder. It came again, equal parts exultant and defiant: "Ah-*ha!*" We bored on. The holes we had dug were filling with water. I distinctly recall one springing a leak, with water curiously gushing upward and into the hole from its downhill side. Instead of clods of clay, sheer geysers of red slurry were flying in all directions. Still we drilled, defying common sense and Nature Herself. But where pride goeth . . . "Whoa! Ah-*ha!*" The Professor slipped and fell. Limbs akimbo, down the muddy slope he slid.

I got to know Professor Vigen Guroian at the University of Virginia in the late 2000s and early 2010s. He cut a distinctive figure there: bespectacled, waistcoated, tweeded, and invariably bow-tied, he was easy to spot, even at the far end of the Lawn. And he was beloved of his students. His courses—on Religion and Literature, Sex and Creation, The Fairy Tale, Theology of the Icon, and (with Dean William Wilson) The Divine Image, for instance—were regularly over-subscribed. A small legion of devoted students, to whom Professor Vigen Guroian was always "PVG," would sign up for nearly any class or seminar he was teaching. I myself had first encountered him directly in the autumn of 2009 at a lecture series hosted

Tiller of Significant Soil

by the Christian Study Center. The theme that term was the Eucharist as celebrated and understood in various Christian traditions. Guroian was of course presenting an Orthodox perspective. Betraying my own ecclesial home, I asked a question about transubstantiation. His response was thoughtful, measured, mirthful, and—in spite of the fact that it culminated in the spirited charge of "Needless scholasticism!"—very evidently full of that pained charity with which, as I would come to know, he would always mourn the divisions between Christians.

Thereafter, at the encouragement of a handful of friends who were already committed members of Guroian's little legion, I set aside my qualms at not being a theologian and enrolled the next year in two of his courses: History of Christianity I, a lecture, and Modern Russian Religious Thinkers, a seminar. The Professor would enter the packed lecture hall the very image of the absent-minded professor, but for some hidden source of mirth that kept a wry smile flitting over his face. It was almost as if he was surprised to be where he was at all. Then it would begin. He might open a lecture with an account of the various woes that had afflicted his garden since the previous session—droughts, floods, and plagues of nearly Biblical proportions—or of the fruits of the last week's harvest, or of his dogs' pre-theological intuitions, or of the latest clash in the cosmic conflict between his innate and ineradicable Luddism and the contrary intransigence of the digitized world. But almost before we noticed, we would find ourselves back with the Apostles, or the Roman martyrs, or the Cappadocians; or we were setting sail with Athanasius, or languishing in the deserts of Egypt or Palestine or Syria with Evagrius and Jerome and Simeon, or sweltering in the white heat of Conciliar controversy, or navigating the perilous designs of Emperors, Popes, and Patriarchs. Guroian moved easily between keys. He spoke with awe for his high theme, which straddled the teachings of the faith and—by human lights—the myriad precarious contingencies by which the Gospel of the God-Man Jesus Christ has been passed down to us. He might grow animated or fall silent in admiration, sorrow, or mirth at the lives of the men and women who sought to understand and to live that message. Now and again he would be visibly struck by a humble, good-humored sense of the absurdity of his office, namely, the charge to teach a thousand years of theology and history in something like twenty lectures of fifty minutes each.

The preambles to Professor Guroian's seminars were similar to those of his lectures. Perhaps he was a bit freer in munching on an end of raw kohlrabi or a rutabaga pulled from his garden that morning. But thereafter he would lean back in his chair to let his students carry the bulk of the discussion. Sometimes he would have a student read an essay to kick things off, a vestige, I later learned, of the old tutorial method that had nearly vanished from academic practice by the time I entered university. In those seminars we students were hardly of homogeneous theological or cultural conviction, and discussions sometimes became heated debates. Guroian knew when to fan the flames and when to cool them. Often, however, it seemed to me that he did not say *enough*. Where was the *answer*? I was an undergraduate, after all, one of a handful in the graduate-dominated seminar, and I was far from the most mature of us. It took me a while to understand that his practice was one of studied restraint, a temperance which created a space in which his students could clash, refine ideas, and, hopefully, draw nearer to the truth. This is where his seminars struck me as being so different from others I had known. Continuous debate is sometimes the ground of cynicism and sophistry. The love of the true and the noble was written too deeply on the Professor's often furrowed brow, tracking our passionate stammering and our faltering arguments, for us to mistake his silence for one of indifference.

That love of the true and the noble was equally clear in the care Guroian took to create a shared ethos for his students beyond the walls of his classroom. Sometimes this was almost imperceptible. The aftermath of a debate had not half the edge it might have had when it was bookended by the carrots or apples from the Professor's garden, and the bread or cakes, for instance, that students had brought to share in imitation of his gesture.

A curiosity in those days at the University of Virginia was the "Take Your Professor to Lunch" scheme, by which the College of Arts and Sciences would reimburse students for lunches shared with their professors at a certain number of local restaurants. A friend and I took Professor Guroian to a pizza parlor called something like "The Magic Mushroom." The décor and menu were predictably psychedelic. Just as predictably, it was very popular with undergraduates. I don't know what possessed us to take the man, in his bowtie and his tweeds, to that grungy establishment, but we did. Guroian, studying the list of pizzas in great perplexity, suddenly lit upon one and burst out, "A 'Cosmological pie'? What! What—well, how about a Christological pie? Do they serve those here? Huh? Well, why not? Ah-*ha!*" I do not think the poor waitress knew what to make of him.

Guroian was and is far more at ease when choosing from the menu offered by his own garden. His book *Inheriting Paradise: Meditations on Gardening* begins as follows: "I am a theologian and a college professor. I like being both. But what I really love to do—what I get exquisite pleasure from doing—is to garden."[1] Speaking of God and calling forth His green and growing things from the soil have been two modes of the same vocation for the Professor. And he was keen to share both with his students. A tour through Guroian's flowering terraces, tidy vegetable beds, and meadow orchard is like following some misplaced Adam through a fallen Paradise: The Professor would gesture at blossoms and roots and shoots and fruit trees, giving everything its name, often in Latin. Guroian is especially proud of his ancestors' connection to the *prunus armeniaca*. "One man's work!" he would shout with a laugh, in a mixture of well-earned satisfaction and something near incredulity at the toll in hours, callouses, backaches, and weary limbs. "One man's work!" "And the students', Vigen!" his wife, June, might add, if she was within earshot. But she was always generous.

If even now you find yourself on such a tour, you may note at one moment the Professor bitterly cursing the industriousness of the weeds in snatches of Armenian or, with special color, in bits of Turkish. The next he may be agog at your inability to distinguish a male mullein from a female. All of a sudden, as if shot straight out of Chesterton's pen, he may chase one of his well-spoiled dogs or dart off-piste to hug a tree in delight at its girth and grandeur. A special treat befalls the visitor if the neighbor's alpacas—yes, alpacas—are out. "Look at you! Ah-*ha!* Look at you, you great woolly beasts!" the Professor will be heard to cry. "Look at you! You're—you're not real, and you don't even know it! You're creations of Dr. Seuss, that's what you are!" Sometimes, munching on a carrot or a radish straight from the soil, he may recount an adventure of Khodja, the great picaresque buffoon of Near Eastern lore.

On some of our walks there have been more somber moments, too. A gardener knows death and the turning of the year. Guroian has buried much-loved dogs in his back field. Once he murmured his hope that he himself would be buried right there in the carefully tended meadow at the edge of his own little not-quite Eden, just a soft step through to the icon's other side. Then, too, that garden always seemed to be growing as if in quiet harmony with the Guroian home's exquisitely decorated interior. That work of art was wrought by Mrs. Guroian, with her genius for the aesthetic.

1. Guroian, *Inheriting Paradise*, 3.

The Hanging Gardens of Culpeper sensed keenly the coming loss of their Mistress and, when it came, they mourned with their Master.

Spring, summer, autumn, winter, spring again: out in his garden, that living sign not of an eternal return of the same, but of a rhythm pulsing toward Resurrection, the Professor could not help revealing to us students an ecstasy and a depth of being that his tweedy form plodding thoughtfully along the white colonnades of Mr. Jefferson's "Academical Village" would not have betrayed.

I recall being invited with a handful of other students up to Culpeper on the occasional Saturday deep into gardening season. We were ourselves an early crop of deracinated millennials, so of course we jumped at the chance to get our hands dirty and to *do* something, even if that was just spending the day pulling weeds. But in principle that could have been done anywhere. The difference was that this weed-pulling was for the Professor and Mrs. Guroian. They held it all together, somehow: the manual, the intellectual, the spiritual, the hospitable, the aesthetic, the domestic. It is unwise to idealize those we admire, still more our friends and loved ones. But for all the wisdom of realism, there simply are those lives, those persons out there, in whom one is able, with some frequency, to glimpse something sacramental, some meeting of the divine and the human, the heavenly and the earthly. Such was the Guroians' terraced homestead on those escapes from Charlottesville. We would work most of the day, and then, with what we had gathered, Vigen and June would fix us a delicious dinner, sometimes featuring a chicken from an aspirational Wendell Berry in the next town over. Mrs. Guroian would generously host the meal around her immaculate dining room table. After dinner we would repair to the back porch for a reading of some short story or a recitation of poetry, followed by discussion well into the night.

That movement—departure from the tiresome city, revivifying struggle with nature, return to the home-as-civilization—was a theme reprised on the excursions Professor Guroian led to Mecosta, a Michigan village which, remote as it is, would be even more obscure had it not been the beloved lifelong home of the great Russell Kirk. Under the auspices of UVA's Edmund Burke Society, which Guroian served as faculty adviser, or of the Intercollegiate Studies Institute, in which he has been active since the 1960s, these weekends were as formative as those in the garden.

We would awake on Piety Hill, Kirk's ancestral home, or at a ranch not far away. The day began with breakfast hot off the skillet, with coffee and grape juice fresh pressed from the ranch's vineyard. In the autumn morning we took mules out over the scrub country past the luxuriant rows of Concord grape vines, haunting in the frost as it lifted into mist. On a summer afternoon we took canoes down the Muskegon River, tracing a route stoically paddled some twenty years before by Kirk, dressed, as ever, in suit and tie—in which attire he had also capsized his canoe before proceeding to the nearest restaurant for a dinner, dripping wet, as if nothing was amiss. Poor Guroian was stuck in my canoe and had to deal with me badgering him with questions most of the way, talking shop when that least of all was called for. Then again, I had to cope with his paddling: his ontological affinity for trees has both conscious and subconscious modes of expression, so I feel sure that by the end we were evenly and equally exasperated. At some point after the paddle or the ride we would return, wash up, and head to Piety Hill or to the library in the old shoe factory down the lane. There we would discuss readings assigned in advance, or sometimes read works aloud together—Eliot's *Murder in the Cathedral* comes to mind. Eliot, Kirk's old friend, comes to mind: Murder in the Cathedral, for one. Years later, after a conference in England, Guroian and I walked the Cotswolds, Quartets and Ordinance Survey map in hand, until we found the Burnt Norton manor, entered the garden by the first gate, sat down by the dry pool (leaves and all), and read.

We students fumbled our way through our ideas. *Something* was happening; there was a *Something* here. If it wasn't always clear what that was, we nonetheless knew it to be good. And here, as in the halls of the University, Guroian's moderating touch was light. "Yes," he might say quietly as we faltered. "Go on . . . What do you mean by that?"

Dinner was in the big house, where our hostess, Mrs. Annette Kirk, the *grand dame* of Mecosta, ever elegant and ever smiling, kept her late husband's legacy with love and verve. She was loquacious, more than I gather he was. But the tall, graceful Mrs. Kirk seemed to glide about the place with an ethereal step that befitted her husband's penchant for the "ghostly tale."[2] Her wit, too, recalls the Kirk I only know from pages and stories. "Oh, marvelous," she said upon catching sight of my necktie and coat. "What a splendid clash. How English of you!" The mismatch was not intentional on my part, for the record. But Mrs. Kirk's remarks, teasing or not, were suffused with genuine delight and had not a shred of malice. For a sheepish,

---

2. Most of Kirk's short stories in this genre can be found in the posthumous *Ancestral Shadows*, a collection that Mrs. Kirk entrusted to Vigen Guroian to edit and introduce.

easily over-awed kid who had turned up to university in sweatpants, to be noticed even backhandedly at what was effectively an introduction into the Great World was an honor.

There were greater wonders ahead to draw the mind. Mrs. Kirk's candlelit dining room is the only time I have ever played Snap Dragon and, had I known what it was, it would have been the last place in which I would have expected to play it. Later in the night the more musical of our troupe would take turns at the piano while the rest of us sang along as well as we could. One mischievous imp struck up "La Marseillaise" before being shouted down. In fair weather, even in the autumn chill, one could count on a nocturnal wander under the Milky Way, on display in all its glory.

Memories shift and fail to find their place. A friend and I wrestled a bronze bust of "Michigan's Man of Letters" into the local library. Did we buckle him into the front seat of Sam's Jeep Cherokee to take him down the hill? How many hours did Kyle, Sam, and I pass in conversation on things human and divine under those stars? I know I spent two weekends in Mecosta, once in my fourth year and once the year after I had graduated. I cannot remember how many Saturdays I spent in Guroian's own garden before the Great Fortification of 2011. The point is that this sort of thing cannot have been too frequent. They were far fewer than the space that they occupy in my memory would suggest. Part of this must be due to the way these excursions, these "reading parties," as the British might call them, drew together a circle of friends and built a sort of world in which virtues of hospitality, work, leisure, honesty, mirth, and faith could be learned, practiced, revived, and enjoyed. If it would be slightly unfair to compare Guroian to his eloquent but superstitious countryman Prohaeresius, it would be monstrously absurd to associate us, his students, with the rhetorician's great Cappadocian disciples. Yet Gregory Nazianzen's poignant recollections of the "university" years he shared with Basil and others at Athens capture something that we felt: a hunger for virtue as keen as that for knowledge, and a sense that we could look not only back into the past for inspiration, exhortation, and encouragement, but also up to the front of the lecture hall, and to either side of us there or in the garden. We had, as he had, "living rules" all around us. The other students of the Guroian Circle taught me so much. Some I would not have known, and others I would not have known half so well, had it not been for the Professor. Though we are now well scattered, and though it has been many years since I have seen most of those extraordinary men and women, I know that we are all at work tending our several gardens, work for which Guroian's own has been the iconographic template.

It was really only in that last year at Virginia that I began to have some inkling of what the study of the humanities was about. That was due above all to the role Professor Guroian played in my formation. That year I was very lucky to find a job that would put a roof over my head and pay my debts. It also taught me a patience which I did not realize lacked, and lacked acutely. But it was not the direction I wanted to follow. As I cast about for other options, the Professor was an ever-generous sounding board. I remember one conversation by phone. It was night, and warm enough. I was flip-flopping my way through Richmond's Museum District. As we spoke of life beyond the cubicle-walled horizon, I floated a plan, par-baked at best, to open a pub. "Well," he said after a pause, "you could do that. I just don't know whether you would be happy. You know, intellectually. But you have to figure that out." Now to this day I think that brew-pubbery is one of the nobler arts and that that could have been a very satisfying path. But as it happens, I am very glad the Professor encouraged me to think of where I was going in the terms in which he did. He gave me the nudge I needed at the moment when I needed it. Over the next decade, he found several such occasions, and judged them well.

Nor has my experience been unique. Guroian has remained a source of practical wisdom and confidence to any number of his old students as we made our way from Charlottesville to the world beyond. Some used to speak of him as a priest or a pastor, or indeed as a father figure. There were certainly aspects of both the pastor and the father in Guroian's professorial vocation, but the office he was exercising when we considered him in those terms was really neither. He was, instead, a *mentor*.

That's a word I had encountered in high school guidance counselling schemes aimed at lubricating college applications. It cropped up again later in on-the-job training, though the more promotion-minded had a preference for the term "buddy." Had the question arisen at the end of my studies, I am sure I would have said I saw the real thing in the Professor. But it never occurred to me to ask what a mentor really was. And for a long time I did not know that Guroian himself had put a great deal of thought into the nature, definition, and practice of mentorship.

The fruits of those reflections can be found in *Tending the Heart of Virtue* (1998). By now it is perhaps the single book for which Guroian is most widely known. This popularity, particularly in the classical Christian education movement to which he has happily devoted so much time and energy since his retirement from academia, encouraged him to add several chapters for a substantially expanded second edition (2023). It seems that everywhere I go I meet somebody whose life has been touched by that book. In fact, while I was writing this chapter, I ran into an Assyrian theologian living in rural Lancashire who had written and lectured on the book years earlier in Rome. She was practically star-struck just to meet someone who knew the Professor: "So he is real, after all!"

Having long been convinced of the Professor's reality, I was nonetheless slow to discover his life in letters. The books on gardening and the essays in *Rallying the Really Human Things* were probably the first of his works that I read. It was years after leaving Virginia before I finally picked up *Tending the Heart*. I wish I had read it earlier.

The subtitle reveals both his sources and his method: *How Classic Stories Awaken a Child's Moral Imagination*. Guroian glides easily from *Pinocchio* to Aristotle, from the *Velveteen Rabbit* to Homer and back, with Christ as the golden thread woven throughout. The book offers us a series of case studies in the titular Burkean anthropological insight as applied to education: that our raw natures are in need of images furnished by culture in order to become and remain most truly what they are.[3] Guroian's gloss on Burke's "moral imagination" is that it is the seat of our ethical lives, the faculty by which we conceive of our relations to other human beings. It is thus inseparable from an account of virtues and vices. Yet the moral imagination is not a storehouse of definitions. Rather, it is "the process by which the self makes metaphors out of images recorded by the senses and stored in memory, which then are employed to find and suppose moral correspondences in experience."[4] Because we cannot and should not experience everything, we rely on culture, and in particular on art, literature, and religion, to stock the "wardrobe" of our moral imaginations. What we read and contemplate will end up setting the points of our moral compasses.

The book takes a number of children's stories in turn, focusing on a handful in each chapter, united around a theme such as "Love and

---

3. Burke, responding to the totalizing destruction of the French Revolution, wrote, "All the decent drapery of life is to be roughly torn off. All the superadded ideas, furnished from the wardrobe of a moral imagination, which the heart owns, and the understanding ratifies, as necessary to cover the defects of our naked shivering nature, and to raise it to dignity in our own estimation, are to be exploded as a ridiculous, absurd, and antiquated fashion" (*Reflections on the Revolution in France*, 170–71).

4. Guroian, *Rallying the Really Human Things*, esp. 54–55.

Immortality" or "Evil and Redemption." In the middle of the first edition is chapter 4, "Friends and Mentors." Guroian first takes Mole and Rat from *The Wind in the Willows* to explore how friendship can call unequal peers out of themselves and to a greater fullness of life. He then looks at the "mentoral friendship" in *Charlotte's Web*, in which two very different but entirely complementary needs bring Charlotte and Wilbur together in ways that give life to both—not automatically, but by the intentional choice of the kindly older spider. Finally, in an act of magnanimity, and overcoming the hatred of his ancient foe, the garden's cloven-footed menace, Guroian sketches an archetype of pure mentorship on the basis of the deer in Felix Salten's *Bambi: A Life in the Woods*. Against the backdrop of the society of deer in general, he examines in particular the relationship between the Old Stag and Bambi. The Old Stag, whose appearances are rare but purposeful and significant, time and again says or does less than the young deer would hope. But his every word and deed—and his very silences—haunt Bambi, spurring him to grow into the stag on whom the rest of the deer can eventually rely for his wisdom and his way of being in the world, just as they had done on the old "Prince" of the herd.

At the risk of speculation, I would suggest that in his portraits of Charlotte and the Old Stag Guroian gives us some insight into his own experience of mentorship, both as mentee and as mentor. Certainly he has always been keen to acknowledge the roles which others played in his own formation. Guroian remembers his middle school English teacher, Helen Rivers, with love and fear. He always spoke in sad awe of John Graham, the lecturer in Rhetoric when that liberal art was still taught at Virginia in the 1960s, who made the English language sing for him and who taught him to write, and who died too young. It was Will Herberg, Guroian's doctoral supervisor, who urged him to cast out into the deep of his Armenian Apostolic Orthodox tradition and to rediscover its riches. And Russell Kirk himself, who served on Guroian's doctoral committee, served also as a model, a guide, and ultimately a friend. The Professor has often spoken of the immensity of his debt of gratitude to all of these teachers and mentors.

At some point the mentee began to teach. I suspect he soon realized that, like his own mentors, he wanted more for his students than merely their academic or professional success, as important as those might be. But if it is difficult to reach a condition of general flourishing, guiding others to that end is an art no more straightforward. Guroian mentions, but does not elaborate, Athena's disguise in the first four books of the *Odyssey*: she appears to the awkward, fatherless Telemachus as the mortal Mentor, who thus quite inadvertently gave his name to the role. Perhaps Homer had some intuition that this sort of guidance is an order too tall for the unaided mentor, however wise he be; that it takes a divine initiative to make us fully human, and that if that divine impetus were to be revealed all at once, it would overwhelm.

By analogy, a human mentor, if he is to succeed, must trust that God is at work, too, and for his own part must show restraint. The mentor, moreover, is not a peer. What he knows has been purchased over long years and often at great price. This means that what he has learned cannot be communicated easily. Guroian frames the mentor's task as follows: "In contrast to the modern educational theory, in the mentor/mentee relationship there lies no distinction between method and content. By means of physical gesture, tone of voice, and behavior, the mentor communicates his special knowledge and skill and also a piece of his own character. There is no such thing in this relationship as being informative without also being formative."[5] To be clear, I do not think the spontaneous proliferation of bow-ties in Guroian's legion was a consciously intended effect of the sort the Professor means here. Nazianzen lamented Basil's many superficial imitators, what with their beards and long faces, and the dearth of those who genuinely imitated him in the asceticism of the heart. Guroian would doubtless have been slightly embarrassed even to notice his students' mimetic frippery. Yet clearly he studied the gestures, voices, and actions of his own teachers and mentors, and the spiritual, ethical, and intellectual worlds behind them, to which the things at the surface served as windows and invitations. I suspect he put no less care into the way he carried himself in the presence of the students and mentees who looked to him.

Guroian explains that what is at stake in such relationships is much larger than either mentor or mentee: "A mentor gives himself over to producing in another essential qualities of character that are not merely private or personal but ultimately crucial to the continuance of a special art or way of life."[6] This self-sacrifice is not of the sort that would allow a mentor to spend all day in office hours, passing the time in pleasant conversation. Precisely because of the paths he has already trod, the Old Stag has other ways still before him, which for the good of his herd he must walk. "He . . . knows the spiritual geography of life and death in the woods," Guroian

---

5. Guroian, *Tending the Heart of Virtue*, 104.
6. Guroian, *Tending the Heart of Virtue*, 104.

writes. "He practices the virtues of attentiveness and watchfulness that extend and deepen life and living for all of the deer."[7] He must keep practicing the art that he knows it is so urgent for others to learn. For both their sakes, the master woodworker needs to keep at his intricate joinery, for which his apprentices are not yet ready, and cannot spend all day with them sawing boards. As Guroian puts it, the Old Stag, the mentor, gives the mentee "as much as he can absorb and not more"; the mentee, for his part, must learn how to "take possession of himself and make independent decisions."[8] All of this demands the distance that we see between Salten's characters. It is a distance, the narrator tells us, that both Bambi and the Old Stag wish they could bridge. At one point the Old Stag rightly refrains from speaking freely, as something close to a peer, at a moment when such familiarity would not have been conducive to Bambi's formation as the next guardian of the deer-herd. But surprisingly, it is only from a sense of awkwardness and bashfulness at the prospect of saying something foolish that the Old Stag holds back. He moves off in silence, seeming as aloof and impassive as ever to a somewhat dejected Bambi.

The urgency of handing down hard-won wisdom, the slow and episodic nature of that intentional transmission, and the long solitudes that the process demands of both parties—with these as its defining marks, mentorship may seem a strange thing indeed. "What kind of friendship is this, if it is friendship at all?" Guroian asks. But mentorship, he argues, really is a kind of friendship, with all its "affection, trust, and mutuality."[9] It is merely the want of exemplars of the type that renders the thing so unrecognizable and so perplexing to us today. I would submit that Guroian's vocation, both in the piety he shows the memory of his own mentors and in the many young men and women he has himself mentored, has had the effect of reviving for a fortunate little corner of the world the image of the mentor and the mentor-friend.

The week we spent building that fence flew by. In blazing heat or torrential rain, our days were full. Upon waking I would read as much as I could from a translation of the *Iliad* I'd found at a library sell-off. At some point Guroian would call us to the kitchen for his "good and grea-zy"—it was always a "z"—breakfast of sausages with scrambled eggs and home-grown thyme. Thus fortified, we would set out for the trenches. We worked

---

7. Guroian, *Tending the Heart of Virtue*, 105.
8. Guroian, *Tending the Heart of Virtue*, 101.
9. Guroian, *Tending the Heart of Virtue*, 104.

hard. But this was no chain gang. Throughout the day we knew we could count on Mrs. Guroian's frequent summonses to ice-cold water, snacks, lunch, tea, and dinner. Evenings were spent in conversation, but, exhausted as we were, we would soon enough fall into happy silence and retire to rest before the next day's labors. Somehow by the end of the week we had raised those posts. Industrial-strength chicken-wire followed. Grape vines, too. I gather the walls have kept the "deer-ly beloveds" largely at bay, and Professor Guroian's garden relatively safe, over the more than dozen years since that week in April 2011.

Guroian knows better than to let spade, or quill, sleep in his hand. He has seeds to sow and harvests to bring in, and much soil to till. "And weeds! Weeds like you've never seen! It's all I can do to stop them from choking out my tomatoes! Don't get me started on the sweet potatoes this year. Now the cucumbers, on the other hand . . ." What can one say? Goad him a bit more, and the Professor will offer again his own cosmic rallying cry, that ecstatic outburst at the absurdity, pain, joy, wonder, and gratuity of being alive in God's Creation. From Culpeper's red hills, from Fort Guroian, from that little memory of Eden, that imperfect anticipation of Paradise, long may we hear: "Ah-*ha!*"

BIBLIOGRAPHY

Burke, Edmund. *Reflections on the Revolution in France*. Vol. 2 of *Select Works of Edmund Burke: A New Imprint of the Payne Edition*. 1790. Indianapolis: Liberty Fund, 1999.

Guroian, Vigen. *Inheriting Paradise: Meditations on Gardening*. Grand Rapids: Eerdmans, 1999.

———. *Rallying the Really Human Things*. Wilmington, DE: ISI, 2005.

———. *Tending the Heart of Virtue: How Classic Stories Awaken a Child's Moral Imagination*. Oxford: Oxford University Press, 1998.

Kirk, Russell. *Ancestral Shadows: An Anthology of Ghostly Tales*. Edited by Vigen Guroian. Grand Rapids: Eerdmans, 2004.

PART FOUR

Faith, Church, Mission

11

The Earliest Surviving Armenian Betrothal Prayers

Michael Daniel Findikyan

One day a good number of years ago, my esteemed teacher and friend, Dr. Vigen Guroian, phoned and, with the cadence of a high school football coach, charged me with procuring the oldest texts of the Armenian Church's betrothal service. He wondered if these medieval liturgical prayers and rituals might prove instructive in thinking through the radical changes affecting the institution of marriage in our day—the waning interest among young couples in partaking in church weddings at all; increasing divorce rates;[1] gay marriage; civil unions; and, in particular, pre-marriage customs and attitudes such as courtship, dating, co-habitation, and unpartnered parenting—all topics that Dr. Guroian has keenly and intrepidly investigated. I ran onto the field and executed the play as best I could. We ended up spending a few hours tackling my very impromptu "translations" of the couple of texts that I had uncovered. I offer here much-improved renderings and observations, a few decades and lost hairs later, in homage

---

1. Statistics on divorce rates in the US provided by any number of government agencies and professional organizations are readily available on-line. These statistics are not unchallenged by various academics and observers. Neither are the precise data my immediate concern here; the overall trends are generally acknowledged.

and gratitude to Dr. Guroian for teaching and inspiring me and countless others, and for tirelessly encouraging me in my vocation and work.

All eastern liturgical rites distinguish, or at one time distinguished some sort of betrothal rite or rites from the actual marriage ceremony, which they refer to as the sacrament of "crowning," the coronation of the bride and groom constituting the culmination of the wedding ceremony throughout the Christian East. Among the various printed editions of the Armenian euchology, known as the *Maštocʻ*,[2] we find several distinct pre-crowning rituals: the blessing and/or exchange of the "sign" or the "cross" (*nšan* or *xačʻ*, respectively);[3] a blessing of the wedding garments (*halawōrhnēkʻ*); an admonitory message by the priest; the joining of the hands of the prospective bride and groom; the braiding of the *narōt* (a plait of red, green and white cords that is blessed, twisted together and placed on the heads of the bride and groom); the exchange of vows;[4] and the blessing and sharing of a cup of wine. No source that I have consulted contains each of these rituals. There is marked diversity among the euchologies, manuscript and print. In fact, today there is no official, canonical betrothal ceremony in the Armenian Church. Priests make use of any number of ceremonies found in modern printed editions of the *Maštocʻ*.

Students of liturgy have long observed that in all traditions, the rites of betrothal exhibit great heterogeneity.[5] This certainly stems from the fact that, in ancient and medieval times, until today in many cultures, ecclesiastical betrothal marked the ritual culmination of deliberations between

---

2. The book is named after Catholicos Maštocʻ Ełivartecʻi (†898), who compiled it. For numerous references in Armenian, see Tēr-Vardanean, *Mayr Maštocʻ*, 11n1. See also Mahé, "L'Eglise arménienne de 611 à 1066," 496–97; Renoux, "Langue et littérature arméniennes," 132–33. Transliteration of Armenian terms follows the Hübschmann-Meillet system in *Revue des Études arméniennes*.

3. Both words are used in Armenian to refer to the instrument of Jesus' execution. In many sources, it is clear that a small cross was exchanged by the bride and groom, as is the custom in the Syriac rites. In other Armenian sources the "sign" or "signs" can refer to any number of symbols such as a ring, bracelet, veil, and/or others.

4. Unlike the Catholic Church and other western churches, vows of commitment and faithfulness by the bride and groom have no place in the Armenian wedding service, nor in the Armenian Church's theology of matrimony. Vows are rather the business of various pre-crowning ceremonies. The vows take the form of questions posed by the celebrant to the prospective bride and groom. Renoux, "Le mariage," 295.

5. For a helpful overview of eastern betrothal and marriage rites with bibliography see Vellian, *Crown, Veil, Cross*; cf. Parenti, "Christian Rite of Marriage," 259–63 for the ever-increasing variety of prayers found in medieval manuscripts of what he calls, "provincial" rites of betrothal and marriage, with respect to the Byzantine rite.

the families concerning the viability of a potential marriage. Such issues as the suitability of the man and woman in age and socioeconomic status; the amiability of the families; the settlement of customary remunerative obligations such as the trousseau and/or dowry all had to be resolved prior to approaching the priest for a sacred seal to authorize the prospective wedding. These indigenous and ancestral domestic customs varied widely from place to place. Many developed ecclesiastical counterparts in the pre-crowning rituals, resulting in a high degree of regional liturgical variance, as we find today in the liturgical books.[6] Furthermore, given that betrothal rites customarily take place outside the church sanctuary, theoretically the inherent canonical and inertial forces that tend to stabilize the churches' authorized rituals would be diminished, thereby facilitating liturgical diversification.

A multiplicity of pre-crowning rituals does *not*, however, characterize our earliest surviving Armenian betrothal rites as found in *Maštoc'* ms. Venice 457 (olim 320)[7] from the library of the Armenian Catholic Mkhit'arean fathers on the island of San Lazzaro in Venice; and ms. Erevan 1001,[8] housed in the *Matenadaran*, the largest repository of Armenian manuscripts in the world. In his monumental edition of the two manuscripts entitled *Mayr Maštoc'*, Gēorg Tēr-Vardanean (†2023) dated ms. Venice 457 between the years 958ad and 964ad, while he cautiously dated the closely-related ms. Erevan 1001 to the eleventh century.[9] The noted philologist's edition presents the complete contents of the two manuscripts as an amalgam. Like all critical editions, it is an artificial construct. The compilation presented by Tēr-Vardanean (and all other services in his edition) does not claim to correspond to the actual liturgical usage of any real worshipping community. To retrieve the original services reflected in the two manuscripts requires the liturgiologist to disentangle the contents of the edition, a process that is made possible thanks to the editor's meticulous critical apparatus. The results of our deconstruction are summarized in the table below.

---

6. See, for example, the cogent analysis of Syriac betrothal rites as reflected in a medieval Chinese manuscript in Brock et al., "Syriac Marriage Ritual"; cf. Barsom, *Order of Solemnization*, 10–12.

7. Sargisean and Sargsean, *Mayr c'uc'ak hayerēn jeṙagrac'*, 3:1–48; Tēr-Vardanean, *Mayr Maštoc'*, 57. For a complete description of the manuscript and his rationale for the dating, see *Mayr Maštoc'*, 50–60.

8. Tēr-Vardanean, *Mayr Maštoc'*, 9–12. Complete codicological description in Tēr-Vardanean, *Mayr Maštoc'*, 60–63.

9. Tēr-Vardanean notes that that the manuscript is in need of "letter by letter" paleographic scrutiny (*Mayr Maštoc'*, 61n136).

The headings for the Armenian betrothal service in both of our manuscripts pertain to a single ritual: bestowing upon, or exchanging between the prospective groom and bride a cross or crosses. The ambiguity in number is due to the fact that the titles use the words *xač'* (cross) or *nšan* (sign, cross)[10] as attributive nouns, which can be understood in the singular or the plural. The titles at the head of the service and in marginal notes in both manuscripts refer to *xač' p'oxel* (to exchange a cross/crosses); *xač'kap* or *xač'kapel* (tying a cross/crosses, thus implying a necklace/necklaces); or *xač'ap'ox aṙnel* (to exchange a cross/crosses).[11] By contrast, all of the references to *xač'* (cross) within the prayers are singular in number. Today the betrothal service is generally known as *nšantuk* (giving of a sign).

The text contains numerous scribal errors, dubious punctuation and incongruous syntactic fragments. Many of these errors are found in both manuscripts, a sign of their codicological kinship.[12] I have not accounted for the textual variants in Tēr-Vardanean's critical edition except in rare cases where they significantly alter the meaning of the text.

Texts placed within square brackets have been supplied by me based on the clear implication of the original text or on conventual language in well-known Armenian liturgical formulas. Rubrics have been placed in italics. Other texts in italics have been highlighted by me for reasons explained in the footnotes.

---

10. See note 3 above.

11. See Tēr-Vardanean, *Mayr Maštoc'*, 234nn18–20.

12. Conybeare, *Rituale*, 108–9, provides an English translation of the service as found in ms. Venice 457, with interpolations from several later manuscripts. See Renoux's criticism of Conybeare's collation of the marriage rite (Renoux, "Mariage," 289) as well as his own French translation of the service from ms. Venice 457 (296–97; cf. Tēr-Vardanean, *Mayr Maštoc'*, 34–40).

The Earliest Surviving Armenian Betrothal Prayers

Venice 457 Canon for Exchanging a Cross	Erevan 1001 Canon for Virgins' Cross-Exchange
*[Responsorial] Psalm 4 [Response] 4:7*
Lord have mercy. Lord have mercy. Lord have mercy.
Proverbs 3:13–18	Ps 111(112):1
	K'aroz[13] Let us beseech the Lord with this holy cross, [that through it he may save us from sin and raise us to life by his gracious mercy. Almighty Lord our God, raise us to life and have mercy on us.]
	Prayer E1 **Prayer E2**
	Again this canon is conducted: *[Responsorial] Psalm 4 Response 4:7.*
Galatians 6:14–18 Alleluia 111(112):1 Matthew 24:30–35
K'aroz Let us beseech the Lord with this holy cross, [that through it he may save us from sin and raise us to life by his gracious mercy. Almighty Lord our God, raise us to life and have mercy on us.]	
Prayer V1 **Prayer V2**	
	Find the Gospel [readings][14] and the Apostle [readings][15] from [the service of] Blessing a Cross.[16] And after the Gospel [the deacon] chants the k'aroz [That we may find this sign . . .].[17]
	Prayer E3

13. The *k'aroz* is a liturgical piece chanted by the deacon and addressed to the people. It always precedes a prayer offered the priest, and serves to invite the assembly to pray together for particular intentions. Sometimes translated "litany," "petition," or "proclamation."

14. John 19:16–22; Tēr-Vardanean, *Mayr Maštoc'*, 171–72; Matt 24:29–36; Tēr-Vardanean, *Mayr Maštoc'*, 187–88.

15. 1 Cor 1:18–24; Tēr-Vardanean, *Mayr Maštoc'*, 170–71; Gal 6:14–18; Tēr-Vardanean, *Mayr Maštoc'*, 187.

16. Tēr-Vardanean, *Mayr Maštoc'*, 168–93.

17. I am unable to identify a k'aroz with this incipit in the service of Blessing a Cross.

E1. Eternal God, and Lord and Maker of all, we beseech you and we entreat you, [for] in your compassion, you care for all creatures. Lord, receive our supplications. Just as you joined the first [man] in matrimony according to the law of Moses, and after the resurrection of your only-begotten and his ascension to heaven, you exhibited *this commandment*[18] by means of your holy cross. In this way, you established your holy church. And by joining your faithful [people] as a couple in marriage, in the name of your only-begotten Son, now again, Lord, give your cross as power and strength for your faithful [couple]. And by means of your all-powerful cross, keep away from them disingenuous musings, insolent thoughts and all dishonesty; and keep them from the darkness that lurks at night, and from obscure paths, and from the filth of adultery.[19] And let their exchange of this cross be considered their inauguration with one another, laying the foundation of a stable base for this edifice *of your holy Trinity,*[20] and of spiritual sturdiness so that they may receive on their heads the noble crown through the blessing of the Holy Trinity, now and forever and ever [and unto the ages of ages, Amen].

> Peace [unto all]
> Let us bow down to God.

E2.[21] *Eternal God, who brought together the nationless and indistinct into a couple in an indestructible union;*[22] you blessed Isaac and Rebecca and *you designated their descendants [as the heirs] of your promise.*[23] [Now], you yourself, Lord, bless this, your servant, and this, your servant-girl, and lead [them] to [do] good works, for you are merciful and you love mankind, *Lord our God, giving peace and praying.*[24] Lord our God, who betrothed your church to the nations, bless this couple and keep this union in peace.

---

18. Or "these commandments." The sentence is awkward.

19. Literally, "mixed beds."

20. Homoioteleuton; cf. the corresponding passage in V1, "of this marriage" (Tēr-Vardanean, *Mayr Maštoc'*, 237).

21. This prayer is a synthesis of the two betrothal prayers found in the oldest surviving Byzantine euchology, ms. Barberini *gr.* 336 (second half eighth century) (Parenti and Velkovska, *L'Eucologio Barberini*, 346; Greek text, 185).

22. The preceding line in the original text is corrupt, lacking a verb.

23. *Zžaŕang noc'a k'o aweteac' erewuc'uc'er.* The Armenian is awkward. Subsequent editions clarify the meaning. See Heb 6:17; Rom 9:8–9; cf. Gen 24:7, 59–64.

24. An erroneous scribal interpolation which is absent from subsequent editions.

And to you befits glory [dominion and honor, now and always and unto the ages of ages. Amen.]

V1.[25] Eternal God, and Maker of all, we beseech you and we entreat you, [for] in your compassion, you care for all creatures. Loving Lord, receive our requests, and as you joined the first [ones in] matrimony according to the law of Moses; and after the resurrection of your only-begotten [and] his ascension to heaven, *the commandment, which exhibited to us your holy cross*,[26] established for the joining in marriage of your faithful [people] with you and with your only-begotten [Son]. Now again, Lord, give this cross, for power and stability, to this [man and woman], who have taken refuge in you, by means of your all-triumphant sign. Keep away from them disingenuous and morose thoughts and all dishonesty. Keep them from abominations and tenebrous paths and from the filth of adultery.[27] And let the mutual exchange of this cross be considered an inauguration; as laying a solid foundation for the edifice of this marriage, [so that they may] receive on their heads the noble crown, by the blessing of the holy Trinity, to whom is due glory, dominion and honor, now and [always and unto the ages of ages. Amen.]

> Peace [to all].
> [Let us] bow down to God.

V2. Holy Father, praised by all, who blessed and sanctified this cross in the name of your only-begotten by the hand of this sinner of yours, [and] by the blessing of the Holy Spirit. And now we beseech you, Lord, send your Holy Spirit on the inauguration of this edifice of mine, which I now establish. Keep [this man and this woman] pure toward one another, and leading them, bring them to the hour when I shall place the glorious crown upon their heads. For to you alone is honor, and to you befits glory, dominion and honor, [now and always and unto the ages of ages. Amen.]

E3. Glory to you, Eternal King, who cultivate your people and fill the church [with faithful who] believe in your holy name. In your loving mercy, bring these [two] together into a loving union, and cultivate them [so that they may] grow to a new stature. Ward off from them the deceit of the evil

---

25. E1 and V1 are slight variations of the same prayer.

26. The Armenian phrase as transmitted here is untenable; cf. the parallel phrase in E1 is also awkward. In both cases, the idea seems to be that marriage comes about by means of the cross (Tēr-Vardanean, *Mayr Maštocʻ*, 237, 235).

27. Literally, "mixed beds."

one, and teach them to submit themselves to one another[28] in love; to walk together along your paths in faith, [and] to fortify themselves in modesty. Keep them steadfast in peace and keep them safe and sound under the protective shelter of your arm so that they may arrive at the bridegroom's chamber, your martyrs' chapel and your holy tabernacle, anticipating the time when they will receive the crown of precious stones, to glorify your unchanging dominion, now and always and [unto the ages of ages. Amen].

* * *

Once unraveled, we find that the respective betrothal ceremonies reflected in the Venice and Erevan manuscripts are closely related, though each contains unique material. The structural core of each service is identical: Psalm 4 with its response; the diaconal proclamation (*kʻaroz*) of the cross; and a double-prayer. A common set of scripture readings concludes this module in the Erevan manuscript, but, more conventionally for Armenian liturgy, precedes it in the Venice manuscript. The Venice manuscript's pericope includes Proverbs 3:13–18, an allegory on the exquisite treasure of wisdom/ *sophia* and the fortune of both the man who finds it/her,[29] and of those who gather around "the tree of life." The latter is, of course, the storied image for the cross in Christian antiquity, a suitable allusion from the perspective of this service.

By contrast, the Erevan manuscript includes a second responsorial psalm and a generic hymn of thanksgiving (Ps 111[112]) with no specific connection to betrothal. It concludes with a rubric that retrieves an additional pericope from the service for the Blessing of a Cross, followed by another prayer, **E3**, which is an elegant synopsis of the service's leitmotifs.

It is not possible to determine the priority of the two forms of the service based on their shape alone. The coherency of the service in the Venice manuscript could suggest a more primitive form, corresponding to the manuscript's slightly earlier date. But it could also signify a more mature evolutionary state, where the service has been edited to bring it into a more polished form. The Erevan manuscript's version exhibits signs of liturgical development in progress: redundancy in psalmody; the unconventional

---

28. Eph 5:21.

29. The Armenian language, lacking gender, cannot express the allusions associated with the Greek feminine noun *sophia* (wisdom), a topos in Greek biblical and patristic literature. Nevertheless, the Armenians employed the Proverbs passage here and grasped the eloquent allegory.

placement of scripture readings vis-à-vis prayer; the addition of an evocative, yet extraneous third prayer; and the seemingly impulsive effort to heighten the service's cross-centered thematic by cursorily lifting scripture readings from an unrelated service via rubric.

With the exception of the concluding prayer of the Erevan manuscript (**E3**), the dual prayers in both manuscripts are configured in the classic "double prayer" euchological form. This ancient form consists of a collect-prayer, followed by a peace greeting, the invitation to bow down; and an inclination prayer. As I have shown elsewhere, this paradigmatic structure remains omnipresent throughout Armenian liturgy, whereas in other traditions it has dissipated.[30]

The collects **E1** and **V1** are variations of one and the same prayer. The prayer establishes marriage on two grounds: first, on the precedent of the first-created man and woman, whom God engineered to be complementary, and whom he joined together "according to the law of Moses," an anachronism that is, however, perfectly viable from the eschatological perspective of traditional liturgical prayer. The prayer asserts, second, that marriage complies with a certain unspecified "commandment" of the Lord, which is associated with the holy cross, and was "exhibited"[31] after the resurrection and ascension of the only-begotten Son. Here both manuscripts are corrupt, implying that scribes struggled to understand the text. It is likely that the intended reference is to 1 Corinthians 7:10–11, where St. Paul recalls a command of the Lord that is not found in the Gospels. Accentuating its divine authority, however, the Apostle emphasizes that "not I, but the Lord" requires that the married woman should not leave her husband, nor the husband, his wife. For the purposes of the betrothal prayer, the sacrosanctity and permanence of marriage are thereby affirmed by divine mandate, but after Jesus' resurrection and ascension, from the lips of St. Paul.

The commandment to join man and woman in matrimony is effectuated by Christ's holy cross. Here again, the incongruous state of the text at this point in both manuscripts suggests that the scribes could not reckon with the passage. Renoux's French translation of **V1** is free and imposes a meaning that may not have been intended: "Après la resurrection de ton Fils unique et son ascension dans les cieux, tu as indiqué que ce rite (se ferait)

---

30. Findikyan, "Double Prayers and Inclinations."

31. *c'uc'er, c'uc'anēr*, according to mss. Erevan 1001, Venice 457, respectively (Tēr-Vardanean, *Mayr Maštoc'*, 235, 237).

avec ta sainte croix."[32] A preferable interpretation derives from the iconic scripture on marriage, Ephesians 5:21–33. Without naming the cross, the Ephesians passage identifies the sacrificial love of Christ for his church, "for [whom] he gave himself up," as the foundation of the "mystery" of marriage. The passage also substantiates the prayer's petitions that the couple be protected and sheltered by the "all-triumphant" or "all-powerful sign," that is, by Christ's love for his people and the prospective bride and groom's selfless love for one another. It should be noted that neither the 1 Corinthians nor the Ephesians passages are designated among the scripture readings for the service of exchanging a cross.

Still, confirmation of this interpretation comes in the succeeding gesture of the collect in both manuscripts, which seizes on the ecclesiological dynamic of marriage, a potent theme in the sacramental theology of the Armenian and all eastern churches. Remarkable is the graphic architectural imagery employed in the prayer: "Let their exchange of this cross be considered their inauguration with one another, laying the foundation of a stable base for this edifice," in the words of **E1**. This terminology unmistakably evokes the prayers and hymns of the Armenian Church's ceremonies for the dedication and consecration of a newly-built church.[33] Marriage serves a purpose greater than the personal satisfaction of a man and a woman, even when their union is bound by Christ-like sacrificial love. In Christian marriage, the couple is crowned to be a building block, a "member" of the Body of Christ. Marriage—*literally* according to the betrothal prayer—is the "foundation" of the Church, as it "builds up the Body of Christ."[34] Betrothal, the exchange of a cross, is the "inauguration" of marriage. It is, consequently, an optional antecedent to marriage only to the extent that laying the foundation of a building is optional for its construction. Without it, like any edifice, the edifice of marriage collapses under its own weight.

---

32. "After the resurrection of your only Son and his ascension into the heavens, you indicated that this rite (should be accomplished) with your holy cross" (Renoux, "Mariage," 296). Fr. Renoux may have had in mind the dramatic ritual in the current Armenian marriage ceremony, whereby the best-man (known as *xač'eghbayr* or "brother-of-the-cross") holds a large cross over the heads of the couple while the celebrant recites the crowning prayer. However, there is no trace of this ritual in the rubrics of the service of crowning in either the Venice or Erevan manuscripts (cf. Tēr-Vardanean, *Mayr Maštoc'*, 243–48).

33. See Findikyan, "Armenian Ritual," 75–121.

34. Cf. Eph 4:11–17.

While the collects of the central double prayer in both manuscripts are virtually identical, the inclination prayers accompanying each are distinct. Most notably, **E2** is a minimally adapted fusion of the double-prayer associated with betrothal in the earliest surviving Byzantine euchology, ms. Barberini *gr.* 336 from the second half of the eighth century:[35]

> Eternal God, you brought together the divided into unity and you placed [between them] an indestructible bond. You blessed Isaac and Rebecca and you made them heirs of your promise. You yourself, bless also these, your servants, leading them to every good work. For you, O God, are merciful, and you love mankind, and to you [we offer] glory...
>
> *And while the deacon says, "[Incline] the head," the celebrant prays:*
>
> Lord, our God, you took from among the nations the pure virgin church as bride; bless this marriage and unite and protect your servants in peace and concord. For to you is due all glory and honor...

The Byzantine prayer invokes yet another paradigm to justify the sacred institution of marriage: the union of the patriarch Isaac with Rebecca. As will be made explicit in the Armenian, Byzantine and other eastern crowning prayers, the new couple is grafted onto salvation history as its most recent heirs, the heirs of God's promises. The second part of **E2** recalls the image of the church as Christ's bride, inspired by 2 Corinthians 11:2, where the Apostle declares, "I betrothed you to Christ to present you as a pure bride to her one husband."

The Byzantine betrothal prayer, in one form or another, will find its way into every Armenian service of betrothal that I have examined except for that of the Venice manuscript. There, the inclination prayer is dedicated entirely to the cross and flows naturally from the spirit of the service for the Blessing of a Cross as found in the Venice manuscript *Maštocʿ*.[36] Just as the sinful priest blessed the (hand-) cross by the inspiration of the Holy Spirit, the prayer beseeches God the Father to bless "this edifice of mine," the couple that has been presented to the church in anticipation, and as the inauguration of their nuptial crowning.

The third prayer of the Erevan manuscript (**E3**), unknown to the Venice text, presents a poignant recapitulation of the themes of betrothal as

---

35. My translation of the Greek text in Parenti and Velkovska, *L'Eucologio Barberini*, 185. On the Byzantine prayer, see Parenti, "Christian Rite of Marriage," 256, 258.

36. Tēr-Vardanean, *Mayr Maštocʿ*, 168–93.

expressed in the prayers of both manuscripts, even if the cross of Christ is not explicitly mentioned.

As noted above, there is ambiguity in the earliest manuscripts regarding the precise ritual around which the service of the exchange of a cross/crosses was built. Based on the prayers and negligible rubrics alone, it is impossible to establish whether a cross or crosses was/were given to the couple; whether a single cross was exchanged between the prospective bride and groom; whether each gave the other a cross or *the* cross; or whether such rituals varied from place to place. Nevertheless, the intent of the ceremony is patently clear. The cross, icon of God's sacrificial love for God's people, is the foundation of the Gospel and the basis of Christian marriage. By receiving and/or exchanging it, the prospective bride and groom dedicate themselves to one another, to Christ, and to the Church without qualification, through the selfless love manifested in the Lord's redemptive death. The cross of betrothal is the foundation of the Armenian Church's theology of marriage, of the church, and of the sacraments. It is therefore essential to the success of a couple's sacred union and the well-being of the church. This obviously raises serious questions for our day, when "engagement" is viewed by most young couples in the west as an intimate and private affair; and the betrothal service, or any pre-wedding church protocol, is considered discretionary, irrelevant, or completely unknown.

Later manuscripts and printed editions of the Armenian Church's betrothal and pre-crowning services contain a profusion of new rituals and prayers that are theologically and liturgically compelling. They are also of interest for the practical issues that they seek to address in pursuit of safeguarding the sanctity of the sacrament of marriage—and of the Gospel itself—against the challenges presented in ever-changing times and socio-cultural circumstances. Could these liturgical developments provide guidance to the church today as she seeks to probe the "great mystery" of God's love for his creatures? It is to this question that I hope to return.

BIBLIOGRAPHY

Barsom, Murad Saliba, trans. *The Order of Solemnization of the Sacrament of Matrimony According to the Ancient Rite of the Syrian Orthodox Church of Antioch.* n.p., 1974.

Brock, Sebastian, et al. "The Syriac Marriage Ritual in the Trilingual Manuscript from Beijing/Taipei." *Orientalia Christiana Periodica* 1 (2023) 33–75.

Conybeare, Frederick Cornwallis. *Rituale Armenorum: Being the Administration of the Sacraments and the Breviary Rites of the Armenian Church.* Oxford: Clarendon, 1905.

Findikyan, Michael Daniel. "The Armenian Ritual of the Dedication of a Church: A Textual and Comparative Analysis of Three Early Sources." *Orientalia Chrstiana Periodica* 64.1 (1998) 75–121.

———."Double Prayers and Inclinations in the Liturgy of the Armenian Church: The Preservation and Proliferation of an Ancient Liturgical Usage." *St. Nersess Theological Review* 9 (2003) 89–104.

Mahé, Jean-Pierre. "L'Eglise arménienne de 611 à 1066." In *Histoire de christianisme des origines à nos jours*, edited by J. M. Mayeur et al., 4:457–547. 12 vols. Paris: Desclée, 1993.

Parenti, Stefano. "The Christian Rite of Marriage in the East." In *Handbook for Liturgical Studies*, edited by Anscar J. Chupungco, 4:255–74. Collegeville, MN: Liturgical, 2000.

Parenti, Stefano, and Elena Velkovska, eds. *L'Eucologio Barberini gr. 336*. Ephemerides Liturgicae 80. Roma: CLV-Edizioni Liturgiche, 2000.

Renoux, Charles A. "Langue et littérature arméniennes." In *Christianismes orientaux: Introduction à l'étude des langues et des littératures*, edited by Micheline Albert, 107–66. Paris: Cerf, 1993.

———. "Le mariage arménien dans les plus anciennes rituels." In *Mariage: Conférences Saint-Serge, LXe Semaine d'études liturgiques*, edited by Achille M. Triacca et al., 289–305. BELS 77. Rome: CLV-Edizioni Liturgiche, 1994.

Sargisean, Barsēł, and Grigor Sargsean, eds. *Mayr c'uc'ak hayerēn jeṙagrac' Matenadaran Mxit'areanc' i Venetik*. Venice: n.p., 1966.

Tēr-Vardanean, Gēorg. *Mayr Maštoc'*. Vol. 1. Vałaršapat, Armenia: Mother See of Holy Etchmiadzin, 2012.

Vellian, Jacob, ed. *Crown, Veil, Cross: Marriage Rites*. Syrian Churches Series 15. Kottayam: Jyothi, 1990.

12

The Truly Human Things
Virtues, Stories & Teachers

By Ani Shahinian

"Human beings are not autonomous but theonomous: this is testified to in the God-man, Jesus Christ, who is no less God than human and in whom all human reality finds its being, its norm, its fulfillment."
—Vigen Guroian

PERSONAL NOTE

I AM PLEASED AND delighted to contribute to this Festschrift in honor of Professor Vigen Guroian. One afternoon in Michaelmas term of 2013 at Oxford, my next-door neighbor learning that I am Armenian came to me in excitement and introduced himself to me as a former student of Vigen Guroian. We spent hours discussing Vigen's works and how they inspired our moral and intellectual lives. That would not be the last time I would run into one of Vigen's students in Oxford, who aspired to explore the worlds of classics, theology, and philosophy, even as they hoped to plumb the depths of the human imagination.

I will not forget the colorful autumn of September 2014, when I drove from Washington, DC, to Vigen and June's home in Culpeper, Virginia. I was full of imaginative anticipation with my hope-filled inquires for Vigen. Three years later, in the fall of 2017, I returned to Oxford for my doctoral studies. I serendipitously met another student of Vigen's at the power-lifting area of the university gym. It was clear that Vigen had influenced men and women across multiple disciplines, inspiring them to become flourishing human beings through their choices, actions, and career paths. Vigen had also achieved one other matter with his students: he left a beautiful impression of an Armenian, and Armenia's Christian history and culture.

In Trinity term of 2018, I collaborated with some of Vigen's students to invite him to Oxford for a symposium on human imagination, morality, ethics, and more. I vividly remember the long walks along the Oxford meadows, the conversations at the British pubs that mimicked the Inklings gatherings of days gone by, the time spent gazing at the Oxford University chapels and cathedrals during long detours, and the flourishing discussions in quaint medieval classrooms of Christ Church. These encounters remain alive in my memory, and even now, I look back fondly on those placid and thoughtful days.

In speaking with Vigen and engaging with his writings on theology, ethics, virtues, scriptural imagination, and the moral imagination over the last decade, I detect parallel thoughts and concepts with the Armenian *Vardapet* (theologian, church father, teacher of human minds and hearts). They both invoke the creative world of the human mind and teach us how to think and write about human affairs. In this small contribution, I will introduce two *vardapets* from the Armenian tradition and their teacher. They have inspired me on matters I have always cherished discussing with Vigen.

INTRODUCTION

The premise that "human beings are not autonomous but theonomous" strikes at the heart of Armenian theological thought on Անձնիշխանութիւն. In other words, self-governance is a result of both the person's ability to exercise will and agency and the person's capacity to participate in divine love and its attendant virtues.[1] The Christian virtues become tools in the hands

---

1. Անձնիշխանութիւն = Anjnišaxutʻiwn = Self-governance. See my preliminary

of the Armenian *vardapet* to teach others how to become *theonomous*, such that they become free agents capable of choosing to do good.[2] The *vardapet* also uses these virtues to teach how to limit the self to serve a greater good. By examining the lives and works of three *vardapets* from late medieval Armenia, I aspire to converse with Vigen's extensive work on engaging with the truly human things. A common thread throughout the paper demonstrates the significance of student-teacher relationship. The ensuing synthesis will illustrate how the Christian virtues, understood with the classical virtues, underpinned the stories of the martyrs and saints which became teaching tools in the writings of the *vardapets* from one generation to the next.

YOVHAN *VARDAPET* OROTNECʻI (1315–1388), THE TEACHER

The life and works of Yovhan *vardapet* Orotnecʻi, *kaxik* (1315–1388), a renowned *vardapet*-theologian and philosopher, remain inaccessible, yet invaluable treasure for scholarship.[3] He was born in the region of Orotn in Syiwnikʻ, in the village of Vaładin, in 1315, to the prince of Siwnikʻ, Iwanē Orbēlean. He was ordained a priest in 1337, and obtained his rank as a *vardapet* at the Glajor Monastery, where he was a student of Esayi Nčʻecʻi (1260–1338) and Tiratur Kilikecʻi (fourteenth century).[4] Some of his earliest works include the writings of Aristotle, Plato, Porphyry, Philo of Alexandria, Basil of Caesarea, Grigor Narekacʻi, to name a few. He was a prolific teacher at Glajor Monastery and established Tatʻew Monastery, where he raised dedicated *vardapets* serving in different monasteries in Greater Armenia. Students from Armenia and the diaspora sought to study under Orotencʻi's tutelage. One of those distant students seeking Orotnecʻi as their teacher was Grigor Tatʻewacʻi who was born in Javaxkʻ (modern-day,

---

investigation of this concept in Shahinian, *Philosophy and Martyrdom*, 106–16. See also Guroian, *Human Things*, 211–20. For the Armenian transliteration, I follow the Hübschmann—Meillet—Benveniste system of transliteration.

2. A *vardapet* = վարդապետ is a reference from the Armenian Scriptural use for Jesus. Its first meaning is simply teacher. In Armenian church history, the term took on a unique meaning to refer to the one who has obtained the highest training to teach scriptures, and the one who is able to speak to the real human issues touching on both the heart and the mind of a person. In short, a *vardapet* is a teacher of the word and a doctor of the church.

3. Orotnecʻi carried the suffix *kaxik*, literally "to hang," because of his dependence on the love of Christ. As of yet, there are no studies on Orotnecʻi in western scholarship.

4. For more on the university in Glajor, see Abrahamian, *Glajori hamalsaran*, 160–76.

The Truly Human Things

Javakheti, Southern Georgia). Orotnecʻi later became the teacher and mentor of the great *vardapet*-theologian and philosopher Grigor Tatʻewacʻi (1346–1409), Mattʻēos *vardapet* J̌ułayecʻi (1349–1411), as well as Grigor *vardapet* Xlatʻecʻi, amongst many others.⁵

In this short contribution, I would like to introduce two students of Orotnecʻi, who went on to become teachers-*vardapets* themselves; composing and compiling some of the most treasured works in Armenian Christianity from the late medieval period. Below, I first look at Grigor Tatʻewacʻi and one area of his extensive study, i.e., the classical and Christian virtues. Thereafter, I introduce Grigor Cerencʻ Xlatʻecʻi, as another exemplary student of Orotnecʻi who embodied the virtues as a *martyrophile* and a martyr himself.

Figure 12.1: Yovhan Orotnecʻi teaching his student Grigor Tatʻewacʻi from the Gospel Matthew (fourteenth-century manuscript illumination, in the public domain [https://commons.wikimedia.org/wiki/File:Hovhan_Vorotnetsi_and_Grigor_Tatevatsi.jpg/]).

---

5. For a summary of Orotnecʻi's life and works in Eastern Armenian, see Minasyan *Yovhan Orotnecʻwy kyankʻn*, 1–19.

Part Four: Faith, Church, Mission

THE SEVEN VIRTUES IN THE WORKS OF GRIGOR *VARDAPET* TATʻEWACʻI (1346–1409)

The life and works of Grigor *vardapet* Tatʻewacʻi have received some attention over the last few decades.[6] The precise date of his birth is unknown, but it is estimated that Tatʻewacʻi was born around 1346 and died in December of 1409. With Grigor Xlatʻecʻi (introduced below), he was a student of Orotnecʻi. In 1371, Tatʻewacʻi was ordained a priest in Jerusalem at the St. James Cathedral (located in the Armenian Quarter of the Old City in Jerusalem). Around the year 1373, he obtained the rank of a *vardapet* in Erzenka (modern-day Erzincan, Eastern Turkey). Upon Orotnecʻi's death, Tatʻewacʻi assumed the responsibilities of his teacher, later passing the mantle to another great teacher of the church, Mattʻēos Ĵułayecʻi. Tatʻewacʻi's rich corpus reflects in an extensive manner the issues and influences prevalent, especially the questions of virtue, in late medieval Armenia.

In 1388, Tatʻewacʻi copied the *Book of the Seven Virtues by Peter of Aragon* for Hovhan Orotnecʻi at Vałatn Monastery near Orotn Monastery in Syiwunikʻ.[7] In his multivolume *Book of Questions* [*Girkʻ harcʻmancʻ*] (1397), Tatʻewacʻi attributed an entire book to the question of the virtues. His treatise on the virtues becomes a pedagogical text for his students and religious leaders of his era. It is written in a formulaic and condensed way, where the person engaging with the text can choose and select sections of the text and elaborate on each point in their teachings. The definitions provided on each virtue draw on the Church Fathers; figures like Dionysus, Philo, John of Damascus, to bring together all that has been said about the divine virtues and the human virtues which adorn the exemplary human being.

Below I present Tatʻewacʻi's teachings on the seven virtues, divided into the divine / theological and human virtues, respectively, with closer

---

6. For a full biography and list of works, see Thomson, *Bibliography*, 134–35. For sources on Tatʻewacʻi's life in English, see La Porta, *Grigor Tatʻewacʻi's Book of Questions*, 6–12.

7. See M46 and M1606, Xačʻikyan, *Hishatakaranner*. [Գիրք Եաւթն Առաքինութեանց Պետրոսի Արագոնացոյ]. The Dominican missions in Greater Armenia, the Fratres Unitores in Kʻrna, and the Armeno-Latin relations become the broader context for this work amongst others during the fourteenth/fifteenth centuries. Tatʻewacʻi's sources (and Peter of Aragon's) go back to Plato, Aristotle, and Philo in their influence and contact with the timeless question of what it means to be a human being. Elsewhere I intend to explore this context and especially the context of virtues and catholic missions with special focus on Yovhan Orotnecʻi.

analysis of what these descriptions of the virtues meant for the *vardapets* in their teachings.

The Three Divine Virtues [աստուածային առաքինութիւնք]

The seven virtues, three theological and four cardinal, are not unique to Tatʻewacʻi, or the *vardapets* in late medieval Armenia. The theological virtues of faith, hope, and love usually refer to the Pauline Epistle to the Corinthians: "But now faith, hope, *and* love remain, these three; but the greatest of these is love" (1 Cor 13:13). Since Paul's time, church fathers and theologians across the centuries have commentated and reflected on the divine / theological virtues. In fourteenth-century Armenia, this topic once again gained traction to a degree where memorization and correct citation of the virtues were esteemed amongst the monks in-training.[8]

Faith [հաւատն]

Tatʻewacʻi begins his treatise with the explanation of faith—*hawatn*, which in the Armenian translates to "trust." In defining faith, Tatʻewacʻi first quotes from Hebrews 11:1, "Now faith is the assurance of things hoped for, the conviction of things not seen."[9] Following the early church fathers, Tatʻewacʻi crowns faith as the "cornerstone of all virtues."[10] Relying on Chrysostom and Methodius, he explains further that faith illumines the individual's reason to distinguish good and evil. Furthermore, he elaborates, "faith is the illumination of the mind through which one comes to recognize the ultimate truth."[11] In order words, a person who possesses *hawat* is, first and foremost, a person with the ability to discern the ultimate good. At the heart of the meaning of this divine gift of faith is the human agency of trust; hence, it appeals the depth of a person's agency and being to respond to the stimuli placed before them.

Moreover, Tatʻewacʻi creates a bridge between truth and faith as he builds on Dionysus (or Pseudo-Dionysius) the Areopagite's definition. He

8. Tʻovma Mecopʻecʻi describes the fervent study of the virtues by monks in this period and how it became a topic of debate and discussion amongst them. See Mecopʻecʻi, *Patmagrutʻyun*, 70–80.

9. Tatʻewacʻi, *Book of Questions*, 589.

10. Tatʻewacʻi, *Book of Questions*, 589.

11. Tatʻewacʻi, *Book of Questions*, 589.

state, "The great Dionysus writes that the divine writings define faith as the steadfastness of the believers, who stand in the truth, and the truth in them."[12] Notwithstanding our modern preoccupations with rationality, or the manners in which the modern mind has tried to create a separation between faith and reason, it actually seems to be the case that reason is central to this definition of faith. Tat'ewac'i continues: "Faith is the capacity poured out by the primal light into the rational being through which one recognizes the spiritual goods."[13] As we shall see, it is the saint-martyr, who is celebrated as an exemplary figure because s/he displayed the rational light present in their actions and words as they discerned and respond to the challenges posited to them.

Hope [Յոյսն]

Unlike modern misconceptions of hope as 'wishful thinking,' hope, according to Tat'ewac'i, invokes the "surety of anticipation." The virtue of hope equipped martyrs, as Tat'ewac'i teaches, to face the societal and familial pressures and challenges. Tat'ewac'i elaborates on hope with this description:

> The inner-workings of the hope are multiple. First, it delivers us from anxiety; second, it strengthens [us], as it is obvious from the Maccabean woman who had seven sons [killed] . . . likewise, all the ranks of the martyrs were strengthened by hope; third, it elevates one's thoughts, as Isaiah said, "those who hope in the Lord will change their strength and receive wings like eagle."[14]

---

12. Tat'ewac'i, *Book of Questions*, 589. [Եւ մեծն Դիոնեսիոս ի գիրս աստուածային անուանց սահմանէ թէ՝ «հաւատն է հաստատ կայումն հաւատացելոց. որ զարդարս կացուցանէ ի մշմարտութիւնն եւ զմշմարտութիւնն ի նոսա].

13. Tat'ewac'i, *Book of Questions*, 589. [հաւատն է ունակութիւն հեղեալ յառաջին լուսոյն ի բանական անձն, առ ի ճանաչել զհոգեւոր բարիս:]

14. Tat'ewac'i, *Book of Questions*, 589. [Եւ բազում է ներգործութիւն յուսին։ Նախ ազատէ ի ներքութենէ. ըստ այնմ «ի քեզ յուսացան հարքն մեր եւ փրկեցեր զնոսա»։ Երկրորդ զօրացուցանէ. որպէս յայտ է ի մակաբայեցւոցն զկնոջէն որ ունէր է որդիս՝ ածեալ ի սպանումն ի միումն աւուր տեսայ. եւ տանէր այնմ՝ յուսովն որ առ Աստուած։ Նոյնպէս եւ ամենայն դասք մարտիրոսացն յուսով զօրացան։ Երրորդ ամբառնայ զմիտս. որպէս ասէ Եսայի «որք յուսան ի Տէր փոխեսցեն զզօրութիւնս. առնուն զթեւս որպէս զարծուի»։ Չորրորդ փրկէ ի քշմանցաց ընդ սադմոսին «որ փրկես զյուսացայս ի քեզ»։ Հինգերորդ տայ զժամանակաւորս. ըստ այնմ «աչք ամենեցուն ի քեզ յուսան». եւ դու տաս նոցա»։]

Tatʿewacʿi grounds his examples of one who displays hope of strength on the Maccabean martyrs and promises from Scripture. He further expands:

> Here certainty [of hope] is not in the sense of proof, but it is certainty of supposition [belief]. And the occasion of hope is first the grace of God, then our own endeavour. Because to hope for things without having done anything is not hope, but presumption.[15]

Here, once again, the *vardapet* speaks directly to the agency and the will of the human being. Hope without action is not hope. Furthermore, hope is twofold: first hope relies on something other than self, that is on God's authority. Second, hope relies on those who have gone before us, as examples to imitate and emulate.

Tatʿewacʿi explains hope in God's authority in three parts: first, hope for the forgiveness of sins; second, hope for God's grace; and third, hope for our salvation. The stories of the saints and martyrs focus on how their character demonstrates their assurance and conviction of the hope of grace and mercy with which they respond and act.

Love *[սէրն]*

The depth of this divine virtue, love, has been central to human desire, agency, and imagination. But, love is not simply a virtue, it is a divine grace and gift. Tatʿewacʿi explains love extensively offering different levels to each explanation. It is noteworthy that the two essential aspects of love, that is love towards God and people, is expounded by Tatʿewacʿi directly. He writes:

> And it is known that love has three parts: natural, moral, gratuitous. Natural love is towards oneself. Morality is towards a neighbour, and gratuitous [love is] towards God. Moreover, there is a differentiation between the love of God and the love for one's neighbour. We love God through himself, and for his own sake. And [one loves] one's neighbour through God and because of God. So when we say love is double, it is double not in terms of its aptitude, but in terms of its functions, because God and one's neighbour are [both] loved through one [and the same] aptitude for love.[16]

---

15. Tatʿewacʿi, *Book of Questions*, 589. [Ստուգութիւն աստ ոչ զապացուցականն ասէ. այլ զստուգութիւն կարծեացն: Եւ պատճառ յուսոյն նախ է շնորհն Աստուծոյ. եւ ապա արդիւնքն մեր: Զի յուսալ յիր ինչ առանց արդեանց ոչ է յոյս. այլ յանդգնութիւն:]

16. Tatʿewacʿi, *Book of Questions*, 580. [Եւ գիտելի է, զի եռակի է սէրն: բնական.

This description of love towards God and others by Tat'ewac'i is fitting for the character of an exemplary human being demonstrated in a saint / martyr, who guided their passions and actions with love towards God and others.

The Four Human Virtues [մարդկային առաքինութիւնք]

Tat'ewac'i expands on and distinguishes the human virtues from the divine virtues. He not only defines each virtue, but also expands on the application of those human virtues quoting from the church fathers. Here he provides how each human virtue relates to the other. Tat'ewac'i writes:

> Again, "virtue is a good aptitude of the mind through which one leads an upright life . . ."; this speaks about the virtue that is poured out by the light of God's grace. Once again, "Virtue is the blessedness and glory of this life here, and it contains in itself light and happiness." In addition, one ought to know, the soul directs itself to its strength through the virtues: the virtue of prudence gives direction to the rational function [of the soul]. The virtue of courage gives direction to the passions of anger of the soul. Sober-mindedness directs the desires. While justice (righteousness) directs all the powers, because it includes the virtues that put in order the human being relative to his neighbour, such as uprightness and generosity, as well as the things that put a person in order relative to oneself, such as penance and innocence, and also the ones that put a person in order towards God, like piety and obedience. This is why justice (righteousness) is called the directive of the will because it is not only a specific power or virtue, but it is common to all of them and contains all of the soul's uprightness.[17]

բարոյական. եւ շնորհական: Բնական սէրն է առիքն: Բարոյականն առ ընկերն: եւ Շնորհականն առ Աստուած: Դարձեալ զանազանութիւն է ի մէջ սիրոյ Աստուծոյ եւ ընկերին: Զի զԱստուած սիրեմք ի յինքն եւ վասն ինքեան: Այլ զընկերն ի յԱստուած եւ վասն Աստուծոյ: Արդ յորժամ ասեմք կրկին զսէրն, այսինքն Աստուծոյ եւ ընկերին. կրկինա այս է ո՛չ է ըստ ունակութեանց. այլ ըստ ներգործունեացն: Զի միով ունակութեամբ սիրոյ սիրի Աստուած եւ ընկերն:]

17. Tat'ewac'i's quotations on these definitions of virtues resembles those of Philo of Alexandria. See Walter T. Wilson's recent translation and commentary in Wilson, *Philo of Alexandria*. Tat'ewac'i, *Book of Questions*, 578. [Դարձեալ՝ առաքինութիւն է բարի ունակութիւն մտաց, որով ուղիղ կեայ. եւ ոչ որ շարշար առնու ի կիր. որ Աստուած ներգործէ ի մեզ առանց մեզ»: Այս խօսի գեղեցալ առաքինութենէ յուսմ շնորհացն Աստուծոյ: Դարձեալ՝ «առաքինութիւնէ երանութիւն եւ փառք աստի կենացս. եւ ունի յինքն լոյս եւ խնդութիւն»: Այլ գիտելի է, զի առաքինութեամբն ուղղի հոգին ի

The Truly Human Things

Righteousness and Justice [արդարութիւն]

Tat'ewac'i's teaching on human virtues unfolds in six parts: "The components of righteousness are six; in other words, discipline, compassion, grace, zeal, defence, and truthfulness."[18] These characteristics are readily observed in the words, choices, and deeds of a saint/martyr. While "discipline is to offer worship and specific service to God," Tat'ewac'i provides an elaborated explanation of zeal:

> Zeal is to be an advocate; by means of this, oppression and injustice and anything harmful is openly rejected. Defence, are those things that merit honours and service of humanity. Truth is to say without alteration the things that are, or have been, or will be.[19]

Tat'ewac'i explains the three ways in which the virtue of justice can be distorted:

> First, love of self or money, as Isaiah says: "Woe to you that justify the wicked for the sake of the bribe." Second, through fear, against which the Lord says, "do not fear those who kill the body." Third, by hatred and jealousy. As [the Apostle] says, "he understood that he betrayed him out of jealously."[20]

While all the other human virtues remain as part of the character of the individual, in eternity, they no longer are in effect in terms of their actions, according to Tat'ewac'i. However, this is not the case with regard to justice and righteousness. These virtue remains in the person's character and

---

գործութիւաս իւր. բանզի խոհեմութիւն ուղղէ զքանականն. արիութիւնն զցասմանականն։ Ողջախոհութիւնն զցանկականն։ Իսկ արդարութիւնն ուղղէ զամենայն գործութիւաս։ Զի նա պարունակէ զառաքինութիւաս որ կարգեն զմարդ ատ ընկերն. որպէս ուղղութիւնն եւ առատաբաշխութիւնն։ Եւ որ կարգեն ատ ինքն. որպէս ապաշխարութիւնն եւ անմեղութիւնն։ Եւ որ կարգեն զմարդն ատ Աստուած։ Որպէս աստուածպաշտութիւնն եւ հնազանդութիւնն։ Վասն այն ասի արդարութիւնն ուղղութիւն կամաց. զի ոչ միայն է առանձնական գործութիւն կամ առաքինութիւն. այլ եւ հասարակ եւ պարունակիչ ուղղութեան հոգւոյն:]

18. Tat'ewac'i, *Book of Questions*, 578. [Եւ մասունք արդարութեան են Զ այսինքն կրօնաւորութիւն. գթութիւն. շնորհ. վրէժխնդրութիւն. պահպանութիւն. եւ ճշմարտութիւն:]

19. Tat'ewac'i *Book of Questions*, 579. [Վրէժխնդրութիւն է շատագով լինիլ. որով բռնութիւն եւ անիրաւութիւն եւ ամենայն վնասակար ի բաց մերժի։ Պահպանութիւն է որք արժանաւորին մարդկան պատուոյ ինն եւ պաշտամանն: Ճշմարտութիւն է որ առանց փոփոխման ասին այնք որ են, կամ լինին, կամ լինելոց են:]

20. Tat'ewac'i *Book of Questions*, 579.

action, whereas the works of prudence, courage, and sobriety are evident in a person's character and actions only in this life.

Prudence [խոհեմութիւն]

In the service of training the earthly life, prudence serves as a person's ability to discern between good and evil. The work of prudence, Tatʻewacʻi teaches, "is when a person does not speak evil against another, nor is he deceived by anyone. For as Christ has commended, 'Be wise like serpents and simpleminded like doves,' such that by wisdom one guards oneself, and by being simpleminded he does not cause harm to another."[21]

Tatʻewacʻi identifies the three parts of the virtue of prudence as wisdom, foresight, and memory. He further elaborates: "By wisdom one is capable of accepting that which is . . . foresight equips the person to see that which will take place as a result of certain actions, and memory equips the person to recall and know that which has taken place."[22]

Sober-mindedness [ողջախոհութիւն]

The deep struggle of creating balance in life requires the exercise of the virtue of temperance or sober-mindedness to response towards one's desires, passions, and needs in the physical life.

> Sober-mindedness is firmness of the soul, through which one controls one's passions, emotions, and bodily pleasure. The deeds of temperance are when one knows how to have less in his state of plenty and how to endure in poverty. As the Apostle says, 'I know (what it means to) grow, I know (what it means) to diminish.'[23]

---

21. Tatʻewacʻi *Book of Questions*, 580; Matt 10:8, 16. [Եւ գործ է սորա՝ որ ինքն ներգործիւն ո'չ առնէ մարդոյ, եւ ն'չյայլ մարդոյ խաբի: Վասն այս հրամայեաց Քրիստոս «եղերուք խորագէտք իբրեւ զօձս եւ միամիտք որպէս զաղաւնիս»: Խորագիտութեամբ պահէ զինքն յայլ մարդոյ. եւ միամտութեամբն այլոց վնաս ո'չ առնէ.].

22. Tatʻewacʻi, *Book of Questions*, 580–81. [Նախ խոհեմութիւն սրտին. եւ այս ի կարգաւորել զներկայն, ի միտ ածել զանցեալն, եւ նախատես լինիլ ապագային, որպէս ասէ յերկրորդ օրէնս «երանի թէ իմանային.» որ է ներկայն. «եւ ի միտ առնուին.» այս է զանցեալն. «եւ նախատեսք լինէին վերջնոցն».].

23. Tatʻewacʻi, *Book of Questions*, 582; Phil 4:12. [Ողջախոհութիւն է հաստատութիւն հոգւոյ. որով արգելու զգանկութիւն զգայական եւ զհեշտութիւն մարմնական: Եւ գործ նորա այս է. յառաւելութեան գիտենալ նուազիլ. եւ ի յարքատութեանն գիտենալ համբերել. որպէս ասէ առաքեալն «գիտեմ առաւելուլ գիտեմ նուազիլ»:]

148

Courage [արիութիւն]

"Courage is the ability whereby one easily bears everything for the sake of the things one loves" writes Tatʻewacʻi.[24] Hence, the deeds of courage, he affirms, are "when a person in difficult times is not broken by adversity nor in times of ease becomes soft in luxury."[25] He further expounds the four parts of courage, which are:

> Doing of great deeds, confidence, endurance, and persistence. The *doing of great deeds* is to do in thought and in action to bring about great and lofty matters with confidence in one's soul. *Confidence* is that by which the soul, in great and in modest matters, is affirmed in itself with certainty of hope. *Endurance* is voluntary and continual vision of great and difficult things in terms of their usefulness and one's own modesty. *Persistence* is firmly and continually examining oneself properly and rationally.[26]

A saint/martyr who is a witness in word and deed rises to the doing of great deeds. Here Tatʻewacʻi defines "the doing of great deeds in thought and action" as a function of the virtue of courage.

These explanations provided by Tatʻewacʻi show how these virtues were understood and embodied in medieval Armenian understanding, commenting on the fullness of what it means to be human.[27]

THE MARTYR, GRIGOR VARDAPET CERENCʻ XLATʻECʻI (1349-1425)

An example of the virtuous character as described by Tatʻewacʻi above is personified in the *vardapet*, martyr in life and death, Grigor Xlatʻecʻi, another student of Orotnecʻi and a peer of Tatʻewacʻi. The great *vardapet*-theologian, Grigor Cerencʻ Xlatʻecʻi [Xlatʻecʻi], influencer of life and culture in late medieval Lake Van region (modern-day Eastern Turkey), remains an unknown figure in western scholarship. Xlatʻecʻi was born in 1349 to

---

24. Tatʻewacʻi, *Book of Questions*, 582. [Արիութիւն է զօրութիւն իմն որով հեշտութեամբ տանի ամենայնի վասն սիրելի իրաց:].

25. Tatʻewacʻi, *Book of Questions*, 582. [Որոյ գործն այս է. ոչ ի նեղութիւնն խորտակի եւ ոչ ի հեշտութիւնն կակղանայ].

26. Tatʻewacʻi, *Book of Questions*, 582. [այսինքն մեծագործութիւն. ապաստանութիւն. համբերութիւն. եւ յարամնայութիւն] (emphasis added).

27. For the full treatment on the virtues, see Tatʻewacʻi, *Book of Questions*, 570-83.

Cer and Xoyand, in Xlatʻ, a city on the north-western shore of Lake Van, in the region of Bznunikʻ. He is known as Xlatʻecʻi from his birthplace of Xlatʻ (modern-day Ahlat, Eastern Turkey).[28]

Xlatʻecʻi began his priestly training at approximately the age of twelve (c. 1361), at the monastery of St. Stepʻanos called Cʻipnavankʻ, in Arckē (modern-day Adilcevaz, Eastern Turkey), a day's walk east of Xlatʻ, on the north shore of Lake Van. For fifteen years at Cʻipnavankʻ, Xlatʻecʻi trained under Vardan the Hermit, who had been a student of Tiratur *vardapet* Kilikecʻi and a classmate of Orotnecʻi. After six years of training at Cʻipnavankʻ, Xlatʻecʻi received the title of *abeła* [monk]. In that same year, in 1367, he moved to the region of Bznunikʻ, the same region where the city of Xlatʻ was located.[29] He spent ten years preaching, teaching, and writing some of his earliest compositions, including a *Čaṙ* əntir [Anthology of Homilies] which is preserved in Xlatʻecʻi's own handwriting at the Mesrop Maštoc Research Institute of Armenian Manuscripts (Matenadaran).

Between the years 1380 and 1387, Xlatʻecʻi travelled to Orotnavankʻ [Orotn Monastery] to study under Yovhan *vardapet* Orotnecʻi (1315–1388), prior to becoming a *vardapet* himself. After Orotnecʻi's death, Xlatʻecʻi settled at the Surb Astvacacni Vankʻ [Monastery of the Holy Mother of God] in Xaṙabast, which was in the region of Kʻaǰ berunikʻ (north-west of the Lake Van region, modern-day Erciš, Eastern Turkey). In Xaṙabastavankʻ [Xaṙabast Monastery], Xlatʻecʻi studied and wrote under the prominent Sargis *rabunapet* Aprakunecʻi (fourteenth century) for ten years, obtaining the rank of *vardapet* in the year 1391.[30] He travelled on a pilgrimage to Jerusalem between the years 1403 and 1405, where he wrote a commentary on the Gospel of John—the only copy of this work is still preserved in Jerusalem. Between the years of 1405 and 1425, Xlatʻecʻi divided his time between two monasteries, serving the communities there at various capacities. In the last decade of his life, Xlatʻecʻi returned to his home monastery Cʻipnavankʻ, where he was martyred on Pentecost Sunday, on May 9, 1425, during the Kara Koyunlu invasions under Iskandar.

In the early days of Xlatʻecʻi's training as a *vardapet*, Armenian Cilicia lost its independence to the pressures of the Mamlūk forces from the

---

28. Mecopʻecʻi, *Patmagrutʻyun*, 70–73; Xalatʻeancʻ, *Kensagrakan Aknark*, 65–72.

29. On Bznuni's history, see Xorenacʻi and Thomson, *History of the Armenians*.

30. Matʻevosyan and Marabyan, *Grigor Cerenc Xlateci*, 28–30. Sargis *rabunapet* Aprakunecʻi discipled over sixty students like Xlatʻecʻi. *Rabunapet* was a title reserved to the very few—they were the teachers of teachers. Orotnecʻi also was a *rabunapet*.

south in Egypt.[31] Xlatʻecʻi's times were marked by invasions and the gradual diminishing of Armenian religious and political life. External invasions, internal rivalries, famine, and harsh winters altered the destinies of the local people. In 1314–1316, the Īlkhānids launched a coup, and established Xlatʻ (Xlatʻecʻi's hometown) as a centre of their rule. The Īlkhānid power in Xlatʻ collapsed between 1345 and 1350, and the region was subsequently incorporated within the administration of Bitlis, from which the Qara Qoyunlu leader Qara Yusuf controlled the region. This greater context involved the reshaping of the religious, political, and cultural boundaries between different communities. It is in this setting that Xlatʻecʻi was born and raised.

XLATʻECʻI, THE TEACHER AND MARTYR

Xlatʻecʻi was a great teacher and apologist of the Christian faith in his times.[32] He drew on past Armenian authors and influencers of faith, culture, and literature, assessing their works and making them accessible to his contemporaries. Xlatʻecʻi, as a teacher, cultivated the minds and hearts of his students, as is evidenced in how his students wrote about him. His students convey in detail his character, along with his qualifications, travel itineraries, pedagogical methods, and his engagement with the issues prevalent amongst the ecclesiastical community at large. One student, Aṙakʻel Bałišecʻi (~1390–1454), who composed Xlatʻecʻi's *vita-martyrology* [the hagiographical martyr text on his saintly life] and a *ganj*[33] on the occasion of his martyrdom, describes Xlatʻecʻi's character utilizing the virtuous language of charity, sober-mindedness, prudence, and his deep faith in God and hope for the lives entrusted under his care. Bałišecʻi details how Xlatʻecʻi made arrangements to earn income by writing manuscripts in order to use those funds to donate them to the poor and needy. Bałišecʻi writes:

> He consoled them with ineffable and inexpressible consolation, with the knowledge of the written Scriptures [Gospels], and with the wisdom of the old and of the new, with exhortation, exhorting

---

31. Kouymjian, "Armenia from the Fall," 57; "Critical Bibliography."
32. Marabyan, *Grigor Xlatʻecʻu Tonakannerə*, 43–46.
33. *Ganj*, literally means "treasure" and *Ganjaran*, "treasury." Abraham Terian defines *ganj* as similar to a kʻaroz, stating that a ganj "is an array of litanic and para-litanic prayers, distinct from litanies or bidding prayers recited by deacons during the Liturgy of the Hours—from which it derives" (Terian, *Festal Works*, xxxiv).

everyone in the true faith of orthodoxy, and in virtuous deeds. Additionally, he made wise the foolish, he called the ignorant to the knowledge of the Lord, he freed the captive, he clothed the naked, he alleviated the sick ones physically and spiritually, he comforted the ones who were mourning, he feed the poor, and all the while, with uneasy vigilance, morning and night, with his own hands, he devoted to the task of writing. He provided for the homeless, and he became desirable to all: to God, to angels, and mankind, to the believers and to the unbelievers, to the point where the Muslims considered the Armenian people fortunate to have a leader such as him.

Xlatʿecʿiʾs unique ability to comfort, teach, and minister to the people of his region, and beyond is celebrated here; especially, he had a distinctive capacity to educate the masses: young and old, literate and illiterate. He was approachable; hence, people of all backgrounds gathered around him to learn.[34] The image conveyed of him in his *vita* is that of Jesus and his disciples, a trope that the author engages to properly situate Xlatʿecʿiʾs character and activities.

Aṙakʿel Bałišecʿi continues to use allegorical references in his estimation of Xlatʿecʿi as a second Vkayasēr = Matryrophile = lover of the saints.[35] The text states:

> In this end time and lattermost age, he was named a second vkayasēr for he collected many writings of ours and of others [of the foreigners], books which were aged and damaged, and brought forth from the darkness into the light the hidden and unknown histories of all the saints, he produced the volumes of the *Yaysmawurkʿ* ... and having stripped off all the deep and incomprehensible discourse, he extracted and wrote simply and clearly the history of the saints. And, all the translation of the God-breathed Scriptures by the holy translators he once again refined, and uncovered the meanings of the holy writings, so that they became comprehensible for everyone.[36]

---

34. For more on the topos of a saint as a learned holy man who is loved by everyone who encounters him, see Brown, *Rise and Function of the Holy Man*.

35. Grigor II Vkayasēr Pahlavuni (1065–1102), was the first to be called "Lover of saints" as he established the practice of collection and arranging the lives of the martyrs and the saints all in one place.

36. Manandean and Ačaṙean, *Hayocʿ nor vkaner*, 264–82. «Եւ զամենայն խորհն եւ զանհասկանալի բանսպերթբեալ եհանի միջոյ. եւ պարզ եւ յստակ գրեացզպատմութիւնս սրբոց. եւ զամենայն աստուածաշունչ գրեանսզքարգմանեալսն իսրբոց թարգմանչացն կրկին յղեաց եւ երաց զմիտս գրոց սրբոց, առ ի հասկանալ ամենայն ումեք»:

The Truly Human Things

Besides being gifted in teaching and speaking to diverse audiences, Xlat'ec'i was ecumenical in his efforts to enrich the Christian communities by making the universal church's writings on the lives of the saints accessible. Here, Bałišec'i describes the development of the *Yaysmawurk'* [Armenian Synaxarion or Menologium where the collection of the lives of the martyrs and saints are written] and the different aspects of the process by which Xlat'ec'i produced the final edition of the *Yaysmawurk'*. Xlat'ec'i's dedication to and preoccupation with the broader question of the Christian virtues and exemplary saintly life is depicted in his careful translation, collection, and compilation of the stories of the men and women who had gone before him and those also in his context. Consistent with the tropes of a learned and virtuous person, the vita-martyr text records:

> The Holy Spirit descended and rested upon him, the spirit of meekness and humility (1 Corinthians 4:21), so that he illuminated all the inhabitants of the province through wisdom and instruction as a perfect teacher.[37]

This language assists the reader and listeners to associate Xlat'ec'i's life and works as analogous with those of Christ, his disciples, and the early church fathers. These embellishments establish a continuity in texts describing how Christian salvific history unfolds in the author's particular context. In the way Xlat'ec'i referred to himself in his own writings sheds light on how he viewed his task and role in his world. In various manuscripts, Xlat'ec'i signs his name as Art'un, an Armenian translation of the meaning of the name Gregory in Greek, Γρηγόριος (Grēgorios), meaning "watchful, alert" (derived from Greek "γρηγορεῖν," *grēgorein* meaning "to watch").[38] As his corpus shows, Xlat'ec'i reflected on the challenges of his times and the need to be alert and awake. The goal and aim of the monk is to be angel-like in the flesh, always awake, creating continuity of consciousness in the body.

---

37. Manandean and Ačaṙean, *Hayoc' nor vkaner*, 264–82. «Եւ էջ հանգեաւ ի վերայ նորա Հոգին Սուրբ, հոգին հեզութեան եւ խոնարհութեան. մինչ զի լուսաւորէր զամենայն բնակիչս գաւառին իմաստութեամբ եւ ուսմամբ՝ իբրեւ զկատարեալ վարդապետ»:

38. See http://www.lgpn.ox.ac.uk.

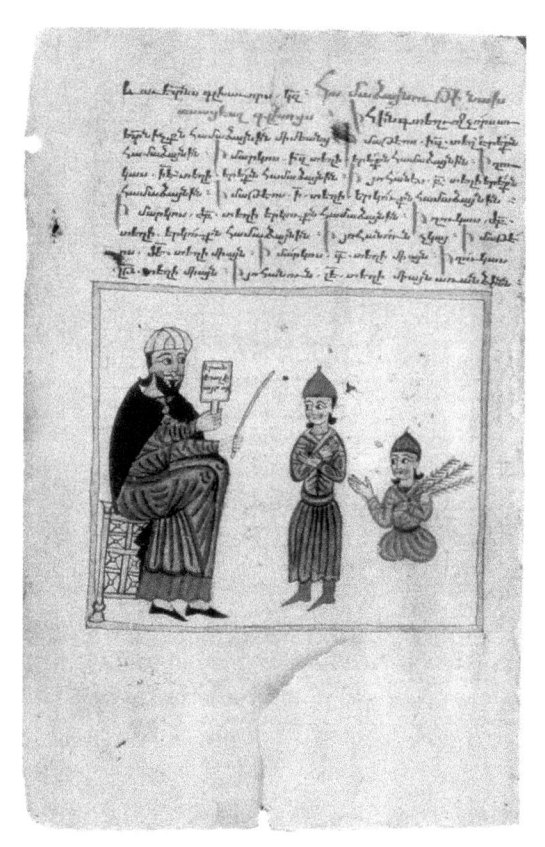

Figure 12.2: Grigor Xlatʻecʻi, teaching from the Psalms: "Blessed is the man who . . ." (fifteenth-century manuscript illumination [M3714], in the public domain).

It is often understandably admirable and worth of celebration for the level of commitment and dedication a teacher like Xlatʻecʻi offered in and through his life. But, what is truly special about him is that because he had exercised the virtuous life of faith he had risen to a place where the virtue of courage was palpable not only in his words and deeds, but also in his choices that brought about his martyrdom. Facing death at the doors of his monastery, Xlatʻecʻi uttered these words:

> For even if they kill me [reference to the Muslim invasions], I believe in my Lord my Jesus Christ; So, together with the martyrs of

The Truly Human Things

God, I shall be found worthy of His incorruptible and unfading inheritance.[39]

Xlat'ec'i was an antiquarian polymath in the eyes of his contemporaries. For the most part, Xlat'ec'i's rich corpus remains hidden with its treasures for scholarly inquiry. His written corpus is large in size and breadth of genres, ranging from copying Gospels, writing homilies, composing hymns, editing the synaxarion of feast days and the saints' lives, to explored his artistic gifts in miniature paintings, composed poetry, and composed letters to his colleagues across the medieval world, to writing riddles, poetry, and letters to his colleagues in monasteries spread around the Lake Van region and beyond. He wrote tirelessly with vigilance for fifty-five years.[40] Xlat'ec'i's most influential collections that have had continual impact and occupied attention in the following centuries were the *Yaysmawurk'*, the *Ganjaran* [lit. Treasury—collection of rhythmic litanies]; *Patmakan ołb* ("Historical Lament"); *Č aṙəntir* [Anthology of Homilies], and *Yišatakaran Ałētic'* ("Memoir of Calamity").[41]

CONCLUSION

Reflecting on what I have proposed here as the truly human things—virtues, stories, and teachers—this paper looked at Tat'ewac'i as the teacher of the divine and human virtues and how they were exemplified in the stories of the saints and martyrs, particularly in the life and death of Grigor Xlat'ec'i. Thus, by gathering together the lives of virtuous people for the benefit of a wide audience, and even more by living a life characterized by the virtues of meekness, humility, love, and righteousness, Xlat'ec'i like his fellow-student Tat'ewac'i proved himself to be both a worthy student of Orotnec'i and a worthy teacher in his own right. May there be many more

---

39. «զիրէ իւնցանէւ մեռանիցիմ, հաւատամ ի Տէր իմ Յիսուս Քրիստոս. Զի րնդ վկայիցն Աստուծոյ անապական և անթառամ ժառանգութեանն արժանաւոր գտայց:»

40. The Mashtots Matenadaran holds over fifty manuscripts of these works. Marabyan enumerates some of these in her work, Mat'evosyan and Marabyan, *Grigor Cerenc Xlateci*, 80–85.

41. There are over two hundred *Yaysmawurk'*s at the Maštoc' Matenadaran Institute of Manuscripts, Yerevan, Armenia, attributed Xlat'ec'i's edition from 1401. Also at the Bodleian, OXL, Marsh 438/I. M8775, Mat'evosyan and Marabyan, *Grigor Cerenc Xlateci*, 26–29.

who, by rallying the virtues in service to others in their own contexts, teach and write diligently to raise up new *theonomous* generations.

Figure 12.3: Photo at Oriel College Chapel, University of Oxford, May 2018 (from left to right: Brian Lapsa, Vigen Guroian, Ani Shahinian, and Rick Yoder; photo credit: Ani Shahinian).

BIBLIOGRAPHY

Abrahamian, A. G. "Glajori Hamalsaran." *Patma-Banasirakan Handes* 1 (1982) 160–76.
Beglarian, Grigor. *Wonders of Armenia*. Erevan: Areg, 2015.
Brown, Peter. "The Rise and Function of the Holy Man in Late Antiquity." *Journal of Roman Studies* 61 (1971) 80–101.
Guorian, Vigen. "Armenian Genocide and Christian Existence." *CrossCurrents* 41.3 (1991) 322–42. http://www.jstor.org/stable/24459946.
———. *Ethics After Christendom: Toward an Ecclesial Christian Ethic*. 1994. Reprint, Eugene, OR: Wipf & Stock, 2004.
———. *Faith, Church, Mission: Essays for Renewal in the Armenian Church*. New York: Armenian Prelacy, 1995.
———. *Incarnate Love: Essays in Orthodox Ethics*. 2nd ed. Notre Dame: University of Notre Dame Press, 2020.

———. *Inheriting Paradise: Meditations on Gardening*. Grand Rapids: Eerdmans, 1999.

———. *Life's Living Toward Dying: A Theological and Medical-Ethical Study*. Grand Rapids: Eerdmans, 1996.

———. "Love in Orthodox Ethics: Trinitarian and Christological Reflections." *Cross-Currents* 33.2 (1983) 181–97. http://www.jstor.org/stable/24458619.

———. *The Melody of Faith: Theology in an Orthodox Key*. Grand Rapids: Eerdmans, 2010.

———. *The Orthodox Reality: Culture, Theology, and Ethics in the Modern World*. Grand Rapids: Baker Academic, 2018.

———. *Rallying the Really Human Things: The Moral Imagination in Politics, Literature, and Everyday Life*. Wilmington, DE: ISI, 2005.

———. *Tending the Heart of Virtue: How Classic Stories Awaken a Child's Moral Imagination*. New York: Oxford University Press, 2023.

Kouymjian, Dickran, 1997. "Armenia from the Fall of the Cilician Kingdom (1375) to the Forced Emigration Under Shah Abbas (1604)." In *The Armenian People from Ancient to Modern Times*, edited by Richard Hovannisian, 2:1–50. New York: St. Martin, 1997.

———. "A Critical Bibliography for the History of Armenia From 1375 to 1605 (1604)." *Armenian Review* 41.1-161 (1988) 39–45.

La Porta, Sergio. "'The Theology of the Holy Dionysius,' Volume III of Grigor Tatʿewacʿi's Book of Questions: Introduction, Translation, and Commentary." PhD diss., Harvard University, 2001.

Manandean, Yakob, and Hračʿeay Ačaṙean. *Hayocʿ nor Vkanerə*. Vagharshapat: Tparan Mayr Atʿoroy S. Ējmiacni, 1903.

Marabyan, Seda, and Artašes Matʿevosyan. *Grigor Cerenc Xlateci*. Erevan: Sargis Xačʿencʿ, 2000.

Marabyan, Seda. "Grigor Xlatecʿow Jeṙagrakan Žšangowtʿ Yownə." *Banber Matenadaran* 15 (1986) 173–90.

———. "Grigor Xlatecʿu Tonakannerə." *Paštōnakan Amsagir Hayrapetakan Atʿoʿṙoy S. Ējmiacni, XB (Ē)* 7 (1985) 43–46.

Minasyan, Anush. *Yovhan Orotnecʿwy kyankʿn ew gortsuneyutʿiwnē*. Yovhan Orotnecʿwy tsnndyan 700-amyakin. Erevan: Yerevan State University Press, 2018.

Shahinian, Ani. "Philosophy and Martyrdom: Contextualizing «Աստմնիշխանութիւն» in the Martyrology of Tʿamar Mokacʿi (1398)." In *Sen Arevshatian 90: Proceedings of the International Armenological Conference, Dedicated to the 90th Anniversary of Academician Sen Arevshatian's Birth, May 22–23, 2019*, edited by the Mesrop Mashtots Institute of Ancient Manuscripts, 106–17. Yerevan: Matenadaran, 2020.

Tatʿewacʿi, Grigor. *Girkʿ harcʿmancʿ [Book of Questions]*. Constantinople: N.p., 1729.

Terian, Abraham. *The Festal Works of St. Gregory of Narek: Annotated Translation of the Odes, Litanies, and Encomia*. Collegeville, MN: Liturgical, 2016.

———. *Moralia et Ascetica Armeniaca: The Oft-Repeated Discourses*. Washington, DC: Catholic University of America Press, 2021.

———. *Philonis Alexandrini de animalibus: The Armenian Text with an Introduction, Translation, and Commentary*. Chico, CA: Scholars, 1981.

Tʿovma Mecopʿecʿi. *Patmagrutʿyun*. Edited and translated by L. S Xačʿikyan. Erevan: Magaghatʿ, 1999.

———. "History of Tamerlane and His Successors." Translated by Robert Bedrosian. https://www.attalus.org/armenian/tm2.htm.

———. *Quelques épisodes de la persécution du Christianisme en Arménie au XVe siècle*. Translated by Félix Nève. Louvain: Fonteyn, 1861.

Thomson, R. W. *The Armenian Version of the Works Attributed to Dionysus the Areopagite*. Corpus Scriptorum Christianorum Orientalium 488–89. Leuven: Peeters, 1987.

———. "The Armenian Version of Ps. Dionysius Aeropagita." *Acta Jutlandica* 57 (1982) 115–23.

———. *A Bibliography of Classical Armenian Literature to 1500 AD*. Turnhout: Corpus, 1995.

———. "The Maccabees in Early Armenian Historiography." *Journal of Theological Studies* NS 26 (1975) 329–41.

———. "Vardapet in the Early Armenian Church." *Le Muséon* 75 (1962) 367–84.

Wilson, Walter. *Philo of Alexandria: On Virtues. Introduction, Translation, and Commentary*. Philo of Alexandria Commentary Series 3. Leiden: Brill, 2011.

Xač'ikyan, Levon. *14. Dari Hayeren Dzeṙagreri Hishatakaranner*. Erevan: Haykakan, 1950.

———. *15. Dari Hayeren Dzeṙagreri Hishatakaranner (1401–1450)*. Erevan: Haykakan, 1955.

Xalatʻeancʻ, Gr. "Grigor Xlatʻecʻi: Kensagrakan Aknark." *Paštōnakan Amsagir Hayrapetakan Atʻoṙoy S. Ējmiacni* KE no (B) (2009) 65–72.

Xorenacʻi, Moses, and Robert Thomson, eds. *History of the Armenians*. Rev. ed. Ann Arbor: Caravan, 2006.

13

The Right Time and the Fullness of Time
"Timefulness" in Orthodox Interpretations of Scripture

EDITH MARY HUMPHREY

ONE OF THE MIXED blessings of teaching in a mainline Protestant seminary is frequent exposure to trends in contemporary Western hymnody, including the compositions and lyrics of Brian Wren. A Reformed composer who retired from Columbia Seminary in 2007, Wren's work has become so popular in some circles that someone has remarked, he is "the most frequently sung hymn writer since Charles Wesley!" One of his better-known hymns begins with a pointed advocacy for the bare Protestant cross, over against the Roman Catholic crucifix, or the cross adorned by the body of Christ in Orthodox worship, especially during Holy Week:

> Christ is alive! Let Christians sing.
> His cross stands empty to the sky.
> Let streets and homes with praises ring.
> His love in death shall never die.[1]

---

1. Wren, "Christ is Alive."

The song then goes on to amplify what the empty cross and the "alive" Christ means in the theology of this poet. Throughout the poem, and not simply in the first verse, the historical moment of the crucifixion, and even Pascha morning, recede to the distant past. Instead, Jesus is now found "daily, in the midst of life," and close at hand. As Christ reigns in this immanent manner, he indeed "suffers still" because of ongoing human "insult" and "war," until that time when "all creation" will learn the ways of justice and peace.

This hymn, then, celebrates the risen Jesus, His ubiquitous presence through the Holy Spirit, and His concern for our ongoing daily life.[2] Anyone singing (or reading) it from beginning to end, however, will also see that it mutes the particularity of Jesus' atoning death, downplays the importance of the Trinity's transcendence, stresses the so-called "social-gospel" over God's call to holiness of life, and suggests that the historical action of God in the Incarnate One was a limitation rather than the focal point where God acted in our world. We can detail these moves as we travel through the hymn: "Jesus suffers still" over our political and social divisions; He rules among us and *not* in the holy place; He was "bound" to Palestine (not, let the reader understand, Israel!) in His human life, but *now* can be alive everywhere by His Spirit. The hymnodist is mostly right in what he affirms but wrong in what he denies. Certainly our LORD is risen—but He has also ascended.[3] Certainly the Spirit has come—but to complete, not undo, the particularity of the Incarnate One. Certainly our LORD continues to be touched by our infirmities and divisions—but His divinity remains unchanged, and His suffering is complete, it is finished. Certainly Christ is among us; yet He is also the only holy One, before whom all creation bows.[4]

---

2. Throughout this essay, I maintain the longstanding tradition of using masculine pronouns for all three Persons of the Trinity and the Godhead, capitalizing "He, Him, His." This is to signal that masculine language for the deity is both normative *and* mysterious—God is not male, but He has revealed Himself in Scriptures and Tradition primarily in masculine terms. For an argument concerning how this is a foundational matter for the Christian faith, see the final chapter in Humphrey, *Further Up and Further In*, and section IIC of Humphrey, *Ecstasy and Intimacy*.

3. I use majuscules for LORD as a reminder that from the earliest New Testament writings, Jesus, soon to be called the God-Man in Christian tradition, was identified with the tetragrammaton YHWH, that sacred name which may be translated "I am," "I will be," or "I cause to be." See St. Paul's reformulation of the Shema (Deut 6:4) in 1 Cor 8:4–6.

4. One of the deepest delights in my career was when I first met Vigen in person and spent an absorbing mealtime with him during a rare quiet moment at a conference in New York. We discovered mutual interests, mutual concerns, and a mutual faith in the Triune God. Though this paper is intended to engage readers from different backgrounds, it is framed as a kind of "in-house" conversation of the sort that Vigen and I

Orthodox Christians may be tempted to fix upon the garden-variety Protestant tendencies apparent in this hymn, such as its over-familiarity with the Lord. However, one critical misperception of the faith that we glimpse in this song is found even in the Christian Orthodox community, which also grapples with the relationship of time and eternity. It would seem that some Orthodox thinkers are, like Wren, too quick to dismiss the importance of time in favor of the eternal, which they assume to be "timeless." A notable contemporary exception to this is seen in the work of our beloved Vigen Guroian who, while delighting in the world of the imagination, and showing deep concern for spiritual formation, also stresses the importance of time and historical memory, both for the faith and for society as a whole. Alongside his plea that children be inducted into the long cultural tradition of fairy-tales and imaginative play,[5] he also has sober words concerning the "keeping alive a nation's collective memory," reminding us that the narrative of political freedom "belongs to a history that needs to be told in order to inspire and ennoble those who possess it and are called to protect it."[6] It is this ability to sing both in the register of mystery *and* of history that marks Vigen's work, and that will be commended in this paper as we explore the concept of "timefulness."

Close attention to the diaconal prayer in the Proskomedia (the solemn preparation for the Orthodox Eucharist) redirects the attentive hearer from an espousal of time*less*ness to the embrace of significant concrete (if mysterious) moments and places: "In the tomb with the body and in Hades with the soul, in Paradise with the thief and on the throne with the Father and the Spirit, wast Thou, O boundless Christ filling all things." Here is the LORD who fills up time rather than obliterating it. This prayer commends the approach to this world that we find throughout the Gospels and letters. Just as our LORD plunged into the spatial elements of this world in His Baptism and Incarnation, so too has He redeemed time, coming at just the right moment (*kairos*, Rom 5:6) and in the fullness of time (*chronos*, Gal 4:4; Eph 1:10). Even despite this consistent perspective that is present

---

shared that evening. I have attempted to avoid too many references to "we" and "us" so as not to alienate those who do not share our presuppositions of the faith, but am well aware that this paper offers mainly a glimpse into a particular Orthodox hermeneutical concern. My hope is that it will nonetheless be intriguing for those outside of Orthodox circles, who also struggle with the relationship between time and eternity.

5. See numerous trenchant presentations concerning the formation of children on YouTube and Ancient Faith, esp. "Tending the Heart of Virtue."

6. Guroian, "America's Freedom Image Problem."

in both Scripture and the ancient liturgies, it is easy for the pious to fall prey to what we might call a *temporal docetism* when they read and interpret the Scriptures. Such over-reactions occur in ethical, theological and liturgical contexts, but more frequently in the way that some theologians have presented the very character of Scripture. For example, it has become commonplace to assert, as a challenge to fundamentalist Christians, that the Scriptures are *only* a signpost to the One who is the Word of God, but that the sacred books are not themselves God's word. Similarly, the claim is frequently made that Orthodox need not enter into Western "Biblicist" and rationalist debates, for they have avoided the infamous Western decline that began in the rationalist Enlightenment, and anyway, the Bible, as a *timeless* document, evading the difficulties of historical demonstration. In this approach, the question of "what really happened" is considered foreign to the intent of the Biblical writers—an assumption that would have astounded, for example, St. Luke, who makes public his intent to "put in order a narrative of the things that have been accomplished among us" (Luke 1:1).[7]

Scripture and ongoing Tradition disclose that such statements about the ahistorical Scriptures are at best exaggerations, and may in fact lead to serious hermeneutical mis-steps. Indeed, Holy Tradition does not uniformly promote a reading of Scripture that neglects the diachronic, that is, the flow of history as revealed to God's people. The aim of this paper is to eschew the polarities of two approaches (viewing Scriptures through either historic*ist* or timeless spectacles) but to sketch instead an appreciation of its time*ful*ness. Though a neologism, "timefulness" provides us with a *tertium quid* that capitulates neither to modernism nor fundamentalism, and that, we shall discover, aptly re-presents how a significant number of key fathers approached their reading and interpretation of the Bible without dismissing time and space.

Of course, many ancient theologians read the Scriptures fruitfully by means of allegory, a method that is not dependent upon historical questions. However, in applying the four-fold method (literal, allegorical, moral, anagogical), the best among them did not destroy the natural meaning of the text when, for example, that meaning had an historical aspect. This principle remains true even of many bits of exegesis performed by what may be called "remedial allegorists," who avoided theological problems in the reading of some Old Testament passages by a turn to allegory. Here, however, we will not probe the exegetical moves of a Clement, a Barnabas

---

7. All Scriptural passages will be rendered by my own translation.

or even the great Origen. Rather, we will consider one of the earliest Christian sermons by the deacon Stephen, then look to Irenaeus's characterization of the *kanōn tēs alētheias*, and finally take our cue from Chrysostom and Athanasius, who fastened upon God's actions in history as an integral part of the Orthodox "hypothesis of Scripture." In all these ancient texts we will note three interconnected features: an awareness of the importance of sequence, a belief that God enters time to bring His plan and our lives to fulfillment, and a declaration that all events find their meaning and *telos* in the God-Man, Jesus, who fully entered human time and space.

We begin with the Protomartyr Stephen and Scripture itself. Though Acts 7:2–53 comes to us in a narrative, we also find ourselves immediately in the realm of interpretation. Stephen's sermon, itself a reading of the Hebrew Scriptures, is refracted to us through the lens of the evangelist Luke, who places before our eyes and ears the apostolic approach to Scripture, modeled by the LORD (or so Luke has told us!), during the 40-day period following the resurrection, when He instructed the two on the road to Emmaus, and the disciples in the upper room. We may be tempted to think that the Hellenist deacon is simply following a rhetorical strategy when he appeals to his Hebraist detractors by fastening upon the hypothesis of the Old Testament meta-narrative: closer attention shows that the medium is the message. Indeed, he follows in a long line of Biblical credos that rehearse salvation history according to a particular shape and for a particular purpose (Deut 6:20–25; 26:5–9; Josh 24:2–13; 1 Sam 12:6–15; Neh 9; Psalms 77/8, 104/5, 105/6, 134/5 and 135/6; Jer 32:16–25; Ezek 20:5–26).[8]

One of the major features of Stephen's history lesson is its explicit concern for the passing of time, marked in various ways—by the adverbs *tote* (7:4), *meta* (7:4b; 7) and *achri* (7:18); by the addition of historical details not necessarily germane to the matter at hand, such as the succession of patriarchs (7:8b), or the reference to a "second" visit (7:13); and by other time markers such as "day" or "days" (7:8; 26; 41; 45) "now" (7:4; 34; 52), or (thrice!) "40 years" (7:23; 30; 36). Especially pointed are the Greek phrases that accentuate time and its fulfillment: "But just as the time (*chronos*) of the fulfilled promise drew near" (7:17); "At which time (*kairos*) Moses was born" (7:20); "When, for Moses, the time *(chronos)* of forty years had been fulfilled" (7:23); "Now when forty years had been fulfilled" (7:30). One

---

8. Olbricht, "Structure and Content," 455–70. Olbright fastens particularly upon Ps 105 (MT), Ps 106 (MT), and Neh 9:6–37 for light on Stephen's speech. (In the text above, where two enumerations are given for Pss, the first is LXX and the second is MT.)

might have thought that in a discourse calling attention to the heavenly *type* of the tabernacle (7:44) and to the sovereign God who does not dwell in houses made by human hands (7:48), that the vertical dimension of revelation would utterly dominate over the horizontal, the timeline. But this is not the case in Stephen's address—nor is it true of the letter to the Hebrews, though some have mischaracterized the book as "Platonic" in that way.

No, the vertical dimension of divine revelation does not eradicate the horizontal dimension of time, nor does the heavenly world erase the importance of the earthly. Instead, space and time are filled up, redeemed, given significance, and put to God's service—as is emphasized in the deacon's sermon. For this is the LORD of heaven and earth, who makes the Sinai rocks holy, and who identifies Himself as the God of the fathers, of Abraham, Isaac and Jacob. He does not dwell in houses made with human hands, but He does dwell with humankind whom His divine hands have created, and He meets with them, appearing in glory in Mesopotamia, in Egypt, in the wilderness. The patriarch Moses, to whom Stephen's detractors appealed, is identified as one raised up by God, "who was in the congregation in the wilderness with the angel who spoke to him at Mount Sinai, and with the fathers, [and who] . . . received living oracles to give" (7:37). In the Torah, God's presence with Moses is palpable in the glory on the lawgiver's face, in signs and wonders, and throughout the wilderness wandering; that same presence finds its focal point in Luke's Stephen, who does great signs and wonders, who pronounces this pointed history lesson, whose face shines, and who will recapitulate the death of the Righteous One, to whom all the prophets pointed. At just the right time, when he is about to meet his death, the Protomartyr sees the Son of Man, the great Glory, and bears witness to those who do not want to hear. Ears, eyes, and time are filled up with the revelation of God.

Luke's point, and Stephen's too, is that the story of Israel and of the world is *God's* story. Yet this can only be seen from the perspective of the One who has finally come, the One who is the true Temple of God, and by Whom God's people have been deeply visited. The Torah was indeed ordained by angels and was received by the first community, says the martyr, but the oracles of God are living, and the divine life moves beyond that time to the "now"—in continuity with the past, even while it brings surprises. The God who in the Hebrew Bible could not be seen by humans without incurring death, now by His death has forged a way by which He can be seen—and adored—by human eyes, in time and in space (cf. Exod 33:20,

John 1:18) The wilderness, the imperfect, the impermanent, says Stephen, gives way to the permanent; if God will dwell not in our houses, we may dwell in His!

Of course, the protomartyr is interrupted, but the tendencies in his homily are clear, directing the hearers to fill in the blanks, and to trace the trajectory, as we see in Stephen's martyrdom the glory of God fully alive in His human vessel, who has the face of an angel, and the mouth and eyes of one, as well! As the Israelites received Torah through angels, now those hearing and reading the words of Luke and the inspired preacher in Acts 7:55–56 receive something far more precious—the identification of the Son of Man as Jesus, present in great glory, pleading for His own, and worthy of worship. The Martyr Stephen's chronicle, though interrupted, continues doing its work, as he prays for God's welcome, and the forgiveness of those who will not (yet) receive: who would have thought that it would eventually make its future mark upon Saul, so-called "least" of the apostles (1 Cor 15:9)? But this is a living oracle, now dwelling in human time and space, and its potency is not exhausted. The historical narrative's respect for sequence (even interrupted) is evident, its timefulness is potent, and its meaning centers firmly upon the One who made our temporal world, who entered it, and who promises to return.

As we move from the first to the second century, much profit is to be found in the work of Justin Martyr, with regards to timefulness. He is well-known for tracing typology in the OT, yet does not spiritualize the Law. Rather, in *Dialogue with Trypho* 40, he but speaks about God's foreknowledge of the future, directs Trypho away from abstract philosophy towards prophets who concentrated upon the events of salvation history (*Dialogue* 7), details the flow of history in chapters 11 and 12 of his *Dialogue*, and in harmony with the creed, emphasizes Jesus' life and death "under Pontius Pilate" (*First Apology* 31). His approach stands in marked contrast to, for example, the *Epistle of Barnabas*, a work that wholly spiritualizes the Old Testament Torah, and that, despite its early popularity, the Church saw good reason not to number with books conforming to the *kanōn alētheias* ("the rule of truth"), comprising the New Testament.

Even more pertinent to our theme is the teaching of St. Irenaeus concerning that *kanōn alētheias*, which we must understand in the light of his critique of the Gnostics, who rearranged the hypothesis of Scripture. This they did, he says, by wrenching details out of their initial position (*Against Heresies* 1.9.4), by having no regard for authorial intent—in this case, that of the evangelist John (1.9.1), and by moving "from a natural to a sense that is against nature" (*ek tou kata phusin eis to para phusin // ex eō quod est secundum naturam, in id quod est contra naturam*) in their rearrangement of the expressions and names in Scripture.[9] Indeed, it is important, Irenaeus tells us, in correcting such heretical eisegesis, to restore to their proper position in the narrative those things that heretics wrench away from the original fabric for their own purposes (1.9.4). John Behr is helpful when he insists that we understand canonicity as not merely a list of approved books, but as also including a way of reading and interpreting Scripture.[10] It is this apostolic approach to reading that most concerns St. Irenaeus. In *Against Heresies*, the author not only points out that the Valentinians had strange and esoteric doctrines, but explains that the reason for this is that they have dismissed the *kanōn alētheias*—the apostolic rule, including an apostolic approach to interpreting Scripture, by which truth can be known. Thus, demonstrates the saint, they do not read the Scriptures with the apostolic eye, a perspective that inevitably includes their natural arrangement and their presentation of history and dispensations. Rather they read it with a light to esoteric mysteries and their own fancies.

In moving on from his critique of Valentinian eisegesis, St. Irenaeus also outlines the faith of the Church in terms of salvation history, filling out the Church's teaching on the Holy Spirit by reference to the dispensations of God (*oikonomiai//dispensationes Dei* 1.10.1), and by tracing the historical flow of the apostolic hypothesis, from creation to the new creation (1.10.1). He speaks of the time-frame of the story, of the different covenants, each with its special character (1.10.3), and of the astonishing grace of God that the Gentiles, "whose salvation was not anticipated," have at last come into the household (1.10.3). In 2:25, he goes on to ask about God's hand in the composition of all things, both in the details as well as in the ordering of names. He entertains the question that someone might ask concerning whether such details really not very important, or "empty" (*in vanum*). His answer is *Non quidum (No, indeed!* Perhaps in the Greek, which is lost, his phrase was the Pauline *Mē genoito!*, cf. Rom 3:4, 6, 31*)*. He then goes

---

9. Irenaeus's work *Adversus Haereses* [*Against Heresies*] may be found in the full Latin version, with the Greek portions that are available to us (from Migne's *Patrologia Graece* 7A), and the traditional English translation, originally published in the *Ante-Nicene Fathers* series, at earlychurchtexts.com. I work here from the Latin and Greek and transliterate the latter.

10. This helpful insight is to be found in the transcript of Behr, "Scripture and Tradition." See also Behr, *Way to Nicaea*.

on to speak about eras, both ancient and current, and the importance of approaching the biblical story with rational thought. By way of illustration, St. Irenaeus explains that created things, in terms of space and time, may be viewed as a musical piece, with various points that may appear inharmonious (*contraria et non convenientia*), but which, when "heard" in terms of the whole, are revealed to be intriguing intervals and suspensions that fit into an integrated whole (2.25.2): there are various notes in God's complex "melody," each of which has its own special character.

For all his keenness to stress the *spiritual* sacrifice that God demands of his people in the vicissitudes of time (4.17.1–6), St. Irenaeus prefaces this theological discussion by admitting that the Law had a proper place in its own time (4.15.1). It was not God's highest will, nor His first choice, but was added for the sake of God's people, rather than because God Himself needed animal sacrifice (4.17.1). Again, this is a far cry from the kind of rhetoric that we encounter, say, in the *Epistle of Barnabas*, which denies that the Torah ever intended to actually demand animal sacrifice or kosher eating.[11] In contrast, St. Irenaeus does not flatten out the words of God by denying their dynamism, and so avoids the temporal equivalent to Tatian's *Diatessaron*. That is, just as Tatian's harmony of the gospels removed all the peculiarities and differences among them, so we can treat time this way, refusing to see the different ways in which God has dealt with humankind, beginning with Noah, then Israel, then the Church. Indeed, despite his era's strong need to differentiate Christianity from rabbinic Judaism, St. Irenaeus does not deny, but acknowledges the propaedeutic place of the Torah, showing that it pointed to Christ, who is its *telos*—both its end and its fulfillment.

We go on to St. John Chrysostom, who is noted for a natural, rather than spiritualized reading of Scripture, since he is frequently cited as the chief exemplar of the Antiochian school, over against the Alexandrian penchant for allegorical reading. His sermons and writings are replete with commonsense interpretations of the Scripture that do not ignore their historical context. We must, however, note the fairly recent challenge regarding the customary scholarly divide proposed between Antioch and Alexandria: this dissent from past scholarship involves (in the words of Margaret Mitchell) a "dismantling of the older dichotomy between allegorical and literal

---

11. See esp. *Barnabas* 10, where the prohibition against eating rabbit is allegorized to refer merely to abstaining from lustful thoughts and actions (*Epistle of Barnabas* 370–441).

exegesis."[12] Frances Young and Christoph Schäubin, explains Mitchell, have suggested that the difference between the two is not a literal interpretation over against an allegorical, but rather a rhetorical approach (Antioch) in contrast to a philosophical approach (Alexandria). As a result, some are now speaking of "the anhistorical character of Chrysostom's [rhetorically framed] exegesis," and explaining his detailed description of Scriptures as a rhetorical move, rather than as a sensitivity to context and history.[13]

In this proposed new schema, any purported historical content is to be dismissed as "exemplary" for the sake of preaching virtue, rather than seen as truly indicative of the saint's concern for time and context. In my view, the question mark that Young and Schäubin put besides the previous scholarly strong dichotomy between Alexandrian and Antiochene methods is worth considering; after all, one finds allegorization in Antioch, and plain-speaking in Alexandria. However, close attention to the manner in which St. John Chrysostom depicts the saints may give us pause before we jump entirely on board—the Golden-mouthed is concerned for what they ate, how they slept, and other historical minutiae by which he displays the biblical characters before the eyes of his hearers as examples of godliness.[14] In reading Scriptures, notably the letters of St. Paul, the Golden-mouthed displays the same devotion to every detail. Indeed, Margaret Mitchell convincingly shows that St. John Chrysostom's rhetorical power and argument depends wholly upon the way that he shows "St. Paul's historical rootedness in real human existence";[15] consequently, we cannot make a dichotomy, as Young has done, between the "historical" and the merely "exemplary."

Of course, it is important not to impose upon St. John's time our own standards of historical discourse! As Raymond Brown has insisted, in commenting upon the nativity narratives of the canonical gospels, these demonstrate a genre between historical reportage and theological invention.[16] Similarly, as Hippolyte Delehaye comments, the ancient Eastern theologians evince "un genre bien tranché, intermediarie entre l'historie et l'invention pure."[17] This idea of something that mediates between history

---

12. Mitchell, *Heavenly Trumpet*, 389.
13. Mitchell, *Heavenly Trumpet*, 390.
14. Mitchell, *Heavenly Trumpet*, 44.
15. Mitchell, *Heavenly Trumpet*, 390.
16. See Brown, *Birth of the Messiah*, esp. the introduction, where he explains why "midrash" does not properly characterize the infancy narratives.
17. Delahaye, *Passions des Martyrs*, 135, cited in Mitchell, *Heavenly Trumpet*, 389.

and invention may lead us to characterize Chrysostom as one who constructs a prose interpretation of Scripture that is akin to the icon. The icon does not capture a historical moment in the detached sense, nor does it *abstract* from the Scriptural text; rather, it shows its deep significance, and how the passage fills up human time and space to overflowing. Similarly, when we read the bishop, we see how the apostle Paul reached out, so to speak, to meet him, and now reaches out to us. History matters, but so does immediate connection with our own time. We may be reminded of the Golden-Mouthed's description of Scripture as containing both tiny nuggets of particular treasure and also flowing with never-ending waters that refreshed our ancestors and still overflow for us, without any risk of our exhausting them (*Homily on Genesis* 3) Scripture both "spoke" and "speaks"—he uses both tenses.[18] The saints in Scripture both lived in their own time, but live and influence us today, for God is the God of the living, not the dead. In the words of Mitchell, "John wished to stress the very earth and time-boundedness of his flesh and blood human example, even as he depicted Paul as a citizen of heaven," since he was concerned with everything from "the historically particular moment . . . to its perduring words for universal readership."[19] Thus, concludes Mitchell, in his writings and sermons, St. John "does not 'merely collapse the time-gap,' (as some have charged) but fully recognizes and *explicitly* bridges it."[20] In St. John Chrysostom, as with the Protomartyr, Justin Martyr, and St. Irenaeus, there remains deep engagement with sequence, a focus upon the God who enters time, and the conviction that all events and persons find their meaning and *telos* in the God-Man, Jesus.

We complete our tour by glancing beyond Antioch, even to Alexandria, for a (perhaps) unexpected example of our "timeful" approach. St. John's younger contemporary, St. Athanasius (c. 296–373), is more frequently noted for his allegorizing techniques. There are, to the ears of a contemporary scholar, bizarre allegorical readings offered by this father, in both his *Discourses Against the Arians* and in his more well-known *On the Incarnation*. On the other hand, one of *his* major criticisms of the Arian exegetes was the way in which they paid no attention to context, topic, authorial attention, or even who was being addressed in the Scriptural text (e.g., *Discourses Against the Arians* 1.12.52). Moreover, his writings demonstrate

---

18. John Chrysostom, *Homilies on Genesis* 3:1 (39).
19. Mitchell, *Heavenly Trumpet*, 391.
20. Mitchell, *Heavenly Trumpet*, 392.

a true concern for history, in the sense of what really happened, and make a concerted effort to struggle with the dispensations of God, rather than to homogenize them or gloss over the differences. A case in point is his *Letter XIX*, in which he speaks about the feast of Passover and Christian Pascha in these terms: "Henceforth the feast of the Passover is ours, not that of a stranger, nor is it any longer of the Jews. For the time of shadows is abolished, and those former things have ceased, and now the month of new things is at hand."[21]

Here we see our principle of historical events and persons being fulfilled in Christ. But how does St. Athanasius fill this out? Not by suggesting that the feast of Passover, or the sacrifices of the Law, were not commanded by the Lord to the Jewish people; rather, these things were both types and the condescension of God to meet the human condition. In this way he explains how it is that Jeremiah (and Amos) can depict God as NOT commanding burnt-offerings to the ancestors, when indeed the Torah says that God required these things. Here is his discussion:

> And what does this mean my brethren? For it is right for us to investigate the saying of the prophet, and especially on account of heretics who have turned their mind against the law. By Moses then, God gave commandment respecting sacrifices, and all the book called Leviticus is entirely taken up with the arrangement of these matters, *so that He might accept the offerer* . . . Now it is the opinion of some, that the Scriptures do not agree together, or that God, Who gave the commandment, is false. But there is no disagreement whatever, far from it, neither can the Father, Who is truth, lie; for "it is impossible that God should lie," as Paul affirms. But all these things are plain to those who rightly consider them, and to those who receive with faith the writings of the law.

St. Athanasius's concern here is for the discrepancy between the prophets and the Law, and indeed, the disdain of some in his own day for the Torah! And, in offering his solution to this problem, please note his humility, as he asks for prayers and *hopes* that his interpretation is correct: "Now it appears to me—may God grant, by your prayers, that the remarks I presume to make may not be far from the truth—that *not at first* were the commandment and the law concerning sacrifices."[22] His solution, then, is to say that the Torah's explicit commands of ritual and sacrifice were not

---

21. Athanasius, *Festal Letter XIX* 2.4.1 (545–56).
22. Athanasius, *Letter XIX* 2.4.3 (456, emphasis added).

God's *first* will. He turns to the flow of time, and the sequence of the story in the Torah, to demonstrate this:

> Therefore, the whole law did not treat of sacrifices, though there was in the law a commandment concerning sacrifices, *that by means of them it might begin to instruct men* and might withdraw them from idols, and bring them near to God, *teaching them for that present time*.... Therefore neither at the beginning, when God brought the people out of Egypt, did He command them concerning sacrifices or whole burnt-offerings, nor even when they came to mount Sinai.... But when they chose to serve Baal ... and forgot the miracles which were wrought in their behalf in Egypt ... *then indeed, after* the law [i.e., the law against idolatry], *that commandment concerning sacrifices was ordained as law*; so that with their mind, which at one time had meditated on those which are not, they might turn to Him Who is truly God, and learn not, in the first place, to sacrifice, but to turn away their faces from idols, and conform to what God commanded. *Thus then, being before instructed and taught,* they learned not to do service to any one but the Lord. *They attained to know what time the shadow should last, and not to forget the time that was at hand.*[23]

St. Athanasius's approach to these matters is sane: first, he recognizes a problem in Scriptures, a problem that is felt because he refuses to allegorize the Old Testament legal requirements. Secondly, he speaks in full humility, offering his words as a theologoumenon, and knowing that he is working through a complex matter: "it is right for us to investigate," "Now it is the opinion of some"; "Now it appears to me—may God grant, by your prayers, that the remarks I presume to make may not be far from the truth."[24] Thirdly, he intends in his discussion to give glory to the God of truth. Fourthly, he makes a suggestion that is not clearly demonstrable in the Torah, but that at least pays full attention to the details and the historical flow of the story. Fifthly, he demonstrates that, in any event, the Old Testament legal requirements were given until "the time of refreshment," until the time that was at hand, when Christ would come.

This approach, along with that of the Protomartyr Stephen, Justin Martyr, St. Irenaeus and St. John Chrysostom, bears out the wisdom of John Behr that there is "no such thing as uninterpreted history."[25] As those

---

23. Athanasius, *Letter XIX* 2.4.3–4 (545–46, emphasis added).
24. Athanasius, *Letter XIX* 2.4.3 (545–46).
25. Behr, *Mystery of Christ*, 16.

of the household of faith, Christians were bequeathed not only Scriptures, but an approach to reading these holy books that comes from the apostles, and, according to Luke 24, ultimately from Jesus. However, to say that history comes to the reader with interpretation is not necessarily to imply that what happened in time is irrelevant. Some may seek to correct modernity's unbalanced fascination with the past; yet we must remember that at least since the time of David Hume, much of modernity (and especially postmodernity) has acquired an *allergy* to the past, coupled with a deep suspicion of the historical enterprise, so that historical writing is described as *all* interpretation, with no verifiable events, personages, or substance. Glib talk concerning "eternal and timeless" truths plays directly into the hands of those who have such allergies and such suspicions. To such antipathies, the passages we have considered offer this correction: history may be only part of God's mystery, but it matters.

The Incarnation itself shows why time is not irrelevant. In accordance the God-Man's assumption of humanity, God knits ordinary events into the fabric of human life, and in them he graces humanity with His very own presence. It is by means of time and space and matter, and on the daily walk with Him to Emmaus (or elsewhere), that worshippers come to be engaged by the Word of the LORD so that hearts burn; it is by means of grapes and wheat, touched by human hands and sacramentally used by the Lord, that believers come to see who He is. But these things happen in dependence upon those earlier moments: we *need* the actual two on the road to Emmaus, *need* the very twelve who saw him on the holy mountain and at table, and *need* the carefully arranged words of the evangelist, who researched, listened and put everything in order. Otherwise, the faith being celebrated is not the Christian faith that touches down in human lives, in time and space. All this is consonant with the central mystery of the Incarnation. The Scriptures and the fathers speak of the true God-Man, who was subject to His parents for a time and learned obedience, who knew when His time had not come, who suffered under Pontius Pilate, and who told His followers to watch the signs of the times. In the fullness of time, and not in timeless abstractions, is He found.

BIBLIOGRAPHY

Athanasius. *Discourses Against the Arians*. In *A Select Library of Nicene and Post-Nicene Fathers of the Christian Church*, Second Series, edited by Philip Schaff and Henry Wace, 4:306–447. 1891. Reprint, Grand Rapids: Eerdmans, 1956.

———. *Festal Letter XIX*. In *A Select Library of Nicene and Post-Nicene Fathers of the Christian Church*, Second Series, edited by Philip Schaff and Henry Wace, 4:544–48. 1891. Reprint, Grand Rapids: Eerdmans, 1956.

Behr, John. "Scripture and Tradition." Lecture given at the University of North Carolina, Chapel Hill, NC, 1998. *Glory to God for All Things* (blog), May 10, 2007. https://glory2godforallthings.com/2007/05/10/scripture-and-tradition-fr-john-behr.

———. *The Mystery of Christ: Life in Death*. Crestwood, NY: St. Vladimir's, 2006.

———. *Way to Nicaea*. Vol. 1. Crestwood, NY: St Vladimir's, 2001.

Brown, Raymond E. *Birth of the Messiah: A Commentary on the Infancy Narratives in the Gospels of Matthew and Luke*. New York: Doubleday and Company, 1977.

Delahaye, Hippolyte. *Passions des Martyrs et les Genres Littéraires*. Studia Hagiographica 13B. 2nd ed. Brussels: Société des Bollandistes, 1966.

Epistle of Barnabas. In *The Apostolic Fathers: Greek Texts and English Translations*, edited by Michael W. Holmes, 370–441. 3rd ed. Grand Rapids: Baker, 2007.

Guroian, Vigen. *Tending the Heart of Virtue: How Classic Stories Awaken a Child's Moral Imagination*. Oxford: Oxford University Press, 1998.

———. "America's Freedom Image Problem." *Imaginative Conservative* (blog), September 25, 2018. https://theimaginativeconservative.org/2018/09/america-freedom-image-problem-vigen-guroian.html.

Humphrey, Edith M. *Further Up and Further In: Orthodox Conversations with C. S. Lewis on Scripture and Tradition*. Crestwood, NY: St. Vladimir's, 2017.

———. *Ecstasy and Intimacy: When the Holy Spirit Meets the Human Spirit*. Grand Rapids: Eerdmans, 2005.

Irenaeus. *Adversus Haereses*. In *Ante-Nicene Fathers*, edited by Alexander Roberts et al., 1:508–953. Translated by Marcus Dods and George Reith. Buffalo, NY: Christian Literature, 1885. https://earlychurchtexts.com/public/irenaeus_on_marcion.htm.

John Chrysostom. *Homily on Genesis 3*. In *Homilies on Genesis 1–17*, edited by Robert C. Hill, 39–50. Fathers of the Church 74. Washington, DC: Catholic University of America Press, 1992.

Justin Martyr. *Dialogue with Trypho*. In *Ante-Nicene Fathers*, edited by Alexander Roberts et al., 1:304–443. Translated by Marcus Dods and George Reith. Buffalo, NY: Christian Literature, 1885.

———. *First Apology*. In *Ante-Nicene Fathers*, edited by Alexander Roberts et al., 1:247–91. Translated by Marcus Dods and George Reith. Buffalo, NY: Christian Literature, 1885.

Mitchell, Margaret M. *Heavenly Trumpet: John Chrysostom and the Art of Pauline Interpretation*. Louisville: Westminster John Knox, 2002.

Olbricht, Thomas H. "The Structure and Content of Stephen's Speech Compared to Old Testament Credos." In *The Language and Literature of the New Testament: Essays in Honour of Stanley E. Porter's 60th Birthday*, edited by Lois Fuller Dow et al., 455–70. Biblical Interpretation 150. Leiden: Brill, 2017.

Wren, Brian. "Christ is Alive." *Hope Publishing*, 1995. https://www.hopepublishing.com/find-hymns-hw/hw1882_52.aspx.

14

Vigen Guroian in the Armenian Church

SHANT KAZANJIAN

IT IS AN HONOR for me to pay tribute to Professor Vigen Guroian, an esteemed American-Armenian Orthodox theologian, teacher, and friend whom I have had the privilege to work with for over thirty years in the vineyard of the Lord, particularly in the context of the Armenian Apostolic Church, under the jurisdiction of the Eastern Prelacy, in my capacity as the Director of Christian Education. But I have another connection with Vigen. For more than three decades, I have been serving as the archdeacon of St. Illuminator's Cathedral in New York City, the church where Vigen was baptized and had his earliest experience of being in an Armenian church. "The sweet scent of the incense, the shimmying of the flabellums, the warm candlelight, the *sharagans* [hymns] sung by the choir, the resonant responses of the priest and the deacon—these are my earliest memories of church," Guroian reminisced during his homily at the Cathedral on Palm Sunday in 1996.[1]

From my earliest days at the Armenian Prelacy, I remember Archbishop Mesrob Ashjian, the then Prelate of the Armenian Apostolic Church, would advise me to invite Guroian to our Christian educational programs as often as possible, and I did. Even a quick review of his writings

1. Guroian, "Palm Sunday Meditation," 6.

and public talks for the Armenian Church community will reveal Guroian's distinctive and significant contribution to the life of the Armenian Church. Given the depth and breadth of his expertise, Guroian has written and lectured extensively on a wide range of topics, including the Armenian Church and nationalism, literature and religious education, marriage and family, sainthood and martyrdom, the Armenian Genocide, diaspora, church unity, ethical issues, creeds, liturgy, prayer, sacraments, and much more. He has addressed and worked with diverse audiences, including the clergy, lay church leaders, church school educators, and the general public, in settings as varied as national conferences and retreats to local church lenten programs.

Whenever I introduced Guroian to our audiences, I often said that Prof. Guroian is more widely known in non-Armenian circles than among Armenians. Already in the late 1980s, Guroian was distinguished in the academic community as a prominent Armenian Orthodox theologian and ethicist. I recall in 1989, a fellow seminarian at St. Vladimir's Orthodox Theological Seminary asked me, "Who is this Armenian theologian?" He had just returned from an interview at a prestigious theological school for a doctoral program where he was asked about Guroian. I told him that I knew of only one Armenian theologian. It had to be Vigen Guroian. After a long and fruitful academic career, Guroian has become far more widely known. But, it is equally true that most non-Armenians know little about Prof. Guroian's prolific engagement over the past four decades in the life of the Armenian Church community.

Guroian's contributions to the Armenian Church are multifaceted and far-reaching. It is beyond our scope to recount all that he has achieved. However, three areas stand out where Guroian has made the most distinctive and noteworthy contributions: (1) nationalism and the Armenian Church, (2) the Armenian Genocide—a religious response, and (3) contemporary ethical issues. I will only reference some of his writings and public engagements here.

NATIONALISM AND THE ARMENIAN CHURCH

In the early 1990s, Archbishop Mesrob Ashjian provided Guroian a platform to speak and write on nationalism and the Armenian Church. Guroian delivered several lectures and published a number of articles in the Prelacy's official publication, *Outreach*. On February 24, 1992, the

Armenian Prelacy sponsored a symposium on "The Armenian Church Facing the Twenty-First Century," a public event held at the Sts. Vartanants Armenian Apostolic Church in Ridgefield, New Jersey, in conjunction with the annual clergy conference. Guroian delivered a thought-provoking lecture on "Church and Armenian Nationhood." At the end of the presentation, as I was making my way through the crowd, I overheard a senior clergyman walking in front of me say, "I guess the Armenian national spirit is much stronger in me than the religious spirit." That may sound strange to most non-Armenians, but that is probably not an uncommon sentiment in the Armenian community.

Here, Guroian lays out his argument to debunk the Armenian religio-national myth and critiques the ideology of a nationalistic church—a considerable feat. He did it cogently and eloquently, standing on the shoulders of an intellectual giant, Archbishop Tiran Nersoyan (1904–1989), who had written an influential essay decades earlier entitled "Nationalism or Gospel." According to Guroian, Nersoyan was the only clergyman who had "exposed this myth."[2] Guroian said:

> Armenians have grown used to describing their church as a national church as if that is always what it was even before modern times and as if that is all it could possibly be in the future. I want to challenge this view . . . The standard apologetic for the church's centrality to Armenian national life has promoted a myth of religious nationalism which replaces the gospel of Jesus Christ. This myth does no real credit to the ancient Orthodox and evangelical faith of our fathers and mothers. The national character of the Armenian church will not disappear. but the Armenian Church must be much more than just a national church.[3]

Guroian traced the development of nationalism in the Armenian Church and highlighted how, in light of the ideological movements that had emerged in nineteenth-century Europe (liberal, romantic, and nationalistic), the Armenian Church leaders had assumed "the role of protector of national identity and exhorter of nationalistic sentiment."[4] And by the beginning of the twentieth century, he asserted, "the Armenian Church generally embraced, often enthusiastically, this role of safeguarding Armenian

---

2. Guroian, *Faith, Church, Mission*, 125.
3. Guroian, *Faith, Church, Mission*, 119–20.
4. Guroian, *Faith, Church, Mission*, 124.

identity prescribed by secular Armenian nationalism."[5] In essence, the Armenian Church became an agency for promoting nationalistic ideology and preserving ethnic identity as an integral part of her mission, something not warranted by the history of the Armenian Church.

However, that is not to say that Guroian was suggesting that we do away with ethnicity or culture in the Armenian Church, as some have wrongly criticized him, as if an acultural Armenian Church can exist. That would be an oxymoron. For Guroian, the church's primary mission ought to be the business of the gospel. He denounced the ideology of nationalism where the church is used as a tool or a platform to advance and promote nationalistic goals and aspirations, pointing out the dangers of such ideology to the witness and the mission of the Armenian Church. Many have recognized that the Armenian Church had assumed the nationalistic agenda simply because of historical circumstances. But even so, now that Armenia is independent, Guroian challenged the Church leaders that it is time to leave that nationalistic task for others to do. The Church should not get sidetracked by non-gospel-related activities and programs, as noble as they may be, which would invariably sap the church's energy and resources. Otherwise, the church would forfeit her mission and vocation as a church. For Guroian, that was the crux of the matter.

Guroian had many supporters, including clergymen. Some churchmen were not happy with the status quo of the Armenian Church vis à vis nationalism. But they did not want to speak out against it because it was a highly charged issue, extremely sensitive and controversial. Guroian was the person to address this issue. He was in a unique position to criticize the church and call her to task as he was a well-established theologian; he was a cradle member of the Armenian Church, not an outsider, and yet, he was independent of the Armenian religious and political establishment. And Archbishop Mesrob, correctly gauging the mood of the times and the community, discerned that this was an opportune juncture in the life of the Armenian people to create a forum to spotlight this pivotal issue, even as he was conflicted between his vocation as a bishop of the Armenian Church and his national responsibilities (as Guroian notes[6]). At the conclusion of the symposium, the Archbishop said, "Let's be honest, no one likes to hear criticism, but if we truly care, we must listen, and we must act. I am grateful that the participants accepted my invitation and had the courage to speak

---

5. Guroian, *Faith, Church, Mission*, 124.
6. Guroian, *Faith, Church, Mission*, xi.

openly about their convictions. We must be self-critical if we intend to meet the challenges ahead." Interestingly, the Archbishop concluded, "the church is too important to be left to the clergy."[7] That seemed to be a tacit agreement with Guroian's criticism.

The proof of that is that, shortly after that, the Prelate authorized the publication of Guroian's book of collected essays, where he critiques the church for her nationalistic tendencies, urging her to remain faithful to her gospel-oriented mission; and the Archbishop continued to publish Guroian's articles in *Outreach*, and invite him to speak on the same topic. Here, I would like to highlight two other high-profile events where Guroian lectured. The first was a lecture that he delivered at the Young Professionals Forum on the Feast of the Naming of our Lord on January 13, 1996, in New York City, on the occasion of the first Pontifical visit of His Holiness Karekin I, Catholicos of *Etchmiadzin*. The second was at the St. Illuminator's Cathedral in New York City on Palm Sunday, 1996, by the invitation and in the presence of Archbishop Mesrob. Both articles were published in *Outreach*.

At the Young Professionals Forum, speaking about a hierarchy of identities—individual, ethnic, national, religious, etc.—Guroian challenged the participants to find their true and ultimate identity in Christ without negating the other identities. He said:

> Armenians have been attracted to a modern form of atheism. It is a nationalism that replaces God with the nation as the highest good that man can achieve. Many Armenians are indeed persuaded that national identity is the only identity the self needs and that the fulfillment of all human struggle and striving is the nation state.[8]

He continued highlighting the widespread identity confusion that is prevalent among Armenians, equating the Christian faith with nationalism, the church with the Armenian nation, and being an Armenian with being a Christian.

He then concluded with a solemn exhortation, appealing to the Young Professionals to challenge His Holiness regarding his dual leadership role that has become the norm in the Armenian Church, in that His Holiness should focus his efforts exclusively on his religious and spiritual domain

---

7. Guroian, "Armenian Church in the Twenty-First Century," 8.
8. Guroian, "Becoming Real," 3.

and relinquish the worldly and secular jurisdiction to others for the sake of the gospel.[9]

A few months later, we learned that Guroian was disappointed with His Holiness's message at the Young Professionals Forum. On Palm Sunday (1996), Guroian delivered a provocative lecture on the mission of the Armenian Church. He expounded the gospel account of Christ's triumphal entry into Jerusalem coupled with Jesus' prophetic symbolic act of entering the temple and driving out those who were selling and buying there, overturning the tables of the money changers and the seats of those who were selling doves. With that narrative as backdrop, Guroian said:

> When Armenian Church leaders play the role of nation builders and neglect building souls—as they have done—they deny Christ and join the priests in the temple and all their kind whom Christ condemned. But our church leaders are not the only ones who are guilty of such behavior. We all share the blame. Our Church leaders have merely taken our cue. They, with our encouragement and support, have courted the ruling powers obsessively, whether Ottoman, Soviet, or now Armenian. In doing so, they have neglected the nurture of faith and let the weed of a secular and idolatrous nationalism choke the garden of the Armenian soul.[10]

He then turned his attention to the message that the newly elected Catholicos had delivered to the Young Professionals Forum in New York City during his first pontifical visit about three months earlier. Guroian's disappointment was that instead of addressing issues that beset the people, "blackening the souls of the Armenian people," His Holiness was about the business of "nation building." That mission befits a secular leader, like the President of Armenia. "But it would have been pleasing," he said, "to have heard more from His Holiness about the building up of Christ's body, the Church."[11]

At the end of this fiery lecture (which sounded more like a powerful Palm Sunday homily), a prominent member of St. Illuminator's Cathedral standing next to me, leaned over and whispered with disdain, "Our clergy don't talk like that!" Precisely! No wonder Archbishop Mesrob used to say, "Vigen is a prophetic voice in our Church."

---

9. Guroian, "Becoming Real," 4.
10. Guroian, "Palm Sunday Meditation," 6.
11. Guroian, "Palm Sunday Meditation," 7.

But myths do not die easily, especially myths like nationalism, which is ingrained in the institutional psyche.

THE ARMENIAN GENOCIDE—A RELIGIOUS RESPONSE

Nationalism also affected how the church responded to the Armenian Genocide. Guroian asserted that the church has failed to speak about the Armenian genocide theologically, particularly from the perspective of the cross of Christ. In the preface of collected essays published in 2005, *How Shall We Remember? Reflections on the Armenian Genocide and Church Faith*, Guroian observed how in all the annual commemorations of the Armenian genocide on April 24, the religious dimension has been conspicuously lacking. In particular, the church has failed to address two interrelated issues: (1) how the Armenian genocide has shaken the foundation of the faith of the people, making it difficult to believe in God, and (2) how the Christian faith might contribute to healing the wounds of the genocide. "For since I have laid down my pen on these matters, neither the church nor any other institution in the Armenian community has shown much interest in what theology and our faith have to say about the genocide."[12] Through his writings and public engagements on the Armenian genocide, Guroian sought to fill that gap while acknowledging that much work lies ahead.

In one of his earliest essays on the Armenian genocide, Guroian argued that it is imperative that the church seek and demand secular and political justice for the atrocities that Turkey committed against the Armenian people; however, the church should not neglect the weightier aspect of her mission and vocation: the opportunity to bear witness to the crucified messiah especially where there is suffering. That is what is at stake.

> I am deeply troubled ... by the obsessive and narrow use to which the genocide has been put in order to reassert Armenian identity and fortify Armenian nationalism ... Having thrown itself into the struggle for justice, the church has neglected its primary responsibility for healing the afflicted nation. It has lacked the courage to faithfully tell the gospel story and cast the suffering of the Armenian people in the context of the story of the only One who was

---

12. Guroian, *How Shall We Remember?*, x.

truly innocent and yet was unjustly nailed to a cross. That crime was not rectified but, nevertheless, opened the way to salvation.[13]

In his essays and lectures, Guroian will point out again and again that the cross of Christ is absent from much of the rhetorics and discourses of the Church on the Armenian genocide. He will continue to remind church leaders and pastors to view the genocide through the lens of the cross, to speak about the sufferings of the people in redemptive terms, and to invite people to embody a cross-shaped lifestyle and discipleship, which would bring much-needed healing to the wounded nation. Now, as then, cruciform living is a difficult message to hear and even more challenging to implement. But Jesus remains the pattern for us to follow, and that pattern is the cross—a foundational teaching of the scriptures. The Messiah suffered and then entered into his glory (Luke 24:21). Apostle Paul similarly writes to the Romans, "If children, then heirs, heirs of God and joint heirs with Christ—if, in fact, we suffer with him so that we may also be glorified with him" (Rom 8:17 NRSV).

A few years later, Guroian registered his dismay again over how the church had fallen short of her mission to bring comfort and to engender hope in the aftermath of the genocide. He attributed the failure to the nationalistic religious ideology, in that the church "wanted to play the role of the leader of both the spiritual people of God and the secular nation."[14] The church has done a disservice to the nation, he said, by associating the resurrection of Christ with the resurrection of the Armenian nation.[15] Instead of advocating a pseudo hope and redemption, challenged Guroian, the church should speak the language of hope and redemption as prescribed in the scripture, which is the message of the cross of Jesus Christ.[16] But, the message about the cross seems foolishness to some and is a stumbling block to others (1 Cor 1:18–25). If the church, however, is to be true to her vocation and mission, she should embrace the scriptural narrative as her own and live by that rather than by some nationalistic narrative.[17] "Yes, on the cross Christ defeated Satan and death. But that victory came at a price.

---

13. Guroian, *Faith, Church, Mission*, 91.
14. Guroian, *Faith, Church, Mission*, 103.
15. Guroian, *Faith, Church, Mission*, 102.
16. Guroian, *Faith, Church, Mission*, 103.
17. Guroian, *Faith, Church, Mission*, 105.

The Church as that community which is forever called to live the form of Christ must also be willing to pay that price."[18]

Guroian returned to the pages of *Outreach* in 2001, providing yet another challenging article, "The Suffering God of Armenian Christology: Toward an Ecumenical Theology of the Cross." He once again spotlighted the church's failure to address the genocide and offered a fresh perspective for the church to speak about the genocide. The failure lies in not communicating a theology of the cross, not relating the sufferings of the people to the sufferings of Christ as somehow people sharing and participating in the sufferings of Christ. "The community needs to know that its protest and suffering is taken up into the life of God and that healing is not solely dependent upon winning earthly justice."[19] He suggested that the church draw upon her traditional sources, not least the Trisagion Hymn, and reclaim her distinctive ancient christology, a tradition that kept the "apostolic insight into the suffering of God in Jesus Christ."[20] "Holy God, holy and mighty, holy and immortal, who was crucified for us, have mercy upon us." He noted that the additional phrase, "who was crucified for us," embraced and accepted by the Oriental Orthodox Churches, aims to underscore "the real suffering of the Second Person of the Trinity."[21] Drawing the implication of this theology and christology and refocusing on the Armenian genocide, Guroian concluded:

> Many of the most sensitive and creative Armenian spirits of this century have been driven to a protest atheism precisely because they have not been able to live the lie of a cheap theology of resurrection or abide the denial in the church's ecclesiastical triumphalism. This triumphalism is unseemly in view of the affliction in modern Armenian experience. And it is inconsistent with the traditional Armenian Christology. This christology requires the church to recover Christ in his humanity, suffering, and compassion on the cross. The Armenocide and its legacy stand as a tragic reminder that the redemptive worth of the Armenian church depends upon whether it practices a sacrificial and cruciform existence.[22]

---

18. Guroian, *Faith, Church, Mission*, 106.
19. Guroian, "Suffering God of Armenian Christology," 4.
20. Guroian, "Suffering God of Armenian Christology," 4.
21. Guroian, "Suffering God of Armenian Christology," 4.
22. Guroian, "Suffering God of Armenian Christology," 4.

This remains one of Guroian's lasting legacies: the need to view the Armenian Genocide within a theological framework, particularly from the perspective of the cross of Christ, the cross that summons us to a cross-shaped life in Christ.

CONTEMPORARY ETHICAL ISSUES

The third area where Guroian has contributed most to the Armenian Church is contemporary moral and ethical issues. He has written and lectured on various moral and ethical topics, such as abortion, euthanasia, surrogate motherhood and other assisted reproduction technologies, same-sex marriage, transgenderism, and the like. Since the 1980s, Guroian has worked with all three Prelates of the Eastern Prelacy but more extensively with Archbishop Mesrob. Again, all his contributions cannot be presented here, but a few highlights will be provided.

In the early 1990s, Guroian presented a cluster of lectures and articles on medical ethics. He was instrumental in designing several innovative programs on "Medical Ethics and the Armenian Church," a first of its kind in the Armenian Church. The Prelacy organized several regional conferences for the community, featuring other prominent orthodox ethicists, Fr. Stanley Harakas and Fr. John Breck, together with physicians and psychologists in the panel discussions. Then, at the beginning of the twenty-first century, Guroian turned his attention to ethical issues pertaining to marriage, gender, and sexuality, addressing diverse audiences and in different contexts, including young adults, church educators, lay church leaders, and the clergy.

Because the Church tradition did not provide specific and clear guidance on these new ethical challenges, Armenian clergymen were not equipped to discuss these hotly debated and charged topics. Archbishop Mesrob acknowledged the gap at one of the conferences on medical ethics, "Most Armenian Church leaders do not really know the church's stances on the issues, let alone the faithful . . . because we are ill-equipped and don't have answers, whenever people approach us with questions regarding the church's position on this or that ethical issue, more often than not, we say 'that is up to the conscience of the individual.' No, it is not so."[23] In hindsight, the Armenian community was fortunate to have had someone like Prof. Guroian to provide a possible response to such issues from an

23. Guroian, "Ethical Issue and the Armenian Church," 8.

orthodox theological perspective and to help guide the faith community through this uncharted territory.

At the height of the same-sex marriage debate in the United States in 2004, Guroian was invited to deliver the keynote address at the National Representative Assembly (NRA) of the Eastern Prelacy of the Armenian Apostolic Church on "Marriage and Family in Brave New America—On Gay and Same-Sex Marriage." Only days before the NRA convened, there were discussions in some parts of the country about granting licenses for same-sex marriage. And as usual, for Guroian, bearing witness to the gospel was his prime concern. "This presents an opportunity for us as a church," said Guroian to the NRA delegates and the clergy, "to recapture the full significance of marriage and to remind ourselves of the difficult witness to the truth that being the body of Christ in the world requires."[24] A lively discussion ensued from the presentation that His Eminence Archbishop Oshagan Choloyan (the then Prelate) yielded his time to Prof. Guroian. Soon thereafter, the Armenian Prelacy commissioned Guroian to write a booklet on "Homosexuality & Same-Sex Union," which was published by the Prelacy in 2007.

Most recently, in November of 2023, Guroian spoke to the Armenian clergy of North American (Eastern, Western, and Canadian Prelacies) at their convention in Washington, DC, by the invitation of His Eminence Archbishop Anoushavan Tanielian, the Prelate of the Eastern Prelacy. This was all the more momentous as it was held under the auspices and in the presence of His Holiness Aram I, Catholicos of the Great House of Cilicia. Guroian delivered a lecture on "Same-Sex 'Marriage' and Transgenderism: The Return of an Ancient Heresy."

Both same-sex marriage and transgenderism, Guroian believes, like other theologians, are "manifestations of a new Gnosticism." Guroian pointed out how this new Gnosticism, much like the ancient Gnostic heresy, challenges the church's understanding of the human person as "a unity of body and soul."[25] Body and soul—they are two sides of the same coin. This new gnostic ideology, he asserted, "subordinates the body, particularly nature's signature of male or female, to the desires of an autonomous self, so that a male body may be used as, even changed to, a female body and vis-a-versa."[26] This ideology undermines the biblical complementarity of

24. Guroian, "National Representative Assembly," 30.
25. Guroian, "Same-Sex 'Marriage' and Transgenderism," 2.
26. Guroian, "Same-Sex 'Marriage' and Transgenderism," 4.

the sexes, male and female, and thus, he argued, it destroys the traditional notion of marriage between a man and a woman. Furthermore, this new ideology, Guroian said, posits that biological sex does not define or determine one's gender. Until recently, one's gender corresponded to one's biological sex. In new Gnosticism:

> Neither chromosomes nor DNA determines gender identity; rather the inner self does, the self that has knowledge of itself that biology or science is not permitted to proscribe.... That means that society is obliged to permit, even to assist, the individual who is one biological sex but identifies himself or herself of another gender, to act upon this knowledge, even to the extent of altering his or her body in order to be biologically the gender that he or she wishes to be.[27]

What is at stake for Guroian is that this new Gnosticism distorts and destroys the foundations of biblical anthropology and all that it entails—a person being both body and soul inseparably, the complementarity of the sexes, being created male and female by God, marriage between a man and a woman, not to mention the whole grammar of faith. As priests, by celebrating the sacraments, whether offering the Eucharist, baptizing an infant, or marrying a man and woman, you act, Guroian concluded, as "guardians of the grammar of Creation."

I have only highlighted some features of the three areas where Guroian has made the most significant and unprecedented contributions to the Armenian Church. To the best of my knowledge, no one in the Armenian Church community, lay or clergy, has addressed these topics as eloquently, courageously, and powerfully as Guroian has, certainly not with his level of clarity and erudition. He has done it with passionate fidelity to "the faith that was once for all entrusted to the saints," with utmost respect for the church institution and its leaders, and with deep love for his fellow sojourners. His teaching ministry has certainly left an indelible mark on the religious and theological landscape of the Armenian Church community.

BIBLIOGRAPHY

Guroian, Vigen. "The Armenian Church in the Twenty-First Century." *Outreach*, April 1992.
———. "Armenian Nationalism and the Ferment of Faith." *Outreach*, March 1991.

27. Guroian, "Same-Sex 'Marriage' and Transgenderism," 13.

———. "Becoming Real: Living the Live in Christ." *Outreach*, March 1996.

———. "Ethical Issues and the Armenian Church." *Outreach*, May 1993.

———. *Faith, Church, Mission: Essays For Renewal in the Armenian Church*. New York: Armenian Prelacy, 1995.

———. "The Ferment of Faith in Post-Soviet Armenia." *Outreach*, February 1992.

———. "Heal Thy People: Reflections on the Church's Mission After the Armenocide." *Outreach*, July 1991.

———. *Homosexuality & Same-Sex Union*. Contemporary Ethical Issues: An Armenian Orthodox Perspective. New York: Armenian Prelacy, 2007.

———. *How Shall We Remember? Reflections on the Armenian Genocide and Church Faith*. Montréal: Armenian Apostolic Church Sourp Hagop, 2005.

———. "National Representative Assembly." *Outreach*, October 2004.

———. "A Palm Sunday Meditation on the Mission of the Church." *Outreach*, July 1996.

———. "Same-Sex 'Marriage' and Transgenderism: The Return of an Ancient Heresy." Lecture delivered at the Armenian Clergy of North American Conference, Washington, DC, November 2023.

———. "The Suffering God of Armenian Christology: Toward an Ecumenical Theology of the Cross." *Outreach*, April 2001.

Index

abortion, 7, 8, 21
   accessibility, 41, 45
accommodationist stances, Orthodox adoption of, 20
Adam, 5
Adam and Eve, 50
adultery, 7, 130, 131
Adversus Haereses (*Against Heresies*), of Irenaeus, 166n9
agape, 44
allegory, 162
Ambrose, 13
American-Armenian Orthodox theologian, Vigen Guroian as, 174–85
Americans, without any religious affiliation, 26
Amos, 170
Amphilochios of Patmos, 70–71
Ancestral Shadows (Kirk), 115n2
ancient literature, on gardens, 50, 52
Antiochian school, 167
antiquarian polymath, Xlatʻecʻi as, 155
Antony, on virtue, 10
His Holiness Aram I, Catholicos of the Great House of Cilicia, presence of, 184
Arian exegetes, criticisms of, 169
Aristotle, 6, 142n7
Armenian Church, 174–85
   Guroian's contributions to, 175
   leaders as nation builders, 179
   neglected its primary responsibility, 180–81
   safeguarding Armenian identity, 176–77
"The Armenian Church Facing the Twenty-First Century" symposium, 176
Armenian Cilicia, lost its independence, 150–51
Armenian euchology, known as the *Mastoc*, 126
Armenian Genocide, 180–83
Armenian Orthodoxy, Guroian driven into the arms of, 108
Armenian religio-national myth, Guroian debunking, 176
Armenian wedding service, 126n4
asceticism, 3, 11, 15
Ashjian, Mesrob, 174, 175, 177, 179, 183
Athanasius, 10, 13, 163, 169, 171
Augustine, 50n6
autonomy, 40, 42
axe, Vigen bringing, xii

Baal, 171
Bałišecʻi, Aṙakʻel, 151–53
Bambi, distance from the Old Stag, 121
Bambi: A Life in the Woods (Salten), 119
baptism, of Jesus Christ, 161
Patriarch Bartholomew, 63–64
St. Basil, on social contingency, 41
beauty, as the heart of creation, 83
Behr, Fr. John, 4, 5
Pope Benedict XVI, 98

betrothal, earliest Armenian prayers, 125–36
betrothal service, 125, 126, 127, 127n6, 128, 132, 136
Bible, as a timeless document, 162
Blood and Earth (Bales), 66
body and soul, as two sides of the same coin, 184
Book of Questions, by Tat'ewac'i, 142
Book of the Seven Virtues by Peter of Aragon for Hovhan Orotnec'i, 142
Madame Bovary, romance leading to disaster, 14
bread and wine, as "natural symbols," 29
bride, calling upon the wind, 55
bride and groom, dedicating themselves, 136
Burke, Edmund, 118n3
Burkean anthropological insight, 118
Byzantine betrothal prayer, 135

Caiaphas, 57, 59
canonicity, 166
"carbon sinks," mangrove trees as, 66
Čaṙentir (Anthology of Homilies), 155
catechesis, 27, 29
catholicity, of a church, 24
cattle, relationship to the plants they graze, 86
celibacy, 9
Chalcedonian formulation, 40, 42
charity, gift of, 87
Chicago, environmental risks and benefits, 64–65
childbearing potential, maximizing, 6
children
    as a blessing from God, 4
    born of the love of husband and wife, 28
    inducting into fairy-tales and imaginative play, 161
    pressure to produce in Rome, 7
    shaping the hearts of, 94
Children's Literature course, Dr. Coupland's, 95
children's stories, taking seriously, 100
Christ. *See also* Jesus
    as the archetype of humanity, 37
    called the Father his own good gardener, 51
    denial of, 78
    empty cross and, 160
    exalting not sex, but marriage, 9
    as the groom of his bride, the church, 29, 135
    as the image of the invisible God, 37, 38
    as *Logos*, 38
    peace of, 23
Christian ecological ethic, Vigen's thought as, 89
Christian ethics, 85
"Christian Ethics in America," 18, 19–20
Christian girls, marrying at an older age, 8
Christian men, marrying younger than pagans, 8
Christianity
    environmental destruction and, 61–62
    on ethics, 84
    model of holiness in marriage, 13
Christians
    critical of society around them, 7
    against a cultural or political movement, 22
    definition of being human, 35
    divisions between, 111
    making an idol of sexual pleasure, 11
    on the purpose of sex, 8
    reliance on rationality, individualism, and perfection, 34
christology, requiring the church to recover Christ, 182
Chrysippus of Jerusalem, on Mary, 55
Chrysostom, John
    on the attitude of St. Paul toward sex, 12n28
    finding value in marriage, 5
    on God's actions in history, 163
    reading of Scripture and the Antiochian school, 167–69
    on the sentence given to Eve, 12n26
    on sexual desire in marriage, 12

Tat'ewac'i relying on, 143
　on the trinitarian character of sexual union, 28–29
Church. *See* Orthodox Church
"Church and Armenian Nationhood" lecture by Guroian, 176
church and state, Guroian not accepting separation of, 20
Church Fathers, 142, 146
Church leaders, courted ruling powers obsessively, 179
Church of God, not needed by the secular world, 20
churches, as free churches, 26
class, Vigen's as a baptism into the cosmic reality, 77
classical antiquity, linking "story" to the divine, 96
climate, contemporary debates about, 90
collections, Xlat'ec'i's most influential, 155
college-day shenanigans, Vigen reminiscing about, 75
commandment, of matrimony, 133–34
commandments, as a way of acting, 70
communion, 29, 45
community
　critiquing collective injustices, 68
　eucharistic, 25
　evaluating structures it builds, 3
　kenosis of persons with disabilities and, 44
　relationship of time and eternity and, 161
　as trusted, 42
　worshipping, 26
concupiscence, marriage as a remedy for, 9
confidence, with certainty of hope, 149
"conjugal union," seeking God's blessing for, 30
conscience, as movement of the whole person, 37
consumerism, 87–88
conversation, passing on, 94
converts, large numbers of presenting challenges, 27

coronation, of the bride and groom, 126
Coupland, Dan, 95
couple being married, 130, 134, 135
courage, 146, 149
courses, taught by Guroian, 110
created order, 72, 102
creation
　all as iconic, 69
　appreciation of, 81–83
　exceptional power over, 86
　as good in and of itself, 85
　human attitudes and behavior toward, 63
　as a marvelous gift, 88
　placed human beings above the rest of the natural world, 62
　respect for, 64
Creator, existence of, 98
creatures, 82, 83, 85, 86
cross
　of betrothal, 136
　of Christ, 181
　exchanged by the bride and groom, 126n3
　giving for power and stability, 131
　as icon of God's sacrificial love, 136
　as power and strength for the faithful couple, 130
　viewing the genocide through the lens of, 181
cross/crosses, exchanging, 128, 129
"crowning," sacrament of, 126
crucified messiah, bearing witness to, 180
cruciform living, as a difficult message to hear, 181
culture, 22, 25, 118
cyclones, mangrove trees and, 66–67
Cypress, sandalwood scent of, 56nn34–36
Cyril of Alexandria, identifying Mary, 13

Dante, on the depths of Hell, 108
death-turned-resurrection, annual rhythm of, 78
deeds, of courage, 149

Index

defence, meriting honours and service of humanity, 147
Demosthenes, on mistresses, concubines, and wives, 6
denominationalism, American as Orthodoxy's challenge, 24
deprivation of love, 42
Dialogue with Trypho, 165
Diatessaron, of Tatian, 167
Dickinson, Emily, 56
Dionysus (Pseudo-Dionysius) the Aeropagite, 143, 144
disability ethic, toward an Eastern Orthodox, 32–45
discernment, 98, 100
disciples of Jesus, 57, 58
discipline, 147
Discourses Against the Arians (Athanasius), 169
dishonesty, 130, 131
disingenuous and morose thoughts, 130, 131
dissidents, arrests of groups of, 57–58
diversity of beings, revealing God as Goodness and Beauty, 82
divine presence, scented gardens associated with, 53
divinity, of Christ remaining unchanged, 160
divinization, God intending for the world, 23
divorce, in Roman society, 7
divorce rates, in the U. S., 125n1
doctor of the church, *vardapet* as, 140n2
doing of great deeds, 149
"dominion," Man having, 51
dual prayers, in manuscripts, 133
dualism, forms of, 20

Earth, as God's own garden, 51
earth auger, for fenceposts, 109–10
Eastern Orthodox ethic, as a virtue ethic, 37
ecclesiology, xv, 64
ecological ethics, xv, 81–90
ecological justice, in Orthodox Christianity, 61–72

ecology
 contemporary debates about, 90
 human dignity and, 63, 64–68
eco-spiritual/ethical visionary, Guroian as, xiv
"ecotheology," 62
Edmund Burke Society, Guroian as faculty adviser, 114
Egyptian "all-year" garden, 53
"enclosed garden," as paradise, 55
Encountering the Mystery (Patriarch Bartholomew), 63–64
endurance, 149
"engagement," in our day, 136
environment, destruction of, 61
environmental harms, 66
environmental health, in Chicago, 65
environmental racism, modern slavery and, 64–68
St. Ephraim the Syrian, reading bits from, 77
Epiphanius of Salamis, 55
Epistle of Barnabas, 165, 167
Erevan 1001, 129
Erevan manuscript, 132–33, 135–36
eros, for one's wife as vulgar, 7
eternal realm, everyday life and, 96–97
ethical dualism, in the life of the Body of Christ, 20
ethical issues, contemporary, 183–85
ethical models, of Guroian, 32
ethical persons, raising children to be, 94–95
ethicist, Vigen's influential legacy as, xiv
ethics, 18–30, 83–85
Ethics After Christendom: Toward an Ecclesial Christian Ethic (1994), xiii, 85, 87
ethnicity, secular religion of, 24
ethnocentrism, compromising to the Orthodox Christian faith, 27
Eucharist, compared to the sacrament of marriage, 4
eucharistic worship, Church providing, 24–25
evil, in children's stories, 102
exchange of the cross/crosses, 134, 136

Index

factual truth, disagreement with normative truth, 97
fairy tales, 100, 101
faith, 143, 180
fall, consequences of, 29
fallen world, imbued with the deep goodness of its Creator, 101
family, 3, 28
fantasy, "joy" in successful, 102
Father, not proceeding from the Son or the Spirit, 83
father figure, Guroian as, 117
fear, distorting justice, 147
fence, week spent building, 121–22
fenceposts, of "Fort Guroian," 109
fields, Vigen contributed to many, xii–xiii
fireworks, at times in Vigen's class, 76
food, creatures providing, 86
For the Life of the World: Toward a Social Ethos of the Orthodox Church, normative claims in, 71–72
foresight, seeing that which will take place, 148
forgiveness of sins, hopes for, 145
Forms of Plato, 97, 98
"foundation" of the Church, marriage as, 134
foundational matters, Guroian appealing to, 20
The Fragrance of God (2006), xiii, 85
free agents, capable of choosing to do good, 140
free church tradition, of Protestantism, 24
freedom, no global narrative of, 19
friendship, 36, 85
fullness of time, God-Man found in, 172

ganj, as an array of litanic and paralitanic prayers, 151n33
Ganjaran (collection of rhythmic litanies), 155
garden(s), 49–60
  of delight in Christ's living community, 55
  as exclusive in the antique world, 52
  growing around him, 74–79
  as images of loving hopefulness, 60
  not a common thing in antiquity, 50–51
  as a symbol, 49–50, 54
  touring Guroian's, 113
  tradition lauding the beauty of, 56
Garden of Eden, 49
gardener, xiv, 79, 113
gardening, 76, 78, 79, 88
Genesis creation account, 69
Genesis garden, compared to Gethsemane, 60
genocide, using to fortify Armenian nationalism, 180
Gethsemane, garden of, 56, 58, 59–60
gifts, from God, 84
global warming, 63
Gnosticism, 184, 185
Gnostics, 165–66
God. *See also* LORD
  beseeching to bless a couple, 135
  can now be seen by human eyes, 164–65
  character of, 99
  creating us to be priests and stewards of creation, 23, 86
  entering time to bring His plan and our lives to fulfillment, 163
  as the God of the living, not the dead, 169
  healing the ruptured relationship between his creation and himself, 21
  hope for the grace of, 145
  knitting ordinary events into the fabric of human life, 172
  loving Creation into existence, 82
  as not male, 160n2
  as the song of resurrection and life, 78
  on the trinitarian structure of love on marriage and family and, 28
  as the true Lord of the universe, 77
  union with perfected only after this life, 84
God's Creation, being alive in, 122

God's haunting, glimmering world, opened through Guroian, 75
God's kingdom, striving to make present, 90
God's story, as the story of Israel and of the world, 164
God-saturated life, evoking Vigen's reverence, 76
good and evil, distinguishing through faith, 143
goodness, 82, 100, 102
grace, 84, 102, 105–8, 145
Graham, John, 119
gratuitous love, towards God, 145
great deeds, doing, 149
"The Great Knock," 75
Greatest Commandment, 70–72
Greek Fathers, on marriage, 5
Greek women, 6
greenhouse effect, 51
Gregory of Nyssa, 5, 54–55, 56nn34–36
Guroian, June, 78, 110, 113–14, 122, 139
Guroian, Vigen
  "active engagement with society" and, 25
  in the Armenian Apostolic Church, 174–85
  assumptions about God, 77
  on the beauty of flowers, 83
  "bring it on" grin of, 106
  on the garden as a theological symbol, 49–50
  on gardening, 88
  in his garden, 79
  on holding together theology, ecology, and human dignity, 64
  on the image of God, 37, 86
  knowing that people tried to exterminate his people, 108
  on marriage, 4, 15
  on the mentor's task, 120
  on moral imagination, 95
  on the Orthodox Church in America, xi–xii
  photo at Oriel College Chapel, Oxford, 156
  on priests no longer serving as agents of the state, 29
  on secular virtues, 23
  on "the shape of our world," 96
  on singing good theology, 78
  as a source of practical wisdom and confidence, 117
  stressing the importance of time and historical memory, 161
  summoned the Church to criticize of injustices, 67
  as a teacher, xi, 75, 105–22
  thesis on Reinhold Niebuhr and Edmund Burke, 19
  understanding creation, 85
Guroian Circle, students of, 116–17

Harakas, Stanley, 183
harmony, sense of, 101
hatred and jealousy, distorting justice, 147
Havilah, closeness to the land of, 51
heart-to-heart communion, 14, 15
Herberg, Will, 119
High Priest's police, ready to arrest Jesus, 57
history, no such thing as uninterpreted, 171
history lesson, features of Stephen's, 163
History of Christianity I course, 111
holiness, 84, 85
Holy Roller, 107, 108
Holy Spirit, 83, 131
Holy Tradition, not promoting a reading of Scripture, 162
Holy Trinity, 30, 130, 131
holy writings, meanings of, 152
home-as-civilization, return to, 114
Homer, on mentorship, 120
homestead, Guroian's Arcadian as, 110
Homilies on the Song of Songs (Gregory of Nyssa), 55
homosexuality, in Roman society, 7
"Homosexuality & Same-Sex Union," Guroian's booklet on, 184
hope, 144, 145
Hopkins, Gerard Manley, 49

Index

hospitality, as the image of God, 36
How Classic Stories Awaken a Child's Moral Imagination, 118
How Shall We Remember?: Reflections on the Armenian Genocide and Church Faith (2005), xiii, 180
human being(s)
  bestowed with power over creation, 86
  in cooperation with others, 42
  as cultivator and guardian of the garden of God, 51
  as God's vice regent, 87
  as icons, 33, 37, 69
  as not autonomous but theonomous, 138, 139
  recognizing God through cognitive processes, 37
  referencing Christ in a dependent way, 38
  as relational, interdependent, and social, 36
  thousands of constituent parts, 40
  vardapet speaking directly to the agency and the will of, 145
  as the very body of Christ, 64
  wellbeing contingent on a myriad of factors, 41
human dignity, 63, 64–68
human nature
  in the community united through divine love, 42
  iconographic representation of, 38
  link between cognitive or rational faculties and, 36
  uprooting atomistic definitions of, 45
human sexual coupling, unique dimension of, 29
humane education, instilling in students, 103
humanities, study of, 117
humanization, God intending for the world, 23
husbands and wives, embracing the monastic ideal of holiness, 10
hymns, 77, 159, 160

icon(s)
  of dependency, 41
  in a dependent relationship, 37
  showing deep significance, 169
  Vigen bringing, xii
  as a way of seeing, 68–70
The Icon and the Axe (Billington), xii
iconographic relationship, between God and humanity, 38
iconography, manifesting the Orthodox ideal of culture, 23
ideas, having consequences for Vigen, 76
identity in Christ, finding, 178
idol, marriage and family as, 3
Īlkhānids, established Xlatʻ as a centre of their rule, 151
"image and likeness," within the patristic and medieval tradition, 86
image of God
  Christ as, 69
  defining inside the human being, 36
  human beings created in, 23
  particular capacity as, 35
  as the second person of the Trinity, 38
images, wardrobe of, 93–103
imagination, as "the organ of meaning," 103
imago Dei, 35
Incarnate Love and The Orthodox Reality, on the creation account in Genesis, 4
Incarnate Love: Essays in Orthodox Ethics (1987), xiii, 84
Incarnation, showing why time is not irrelevant, 172
inclination prayers, 135
individual, protecting the rights of, 21
individual model, of disability, 34
individuated person
  distinctiveness of, 43
  functioning for Guroian, 40–41
industrial medical apparatus, Vigen's frustration with, 78
infanticide, in Roman society, 7
Inheriting Paradise: Meditations on Gardening (2000), xiii, 85, 88, 113

injustice, elevating, 45
inner self, determining gender identity, 185
intellectual disabilities, persons with, 36
Intercollegiate Studies Institute, Guroian active in, 114
interdependency, as human nature, 41
"Inversnaid" poem (Hopkins), 49
Irenaeus, 163, 165–67
Isaac and Rebecca, 130, 135

jealousy, distorting justice, 147
Jeremiah, 170
Jesus. *See also* Christ
  as the basis or foundation for icons, 69
  chose to protect his loved ones, 59
  commanded the disciples to set a watch, 58
  identified with the tetragrammaton YHWH, 160n3
  overturned the coin dealers' tables, 57
  prayed in a torment of agony, 58–59
  remaining the pattern for us to follow, 181
  suffering over political and social divisions, 160
John (Gospel of), Xlatʻecʻi wrote a commentary on, 150
John of Damascus, 69
joy, 13–14, 108
Judas, betraying Jesus, 57
Juɫayecʻi, Mattʻēos *var*, 141, 142
justice and righteousness, 146, 147–48
Justin Martyr, 165

kanon aletheias, "the rule of truth," 165
Karekin I, Catholicos of *Etchmiadzin*, first Pontifical visit of, 178
kʻaroz, chanted by the deacon and addressed to the people, 129n13
kaxik, dependence on the love of Christ, 140n3
kenosis, 43, 44, 45
Kilikecʻi, Tiratur, 140

Kingdom of God, marriage preparing for, 4
Kirk, Annette, *grand dame* of Mecosta, 115–16
Kirk, Russell, 94, 114, 115, 119
knowledge of God, prizing, 35
Koreans, care toward trees, 70
St. Kosmas the Aetolian, 70

Lapsa, Brian, 156
Last Supper, in a room near the house of Caiaphas, 57
law of Moses, joining together according to, 133
legal and sacramental marriage, separating in America, 29
leisure, as essential part of gardening, 76
Letter XIX (Athanasius), 170
Lewis, C. S., 75
liberal arts, codified in late Roman antiquity, 99
"liberation theologians," 62–63
life expectancy, in Roman times, 7
life in letters, of Guroian, 118
Life of Antony (Athanasius), 10
literary conversation, of Vigen in *Tending the Heart of Virtue*, 93
literature
  intertwined with the garden, 79
  moral imagination feeding with good, 96
  as not one of the seven liberal arts, 99
  purpose of all, 103
  as a study of human nature, 98
  unique properties of normative, 101
"little church," family constituting a kind of, 3
liturgical prayers and rituals, medieval, 125
liturgy, 85
LORD, 160n3, 161, 164. *See also* God
love
  as a divine grace and gift, 145–46
  of God and of neighbor as at the heart of ethics, 89
  at the heart of all Christian ethics, 90

requiring self-sacrifice and elevation, 44
sacrificing for another's benefit, 43
of self or money, 147
of the true and noble, 112
uniting persons, 42
love for trees, 70, 71
loving union, bringing two together into, 131

male and female, in the sacrament of marriage, 29
male body, changing to a female body, 184–85
man
  attraction of to a male youth, 8
  expected to be sexually experienced, 6
man and woman
  keeping pure toward one another, 131
  precedent of the first-created, 133
mangrove trees, destruction of, 66
Manichaean dualisms, 22
marriage
  in antiquity, 6–9
  applying liturgical prayers and rituals to, 125
  as a couple in, 130
  establishing a common household and producing offspring, 5
  by means of the cross, 131n26
  "natural" sacramentality in, 27–28
  Orthodoxy and the transformation of, 3–16
  purpose greater than the personal satisfaction, 134
  recapturing the full significance of, 184
  as a sacrament, 29, 136
  as "a sacramental sign, 30
  sacrosanctity and permanence of, 133
  strength in continuity, 4
  symbolism that God ordained for it, 29
  of two equals, 6–7
  understanding the Orthodox transformation of, 6
"Marriage and Family in Brave New America – On Gay and Same-Sex Marriage," 184
married sexuality, 12
married woman, should not leave her husband, 133
martyrdom, 4n7, 144, 154–55, 165
Marx, Groucho, 52
masses, capacity to educate, 152
Mastoc, modern printed editions of, 126
Matenadaran, repository of Armenian manuscripts, 127
materialist view, 81, 83
Maximus the Confessor, 5, 40
Mecop'ec'i, T'ovma, on the study of virtues by monks, 143n8
Mecosta, excursions to, 114
medical bias, people with disabilities facing, 39
medical ethics, Guroian's lectures and articles on, 183
"Medical Ethics and the Armenian Church," programs on, 183
medical model, disability defined by, 34
"melody," various notes in God's complex, 167
The Melody of Faith: Theology in an Orthodox Key (2010), xiii, 78, 82, 85
memory, 148
mentee, 121
mentor, 117, 120
"mentoral friendship," in *Charlotte's Web*, 119
mentorship, 117–18, 119, 121
Messiah, suffered and then entered into his glory, 181
Methodius, Tat'ewac'i relying on, 143
Michigan, excursions to, 114
Modern Russian Religious Thinkers seminar course, 111
modernity, acquired an allergy to the past, 172
modesty, 132
"monastic asceticism," 27

monastic life, 11, 11n23
monastic movement, Mary playing a central role in Christian devotion, 13
monastic revolution, 9–12
monasticism
  began as a demanding lay movement, 24
  relevance to marriage, 10
moral and ethical issues, contemporary for the Armenian Church, 183–85
moral imagination
  always feeling that there should be goodness, 101
  beginning with stories that children learn, 100
  extending Vigen's work on, xv
  guiding principle of Guroian's, 95
  Guroian on, 100, 102, 118
  lessons in the well-stocked "wardrobe" of, 103
  making metaphors out of images, 99
moral judgments, 99
moral virtues, 84
morality, 84, 145
Moses, 69, 164
ms. Erevan 1001, 127
ms. Venice 457, 127, 128n12
Murder in the Cathedral (Eliot), 115
Muses (mythological Greek goddesses), as the source of all stories, 96
music, Vigen giving his students, 78
musical piece, viewing created things as, 167
mutual consent, of husband and wife, 9
mutual exchange, of the cross, 131
mystery
  of Christ, 89
  letting it be, 77

narrative, supplying imagination with "symbolic information," 96
narrative fiction, portrayals of evil and beauty, 101
nationalism, Armenian Church and, 175–80
"Nationalism or Gospel," by Tiran Nersoyan, 176

nationalistic religious ideology, failure attributed to, 181
nation's collective memory, keeping alive, 161
natural love, as towards oneself, 145
natural world, immense and sacred beauty, 50
Nazianzen, Gregory, 116, 120
Ncʻečʻi, Esayi, 140
neighbor, serving, 72
Nersoyan, Tiran, 176
Noble Lie, of Socrates, 98n11
non-human creation, 69, 85
normative truth, 99, 101
normatively true stories, 97–98
"Notes Toward an Eastern Orthodox Ethic," 32

Odyssey, Athena's disguise in the first four books of, 119–20
Old Stag, 119, 120–21
olive grove, at the foot of the slope of the Mount, 56
On the Incarnation (Athanasius), 169
On the Making of Man (Gregory of Nyssa), 54
one flesh, becoming, 8–9
one human nature, united in love with Christ, 42
Orbēlean, Iwanē, prince of Siwnikʻ, 140
ordered cosmos, 98
Origen, 50n7, 54
original sin, as man's choice, 87
Orotnecʻi, Yovhan *vardapet*, 140, 141, 155–56
Orthodox Christianity, xii, 19, 24, 25, 30, 61–72
Orthodox Church
  brought romance into the world, 15
  as complicit in justifying barriers, 34
  cross adorned by the body of Christ, 159
  on the Eucharist, 111
  garden as a metaphor for, 55
  Guroian calling upon to manifest the presence of God's kingdom, 20
  interest in the ethics of, 18
  large numbers of converts to, 26

needing "exemplars and catalysts of human flourishing," 26
not needing to enter into Western "Biblicist" and rationalist debates, 162
presence of icons, 68
preserving cultural identity, 24
role of, 25
wedding service, 4n7
Orthodox ethics, 18, 33
"Orthodox reality," Vigen's, xii
The Orthodox Reality: Culture, Theology, and Ethics in the Modern World (2018), xiii
Orthodox social ethic, 22, 32, 43
Orthodox theology, 41–42, 63
Oxford, 138–39, 156

pagan deities, as personifications of nature, 14
Pahlavuni, Grigor II Vkayasēr, first to be called "Lover of saints," 152n35
Palm Sunday lecture, of Guroian, 179
Paradise Garden, unusual features of, 50–51
participatory body, 39–43
passion, of Vigen as promethean, 76
passionate desire (*eros*), 7
Patmakan ołb ("Historical Lament"), 155
Paul, on Christ as "the image of the invisible God," 69
peer, mentor as not, 120
people with disabilities, suffering of, 43
Persian Satraps, *paradizai* of, 52
persistence, as continually examining oneself, 149
the person, in Guroian's social ethic, 40
person with intellectual disabilities, participating in the community, 42–43
personal transformation, facilitated by a community in an ethic of love, 33
Peter of Aragon, 142n7
philia, as affection coming of living and laboring together, 7
Philo of Alexandria, 142n7, 146n17

Piety Hill, Kirk's ancestral home, 114–15
pizzas, Guroian selecting a "Cosmological Pie," 112
plants, relationship to the multitude of soil organisms, 86
Plato, 8, 98, 142n7
Pliny, 53
Plutarch, 53
poets, relationship with truth, 97
police force, of Caiaphas, 57
policy, effecting the greatest good for the greatest number, 89
political agendas, 22
political freedom, narrative of, 161
political orders, illusory claims about, 20
politics, reforming as the Church transfigures, 23
Politics (Aristotle), 6
"Politics and the Moral Life in the Writings of Edmund Burke and Reinhold Niebuhr," Vigen's dissertation on, xiii
pollution, 63–64, 65
Pompei, small walled garden in, 53–54
the poor, trapped in Chicago, 65
poor as poor, as sinful, undisciplined, or lazy, 62
poverty
escaping by loving trees, 70
social problem of, 64
power, of humanity over creation, 86
Prayer E1, 129, 130
Prayer E2, 129, 130–31
Prayer E3, 129, 131–32, 135–36
Prayer V1, 129, 131
Prayer V2, 129, 131
prayers, 13, 85
pre-crowning rituals, 126, 127
priests, acting as "guardians of the grammar of Creation," 185
Prohaeresius, comparing Guroian to, 116
Proklos of Constantinople, 55
prophets and the Law, discrepancy between, 170

Proskomedia (preparation for the Orthodox Eucharist), diaconal prayer in, 161
Protestant free church example, Guroian on, 25
prudence, 146, 148
publications, of Vigen Guroian, xiii

Quasten, describing Severian, 54

rabunapet, as a teacher of teachers, 150n30
racism, environmental, 64–68
Rallying the Really Human Things, 118
rationality
    approaching the biblical story with, 167
    defining personhood, 35
    as not a particle or trait, 38–39
    providing moral infrastructure for other image types, 36
    tied up with self-sufficiency and self-reliance, 34
Rawson, Beryl, 7
"reading parties," drawing together friends learning virtues, 116
reality, 99, 101, 102
reason, as central to definition of faith, 144
Rebecca (wife of Isaac), 130, 135
reconciliation, 14–16
redemption, 56
relational interdependency, 39
relational model, 35, 39
relationality, 36, 38
religion, 23, 108
Religion in Children's Literature college course, taught by Guroian, 94
religious lobby, serving a secular agenda, 27
religious nationalism, myth of, 176
religious secularism, becoming forms of, 22
"remedial allegorists," avoided theological problems, 162
renunciation, of sex, 8
Republic, Plato's, 97

Republic of Korea, Environmental Justice in, 66
"Restoring the Senses: Gardening and Orthodox Easter" recording, for *On Being* (2012), xiii
resurrection, 89, 163
Resurrection (*Anastasis*), 50
revelation, 28, 88–89
revelatory relationship, between icon and archetype, 38
rhetorical approach (Antioch), 168
righteousness, components of, 147
rights, secular accounts of, 21
rites of betrothal, 126, 127n6
Rivers, Helen, 119
Roman Catholic crucifix, 159
Roman garden, 53
Roman marriageable women, dearth of, 7
romance, courting disappointment, 14
Romans, taste for formal garden layouts, 53
rose bush, marveling in the beauty of, 88

"sacred groves," Greek, 53
sacrifice, marriage often requiring, 4
sacrificial love of Christ, for his church, 134
saint-martyr, as exemplary, 144
saints, 11, 152
salvation, hope for, 145
salvation history, Biblical credos rehearsing, 163
same-sex marriage, 28, 184
"Same-Sex 'Marriage' and Transgenderism: The Return of an Ancient Heresy," Guroian delivered a lecture on, 184
Saul of Tarsus, 165
Schmeman, Alexander, 87
Schwartz, Rebecca, 95
Scripture
    approach to reading coming from the apostles, 172
    as at best exaggerations, 162
    as only a signpost to the One who is the Word of God, 162

reading with the apostolic eye, 166
"timefulness" in Orthodox interpretations of, 159–72
secular assumptions, 26
secular culture, 27
self-emptying, theologies of, 43–44
self-governance (Anjnišaxut'iwn), 139, 139n1
self-sacrifice, 44, 120
self-sufficiency, 40
seminars, preambles to Professor Guroian's, 111–12
"sequestration," by mangrove trees, 66
sermon, of Stephen, 163–65
Severian the bishop of Gabala in Syria, 54
sex traffickers, purchasing shrimp farm recruits, 67
sexual drive, as tainted, 3
sexual love, aspiring toward perfect union, 4
sexual morality, as a set of rules, 15
sexuality, 5, 9, 27
Shahinian, Ani, 156
shape of our world, 96–99, 103
shrimp farms, 66, 67
"sign" or the "cross," blessing and/or exchange of, 126
sin, holy cross saving from, 129
slavery, 62, 63, 64–68
Snow White, as a sacrament, 79
sober-mindedness, 146, 148
social environments, producing barriers to access, 33
social ethics text, groundbreaking Orthodox, 71–72
Social Gospel, 19–20
social model, for disability, 34
social obligations, to persons with disabilities, 44
social reform movement, Christianity as not, 8
social structures, theologians and, 62
social transformation, *theosis* as, 33
"social-gospel," stressing, 160
society, culture forming and shaping human, 22
Socrates, 97, 98

soil, tiller of significant, 109–22
sole authorship, Muses precluded, 96
solidarity with Christ, as the image of God, 36
Son of Man, identification of as Jesus, 165
soul, 10, 56
space and time, God's service and, 164
Spirit, come to complete, not undo, 160
spiritual ethos, Orthodox communities needing to cultivate, 26
spiritual radiance, 55
spiritual sacrifice, Irenaeus stressing, 167
spiritual transformation, of the person, 40
spiritual undertaking, marriage as, 11
"spontaneous" behaviors, of Vigen, 107
St. Illuminator's Cathedral in New York City, 174
St. Vladimir's Orthodox Theological Seminary, 175
Stark, Rodney, 7
Stephen, 163–65
stories
　for children suggested by Kirk, 94
　comprehending both the world and ourselves, 98
　in "harmony with the fundamental realities," 101
　Muses provided inspiration for all, 96
　training a student's affections, 99
students, developing a sensitivity to goodness, 100
student-teacher relationship, significance of, 140
submitting, in order to know, 99
substantialist model, on the image of God, 35
suffering, 44, 62, 182
"The Suffering God of Armenian Christology: Toward an Ecumenical Theology of the Cross" (Guroian), 182
"symbolic information," 97, 98

"Take Your Professor to Lunch" scheme, at the University of Virginia, 112
Tanielian, Anoushavan, 184
Tatʿewacʿi, Grigor *vardapet*
   definitions of virtues, 146n17
   sought Orotnecʿi as teacher, 140–41
   sources on, 142n7
   teachings on the seven virtues, 142–49
   worthy student of Orotnecʿi, 155
teacher, Xlatʿecʿi as, 151
teacher and friend, Vigen Guroian as, 105–22
teacher of the word, *vardapet* as, 140n2
Telemachus, mentor of, 120
temperance. See sober-mindedness
temporal docetism, falling prey to, 162
"tending a heart," act of, 103
Tending the Heart of Virtue: How Classic Stories Awaken a Child's Moral Imagination (1998, 2023), xiii, 93, 94–95, 100, 103, 117–18
Ter-Vardanean, Georg, 127
Theodore the Studite, 55
Theodotus of Ancyra, 13
Theogony, Hesiod's, 97
theologians, reading Scriptures by means of allegory, 162
theological framework, viewing Armenian Genocide within, 183
theological integrity, of Vigen Guroian, 18
theological virtues, 84, 143
theological-ethical tradition, of Orthodox Christianity, 68–72
theology
   connection to ecology, 61
   creating accessible, 45
   Guroian scaffolding using conditional language, 32
   liberating oppressed and enslaved persons, 62
   naming our best efforts to grapple with God, 77–78
   Orthodox, 41–42, 63
   seeking after the Almighty, 74–75
   as a story that lays a claim on you, 79

Vigen's lifelong immersion in Eastern, 78
theonomous generations, raising up new, 156
theosis, 33, 40, 43–45
Theotokos, 13, 14, 15
things, acquiring without exploiting, 89
Thomas Aquinas, 35–36, 82, 83
threnody, 50
"throw away culture," consumerism encouraging, 88
time (*chronos*), 163
time (*kairos*), 163
time and eternity, relationship of, 161
"the time of refreshment," Old Testament legal requirements given until, 171
"timefulness," in Orthodox interpretations of Scripture, 159–72
Tolkien, J. R. R., 101, 102
topiarius, Latin word for a gardener, 53
Torah, 164, 170–71
"Toxic Release Inventory (TRI)," in Korea, 66
transformation, participatory model for, 40
transgenderism, 184
transliteration, Armenian, 140n1
transubstantiation, as "needless scholasticism!" 111
Tree Hugger, Vigen as a *bona fide*, 107
"the tree of life," as the image for the cross, 132
Tree of Life, fruit trees clustered around, 51
trees, emphasis on, 70, 71
Trinitarian ecological ethics, Vigen's approach as, 87
Trinitarian reading, of reality of Vigen, 88
Trinitarian relations, 41, 84, 86
Trinity
   divine attributes of, 82–83
   faint reflection of in creation, 86
   masculine pronouns for, 160n2
   transcendence of, 160
Trisagion Hymn, 182
triumphalism, xiv, 182

Triune God, mutual faith in with Vigen, 160n4
trusted others, 40
truth, 98
tsunamis, mangrove trees providing a natural barrier during, 66–67
tutorial method, of Guroian, 112

union
   of the patriarch Isaac with Rebecca, 135
   as the primary good of marriage, 4
utilitarianism, 89

Valentinians, dismissed the *kanon aletheias*, 166
Vardan the Hermit, Xlatʻecʻi trained under, 150
vardapet, 140, 140n2
vardapets (theologian, church father, teacher of human minds and hearts), 139, 140
vegetables (*olera*), in a Roman garden, 53
Venice 457, canon for exchanging a cross, 129
vertical dimension, of divine revelation, 164
Vigen. *See* Guroian, Vigen
Virgil, 100
Virgin Mary, 13, 14
virtue(s)
   Christian ecological ethic and, 89
   divine, 143–46
   entire book on the question of the, 142
   holding fast according to nature, 10
   seeds sown when a child reads or hears a true story, 100
   tending the heart of, 99
   as tools of the Armenian *vardapet*, 139–40
virtue ethics, 33, 34–39
vita-martyr text, on the Holy Spirit, 153
voluntary organizations, churches as, 26
vows, in pre-crowning ceremonies, 126n4

"wardrobe," 102–3
water, in a well irrigated garden, 54
weed-pulling, for the Professor and Mrs. Guroian, 114
weeds, Guroian cursing the industriousness of, 113
well-lived life, seeing in Vigen Guroian, 79
"whitewashed sepulchers," 58
Wilken, Robert Louis, xi
Wilson, William, 110
The Wind in the Willows, 119
wisdom/*sophia*, 121, 132, 148
the Word, 56, 83, 88
work, xii, 50n4
world
   converted into a carnival, 76
   as a good world, 101
Wren, Brian, 159–60

Xlatʻecʻi, Grigor Cerencʻ, 141, 142, 149–55

Yišatakaran Alēticʻ ("Memoir of Calamity"), 155
Yoder, Rick, 156
Young Professionals Forum, 178–79

zeal, 147